geographies of learning

geographies of learning

Theory and Practice, Activism and Performance

Jill Dolan

Wesleyan University Press
Middletown, Connecticut

Wesleyan University Press

© 2001 Jill Dolan
ISBN 0-8195-6467-3 (cloth)

ISBN 0-8195-6468-0 (paper)

Printed in the United States of America

Design and composition by Chris Crochetière,

B. Williams & Associates, Durham, North Carolina

5   4   3   2   1

CIP data appears at the end of the book.

contents

For Stacy,
happily, my fellow-traveler across the terrain

acknowledgments

Geographies of Learning reflects five years of my life as an academic scholar, administrator, and activist. In that time, I've worked and talked with many people whose ideas and experiences inspired and influenced my thinking. In earlier drafts, several of these chapters were given as lectures at various conferences and universities. I'd like to thank my smart interlocutors at the "Forms of Desire" and the "Queer Theater" conferences at the Center for Lesbian and Gay Studies (CLAGS); the "Theory/Practice" conference organized by Adrian Kiernander in Sydney, Australia, and the gallery lecture organized by Peta Tait in Melbourne, Australia; and audiences at the University of Calgary, University of California–Riverside, University of California–Irvine, Louisiana State University, University of Arizona, Arizona State University, and the University of Texas at Austin for their useful responses to pieces of this work. I'm grateful to Susan Bennett, Sue-Ellen Case, Robyn Wiegman, Jennifer Jones, Miranda Joseph and Janet Jakobsen, Margaret Knapp, and Desley Deacon respectively, for extending invitations for me to visit these universities and present my work.

The Governing Council of the Association for Theatre in Higher Education (ATHE) saw me try out many of the ideas about theater studies that I describe in these pages. I want to thank them for encouraging me, and for giving me such a wonderful platform for my revisionist thinking. I'm also grateful to the members of ATHE who, during my term as president, supported my efforts to make it an activist organization with a national profile in arts and education advocacy. My work with ATHE motivated me in numerous ways, and I continue to be inspired by my work with this organization. I particularly want to thank Ann Marie Costa, Nancy Erickson, Barbara Grossman, Mark Heckler, Richard Runkel, Meg Swanson, Bob Vorlicky, and Mark Weinberg for their engagements with me around these ideas.

Likewise, the Women and Theatre Program (WTP) continues to offer a place for my thinking, even though other obligations in the last six or so years have kept me from participating actively in its conferences and programs. Knowing that the WTP perseveres in providing an intellectual site for cutting-edge feminist performance theory and practice lets me know I always have a home to which to return.

I want to thank my women's studies friends and colleagues at the University of Wisconsin–Madison, especially Dale Bauer, Susan Bernstein, Julie D'Acci, Betsy Draine, Nancy Kaiser, Elaine Marks, Mariamne Whatley, and Nancy Worcester, for being supportive of my teaching and my research in feminist theory and in feminist performance. My colleagues in the Department of Theatre and Drama at Wisconsin—Mary Karen Dahl, Jim Moy, Bob Skloot, and especially Sally Banes and Phillip Zarrilli—provided me with a wonderful intellectual and social community during my six years teaching there. My work with them and my colleagues in the practical side of the department shaped my thinking about how theory and practice really can be combined in theater studies.

The board of directors of CLAGS at the City University of New York (CUNY) also supported my quest to meld theory and practice in lesbian and gay studies and activism. I want to thank everyone who served on the board during my tenure at CLAGS (1996–1999) for their flexibility and generosity and patience as I tried to understand what it might mean to be the executive director of such an important, historic organization. I particularly want to thank Arnaldo Cruz-Malavé, Paisley Currah, Marty Duberman, Lisa Duggan, David Eng, Licia Fiol-Matta, Stephanie Grant, Carol Kaplan, Martin Manalansan, Framji Minwalla, Oscar Montero, Ara Wilson, and extend my gratitude and affection to Paula Ettelbrick and Alan Yang for their support and their influence and for what I learned from them intellectually and politically. I also want to thank John D'Emilio and Esther Newton, with whom I spoke frequently during my years at CLAGS, for their insights and inspiration. I especially want to thank my friend Alisa Solomon, my successor as executive director of CLAGS, for her response to much of this work, in theater studies and in gay and lesbian studies and activism, often while it was happening around us. I continue to learn quite a lot from the example she sets as a public intellectual and an activist academic. The CLAGS staff, Rachel Cohen, Heidi Coleman, and Jordan Schildcrout, made my life at CLAGS a pleasure. They staunchly supported my effort to meld queer theory and queer practice, both intellectually and practically, executing the vision in which I believed while helping me maintain perspective and my sense of humor. I'm pleased that in the process, they also became my friends.

My colleagues at the CUNY Graduate Center provoked much of my thinking about working in institutions of higher education, especially Jane Bowers, Marvin Carlson, George Custen, and Francesca Sautman. President Frances Degan Horowitz, Assistant to the President Steve Gorelick, Provost

Bill Kelly, Vice Provost Stephen Brier, and Dean Alan Gartner administratively and politically supported my work in the Theatre Program and with CLAGS in ways that mattered quite a lot at CUNY. My program assistant, Lynette Gibson, both supported me and protected me, and made possible my work with the Theatre Program and with CLAGS; I so appreciate her level-headed good humor and her knowledge. My colleague Nancy Miller provided my connection to feminism at the Graduate Center and, more important, became my friend and confidante. I treasure the memory of our alcohol-free dinners.

My CUNY graduate student dissertation-reading group—Sharon Green, Jay Plum, Beth Schachter, Maurya Wickstrom, and Jim Wilson—kept me intellectually connected while I was mostly serving as an administrator and were always willing to listen to my institutional quandaries. Thanks, too, to my other dissertators, Julie Jordan, Bruce Kirle, Rose Malague, and Alisa Roost. Engaging with my students' work gives me opportunities to learn that I always appreciate.

My colleagues in the Department of Theatre and Dance at the University of Texas at Austin have already been supportive of the ideas in this book, though I've been at UT only a short time. I'd particularly like to thank Richard Isackes, who arranged a research leave in spring 2000 that allowed me to finish the manuscript, and Oscar Brockett, Charlotte Canning, Ann Daly, Sharon Grady, Joan Lazarus, Lynn Miller, and Suzan Zeder for their conversation and friendship.

Dwight Conquergood, Erin Hurley, Danny Kleinman, Susan Leonardi, Vicki Patraka, and Tamsen Wolff read drafts of parts of this material in various stages of its development, and gave me enormously useful feedback. Laurie Beth Clark shared experiences, opinions, and ideas with me through her years of chairing at the University of Wisconsin–Madison. Kate Davy read drafts and most helpfully, talked through institutional and administrative issues with me from her own experiences as dean and provost. Miranda Joseph shared facts about the situation at the University of Arizona that would have been much more difficult to find on my own.

Several people read and commented on the entire manuscript of *Geographies of Learning* at various stages. An anonymous reader for Wesleyan provided very detailed, specific suggestions, many of which I was happy to incorporate. My friend and CLAGS colleague Harriet Malinowitz gave me tough criticism that provoked my further thinking. Robyn Wiegman suggested numerous helpful structural improvements in her two separate, very generous readings of the manuscript. My friend and colleague at the University of Texas at Austin, Lisa Moore, helped motivate me to complete the book with her enthusiastic comments and suggested that each chapter end with a set of "ten commandments." Ann Pellegrini, in addition to being my friend and buddy on the CLAGS board (and a fellow scotch aficionado), gave me very smart, detailed feedback that propelled me toward the final revisions. She also suggested that I write more explicitly about pleasure, which I happily attempted to do.

Holly Hughes, Deb Margolin, Tim Miller, Peggy Shaw, Alina Troyano, Lois Weaver, and Paula Vogel inspire me with their art and their activism. This book is written to honor their lives and their work.

Ramon Rivera-Servera, my research assistant and dissertation student at the University of Texas at Austin, helped me finish the bibliography and provided the most helpful resource list. I wouldn't have been able to complete this project without his generous help and his fine labor.

I'm grateful to Lisa McGrath for being smart and exacting and generous with her support. She kept me sane and helped me to think in complex, self-reflexive ways during the very complicated two years when I was finishing this manuscript. Her insistence that I, too, am an artist, was a lovely gift, one that encouraged and enabled my writing.

Peggy Phelan was a continually clever and comforting source of companionship and advice during my stint as an administrator, especially when we were both chairing our separate departments. I want to thank her for letting me vent and for venting with me, with humor and intelligence and clear-sightedness. Her friendship and her scholarship make these often impossible struggles seem worthwhile.

Suzanna Tamminen and Tom Radko, at Wesleyan University Press, have been continually supportive of this project. I appreciate their interest in and commitment to my work.

Finally, Stacy Wolf read every word of this manuscript more times than I can count. Her insightful comments and suggestions, her smart engagement with my arguments and ideas, her support for my polemics, carried me through every moment of my writing. She's my constant source of motivation, inspiration, and delight.

:

I want to thank the publishers of these journals for permission to reprint the following articles, which have been incorporated, extended, revised, rearranged, and in some cases rethought for publication here. "Geographies of Learning: Theatre Studies, Performance, and the 'Performative'" appeared in *Theatre Journal* 45.4 (December 1993): 417–441. "Building a Theatrical Vernacular: Responsibility, Community, and Ambivalence in Queer Theatre" appeared in *Modern Drama* 39 (March 1996): 1–15. "Producing Knowledges That Matter: Practicing Performance Studies through Theatre Studies" was published in *TDR (The Drama Review): The Journal of Performance Studies* 40.4 (winter 1996): 9–19. "Advocacy and Activism: Identity, Curriculum, and Theatre Studies in the Twenty-First Century" appeared in *Theater Topics* 7.1 (March 1997): 1–10.

chapter one
Laying Out the Terrain

As a scholar and an administrator whose primary work has been to translate theory into practice and back, I've found that each of my three academic locations—theater and performance studies, lesbian/gay/queer studies, and women's studies—is fraught with remarkably similar divisions around these terms, each of which challenges its scholars in a slightly different context. Each field is shaped by tensions between those who purportedly "do" (as if one could "do" without thinking) and those assumed only to "think" (as if thinking could ever be merely so). Practitioners and activists disparage the work of scholars, especially "theorists," and some academics remove themselves from more direct action in a larger public sphere. All three fields are riven with conflicts over the value of theory versus practice and over the value of poststructuralist theory versus empiricist scholarship. Working together, these two sets of conflicts produce an unwitting alliance between radical activists and conservative scholars against progressive scholarship. This alliance, I argue, is dangerous because it puts the future of public education, and especially radical work on social relations within it, at risk. In these pages, I argue that it's vitally important that activists and academics, theorists and critics and more positivist scholars, find ways to interrupt our repetition of these debates and learn to work together productively.

The disdain and distrust with which academics and activists in the feminist and lesbian/gay/queer movements and artists and critics in theater studies sometimes hold one another is counterproductive, if not destructive. Working together, we might enhance our mutual progress toward social justice, more liberal democratic education, and the flourishing of the arts as a social entitlement and a rich site of critical engagement. Those of us who focus on intersecting issues of gender, race, sexuality, nation, ability, transculturalism, citizenship, and more, labor in a conservative social context. We can hardly afford to alienate ourselves from one another, when our desire for social change is more often than not the same. In *Geographies of Learning*, I share my own experience of these frustrating divisions and suggest concrete ways to overcome them. My concern here is to trouble how the theory/practice divide has hobbled academics' and activists' and artists' thinking about their work.

Although my focus here is quite specific, this conflict erupts in many disciplines between theorists and historians or between cultural studies scholars and more textually inclined critics. In the 1990s, the Association of Literary Critics and Scholars was established as an alternative to the Modern Language Association, and the National Association of Scholars was founded as a professional organization for conservative faculty. These groups exemplify the contentions between those who use their skills to look at knowledge in contexts often forged by identity constructs, and those who want to study texts or history or any form of knowledge outside of social (or what they consider "political") considerations.

These debates occur regularly in theater studies and performance studies, when academics dispute one another's methods, and when poststructuralist theorists and cultural studies scholars lock horns with more positivist historians and with those whose preferences run to new criticism. At the same time, those who teach the practical business of theater and performance—acting, directing, playwriting, speech, voice, design, movement—are often simply hostile to theory, regardless of its particular method or inflection, and privilege a more utilitarian view of knowledge in the field.

If theater academics and practitioners worry over the primacy of theory versus practice in how their departments allocate resources of time and money, women's studies and lesbian/gay/queer studies programs suffer these and other struggles because of their relatively recent status as established academic programs or departments. Many women's studies programs were founded beginning in the mid- to late seventies in colleges and universities around the United States. The civil rights and feminist movements lead women to advocate for a rigorous study of gender across disciplines as well as in separate programs set up to counter the historical absence of a focus on women in academic study. Likewise, lesbian/gay/queer studies programs, in the late eighties and nineties, although there are fewer of them relative to women's studies programs, were established to redress a glaring absence of attention to sexuality at the heart of academic curricula. Lesbian/gay/queer studies, too, found its roots in a social movement, as queer civil rights activism in the eighties and nineties became more publicly visible. Both women's studies and lesbian/gay/queer studies began with a concern for adding to the store of knowledge information about populations that hadn't before been considered. As they have matured, these fields have moved on to investigate the methods of producing knowledge, offering feminist theory and queer theory as ways of looking at any content matter through the explanatory, investigatory lenses of gender and sexuality.

Women's studies and lesbian/gay/queer studies, too, struggle with tensions between their incarnations as academic fields of knowledge and their origins in and connections to social movements in which their intellectual work might actually reshape cultural meanings. The difference between vernacular and expert knowledge in both fields has become a site of contention, as activists accuse academics of producing ideas irrelevant to the concerns of those still working at the "grassroots" level on issues of policy, legislation, and civil rights.[1]

In lesbian/gay/queer studies, the theory/practice split opens a divide between academics and activists, especially since, in the late nineties, "queer theory" has become so prevalent in what were once simply lesbian and gay studies. Queer theory has now gained a kind of radical chic and has been both profiled and disparaged by mainstream media. But activists more and more dismiss the pursuit of theoretical insight as elitist and irrelevant to the direct action they engage around issues like AIDS funding, domestic partnership benefits, the possibility of same-sex marriage, and other social issues.

Women's studies has suffered similar tensions between feminist theory and feminist practice. Ironically, the American feminist movement has splintered and faltered, thanks, among other things, to hostile representations in the mainstream press, and to a new generation of "postfeminist," highly noticeable young women writers such as Katie Roiphe and Naomi Wolf. But women's studies has consolidated its gains as a program or department on many college campuses. Majors, minors, and in some cases graduate degrees in the field have proliferated although in many (but not all) cases, programs have moved away from a direct connection to what remains of the feminist movement. Feminist theorizing or feminist methods are now ubiquitous across disciplines, in some cases obviating the need for separate departments for the study of women. But tensions about using certain kinds of continental theories still inflect teaching and learning in women's studies.

I want to mediate these tensions in *Geographies of Learning*. My aim, in this book, is to describe the theory/practice divide in all three interdisciplines, while crafting an argument toward its profitable resolution. I'll argue that progressive academics need to translate and promote the usefulness of their work to wider audiences, and that activists need to respect and engage the potential of knowledge generated in academic settings. "Theory" itself is not always political. But the poststructuralist brand of theorizing that galvanized the American academic community in the eighties and nineties has always been inflected with radical ideologies, since it was cut on the teeth of identity politics that had in many cases fought to establish identity area studies (women's studies, African American studies, other critical race and ethnic studies, lesbian and gay studies) on college campuses. Because of its political inflections, poststructuralist theorizing has become a flashpoint for disputes internal to disciplines, and for conservative mass media commentators eager to deride what they see as a too politicized, activist academy. On the other hand, poststructuralist theory is often dismissed as antiutilitarian and perhaps even antithetical to the goals of political work by those doing community activism, and even by some progressive teachers. Students often resist poststructuralist theory, as I explain here in chapter 6. My women's studies students at the University of Wisconsin–Madison much admired bell hooks's suggestion that they go door to door, talking revolution, and railed against the necessity that they learn complicated vocabularies that they felt would make them unable to speak with anyone.[2]

Contestations over theory versus practice are particularly pernicious in the arts, because of historical frictions between artists and critics, and the romantic presumption that thought ruins creativity. While poststructuralism is often deplored, "theory" also becomes shorthand for research, analysis, scholarship, or any kind of academic work or critical thinking. For example, at a conference in March 1998 on women and film at Barnard College, scholar Patty White remarked that her students often claim that learning feminist theory ruins their film-viewing experiences.[3] Once they know how film works, and once they have the ideological tools to engage it critically, the unalloyed pleasure they once took from representation is tarnished by insight, by perspective, and by new knowledge. Similarly, in a feminist theater course I taught at UW–Madison, I recall one of my students bemoaning the fact that she could now no longer watch reruns of *Little House on the Prairie* without noticing that there were no Jews or people of color in Michael Landon's neighborhood. The student mourned her loss of innocence, along with what she felt as the corruption of her pleasure. My job, as her teacher, was to persuade her that critical thinking has its own pleasures.

In November 1997, at a conference in New York City sponsored by the Women's Project and Productions on women in theater, very few of the panelists used feminist theory or analysis to trace out the situation of women in the field or their status in (and as) representation. Feminist theories could have answered some of the questions that were posed throughout the two-day event, but instead, feminism was dismissed as an old-fashioned, historical, intellectual exercise, and the participants were for the most part resoundingly anti-intellectual.[4]

But theory is not antiaesthetic or anticreative, and *thinking* about theater might actually enhance its value within American culture. My own work in feminist theory empowered me intellectually, politically, artistically, and creatively, making me a more appreciative spectator of more diverse performance work and a more conceptually oriented theater director. My theoretical reading also allowed me to see theater as even more central to the project of culture. Materialist feminism, deconstruction, and poststructuralism suggest that what people make of representation is historical, contextual, changeable. Theater is an ideological project, a place at which resistance is possible. Given the right critical and creative tools, active, rather than passive, consumption of theater and film and dance and performance contributes to a richer conversation about art and its efficacy. Teaching critical reading skills and theory is enormously important, because students need tools to intervene in representation, or even just to consume it critically and passionately. My goal, as a feminist teacher, is not to force my students toward some artificial consensus; they won't always use the critical tools I'd like to share with them in the same ideological or practical way. But giving them tools empowers them, regardless of how students use them. And rather than dampening their enthusiasm for art, critical tools can enhance their understanding.[5]

A widespread backlash against poststructuralist theory in the humanities (especially against queer theory) has been strong in the last several years, as critics complain that academics who use certain kinds of theoretical vocabularies have created an insular, self-referential elite whose work has no currency outside its own sphere.[6] But new ideas need new languages. The academics I most admire are trying to reinvigorate language to describe new possibilities for social relations. Some high theoretical work is often too opaque to be readily or widely useful, but that's not its purpose. It has been generated in an academic context that deserves its own language and the significance of completely new (and newly articulated) ideas.

The specific attack on queer theory appears to be about jargon and language, but it also exemplifies the academic/activist divide. Hate crimes legislation, the press forward for gay and lesbian marriages, the complexities of immigration and citizenship for queers and queer couples, and the need for further funding for AIDS research are urgent issues that steer lesbian and gay politics. Activists often become impatient with academic work that appears to have no immediate use value. But theoretical work pushes at the boundaries of knowledge, expanding understandings of lesbian/gay/queer subjectivity and experience that will ultimately find their place in the social movement.

People rarely take scientists to task for their jargon, which is considered necessary to the advancement of specialized knowledge. But scholars in the humanities who use high theory regularly find themselves challenged by commentators who resent or despise the density of the language. The presumption in the humanities is of wide accessibility for "humanistic" knowledge and for art objects prided for their "universality." On the other hand, some scientists do write for popular audiences, because science matters to people's daily lives in real ways. In the arts and humanities, only reviewers or essayists tend to write for mainstream trade presses. As a result, very little cultural criticism is published that's accessible, sophisticated, and theoretically inflected. Progressives in academia have recently moved to reinvigorate and expand a discourse of "public intellectuals" who can speak authoritatively in trade presses, largely in response to their perceived lack of connection to a wider audience for their ideas. Some academics are interested in translating their theory into the vernacular, so that it can be useful to activists doing a different kind of work and so that it can engage a wider public conversation. Not every scholar writing high theory will be interested in or able to do the work of mediating among various constituencies at once; but for some people, such translations will be invaluable.

In *Geographies of Learning*, I argue that it's possible to use high theory to develop and extend new knowledge in the arts and humanities and at the same time (or later) translate it for readers and artists and critics to whom it might be useful in other, nonacademic contexts. Most scholars translate regularly to students when they introduce them to theoretical concepts for the first time in class. If progressive thinking takes public pedagogy as a common goal, such translations might become routine in practical, political ways in wider contexts. The onus is on progressive academics to maintain several audiences.

For whatever reason, I've always seen myself as a translator and mediator of the theory/practice debate. My scholarship for the last twenty years has addressed issues of theory to practitioners and vice versa, as a theater critic speaking to artists, as a lesbian scholar speaking to activists, and as a feminist looking at theories of social change as they happen in performance and representation. In the last seven years, I've worked as chair of a large theater department on a Midwestern state university campus; as chair of a Ph.D. program in theater studies in New York City; as executive director of a center for queer studies, also in New York; and as president of a national association for theater educators. In every case, these theory/practice debates pressed daily on my work. And given my concurrent administrative positions, issues raised in theater and performance studies have been inseparable from those raised in lesbian/gay/queer studies or women's studies. In *Geographies of Learning*, I map these congruities and divergences, speaking to both sides of all three divides.

Servicing the Field: Academics, Advocacy, and Activism

Professional service has been a way for me to contribute to shaping my fields, and what they mean to both academic and public culture. I've also come to see university service as a place to do activist work. For example, as chair at the University of Wisconsin–Madison's Department of Theatre and Drama from 1993 to 1994, I could articulate the value and idiosyncracies of an arts degree in a research institution and work to actualize some of my ideas about theory and practice mingling at the site of theater studies. As deputy executive officer and then executive officer (chair) of the Ph.D. program in theater at the Graduate Center of the City University of New York (CUNY) from 1994 to 1999, I was able to argue the value of theater studies as an interdisciplinary research site and to agitate for continuing ties to the professional and community theater resources in the city. As the executive director of the Center for Lesbian and Gay Studies (CLAGS) at CUNY from 1996 to 1999, I learned a great deal about the relationship between academics and activists. I worked to sharpen CLAGS' mission as a research center that makes a direct and useful contribution to gay and lesbian communities, as well as creating a space for more rarified and theoretical ideas to flourish. As the president of the Association for Theatre in Higher Education (ATHE), I used my public position to write letters to editors about arts defundings around the country and to rally our membership toward a proactive, activist stance on national arts advocacy issues.

Coming to the academy from the social movement and moving from faculty to administrator and back have prompted my own musings about whether it's possible to maintain radical, oppositional politics in institutions that are becoming increasingly conservative. Universities and colleges are run more and more on corporate models, with an eye on the fiscal bottom line. Public institutions fight for increasingly smaller shares of state or city budgets and often operate under the stewardship of politically conservative activist trustees. I'm interested in how faculty and administrators who would maintain progressive politics can function in these environments. I watched first UW and then CUNY conduct downsizing exercises that reduced their liberal propensities, experiencing firsthand at CUNY, especially, the ways in which conservative fiscal and ideological policies can deeply influence educational decisions. In 1998, the CUNY board of trustees purposefully ended nearly twenty-five years of open admissions on its campuses and banished remedial education from its senior colleges. Under the banner of a return to "excellence" and of fiscal prudence and responsibility (which some see as an excuse for racist policies of exclusion), the CUNY trustees dimmed educational opportunities for the city's most impoverished students, who need the career possibilities that university degrees and higher education bring. The CUNY trustees have compromised the chance for immigrant and poor youth to educate themselves in an American university system that could let them influence and be shaped by cultural norms and subcultural resistances. Now that they've reduced the student population, some predict that the CUNY trustees will reshape the curriculum next, intent on reestablishing a conventional, canonical core of knowledge.

I taught women's studies just as it was being institutionalized as an academic area, and I've recently witnessed the arrival of lesbian/gay/queer studies into the academy in a similar fashion. Some activists believe that academics in once outlawed fields now lead privileged lives, with livable wages and decent benefits and the job security of tenure. Many of us do boast of such lives. But often, these sharp criticisms of academics are founded on generalizations and fail to account for the ways in which context determines how individual academics fare. For example, this critique disregards the academy as a working environment with its own discriminatory practices.

Many gay and lesbian academics are on the front lines of social change in their institutions. They risk their jobs and sometimes their lives to be out, to establish programs, to teach their courses, to raise the issue of sexuality to administrators and students who would rather rest secure in their own often heterosexist, if not homophobic, misperceptions. After all, most colleges and universities are not located in more liberal, urban, coastal cities. And institutions tend to mystify their practices and their methods of decision making. As a result, it's sometimes hard to prove that, for instance, a faculty person didn't get tenure not because his or her publications were inadequate, but because he or she is lesbian, gay, or queer, or because his or her committees or administrators didn't like his or her politics. Many academics work purposefully to generate knowledge that can be useful to the activist movement, and others generate theory that will lead people to see social relations differently, to imagine them radically transformed and equitable. If knowledge in the field and knowledge of labor conditions in the academy is shared, translated, and contextualized, then although they work in necessarily separate spheres, the work that academics and activists do might become common currency, with use value across the academy and the movement.

Academics and activists, and artists and critics need each other even more in this particular historical moment. Increasingly, the dissension between progressive academics and conservative boards of trustees means that academics work in hostile climates similar to the ones progressive artists face in this country. Boards of trustees at state universities are becoming conservative and vocal in their activism, interfering in academic conferences and challenging faculty rights to tenure. Likewise, federal, state, and local arts funding organs are becoming more and more conservative in their decisions. As I'll describe in chapter 3, theater-producing organizations as diverse as the Charlotte (North Carolina) Repertory Theatre, Out North in Anchorage, Alaska, the Manhattan Theatre Club in New York, and the Esperanza Center for Peace and Justice in San Antonio have all seen their funding cut or their work vilified by activists on the conservative right. These legislators or city council people or granting organizations refuse to acknowledge the impact and import of especially gay and lesbian theater, but really of any theater or performance that deviates from a white, middle-class, heterosexual norm, or that engages bodies in direct and visceral ways.

Charting the State of the Profession

This book extends conversations begun by other writers, primarily in English departments in the United States (Cary Nelson, Michael Bérubé, Gerald Graff, Richard Ohmann), who have commented on the state of the profession from a largely politically invested, mostly leftist orientation. I can only speculate about why these conversations haven't been publicly staged in other disciplines, such as the ones I'm addressing here. English departments are often the largest, best supported departments in colleges and universities; tenured faculty in their ranks can afford to launch institutional critiques, because they speak from relatively secure positions. Tenured faculty in, for instance, theater studies, are less sanguine, however, since their departments are often in danger of being cut off from resources or exiled from the curriculum. Because of their charge to teach composition and critical reading skills, as well as to offer "core" knowledge in literary studies, English departments often employ many adjuncts and part-time lecturers. As a result, labor issues are visible and central to faculty discussions, especially when progressive faculty see part-timers *as* workers, whose labor is often alienated and exploited. Finally, the Modern Language Association, which comprises faculty and graduate students in English and foreign language departments, provides a national professional forum in which institutional issues about knowledge production, about the condition of faculty as laborers, about the corporatization of the academy, and about the other pressing concerns I touch on here can be debated rigorously and visibly. The MLA has, in fact, presented several resolutions to its members for voting over the last several years that explicitly address the status of graduate students, unionization, and other labor-based concerns.

I'm concerned about academics as workers and with the university as a marketplace in which ideas become commodities. The market moves writers to value certain ideas, to choose certain topics over others, or to orient their materials in particular ways to appeal to the widest possible readership. Where the single-author monograph could once be a model of original, sometimes esoteric thinking, the increasing financial pressure under which university presses operate means that these books are more and more difficult to produce. Marketing needs often determine content, method, and style in university press publishing, which in turn influences research and scholarship decisions from the outset. And because achieving tenure requires more and more publications, especially at larger research institutions, junior faculty are immediately compelled to slant their work toward the markets of the university presses that will publish them and facilitate their drive toward job security.

At the start of the twenty-first century, any responsible academic needs to be self-conscious about the context in which they teach and work and to understand the politics that influence the academy. We have to think continually about labor issues: the prevalence of exploitative, low-paying adjunct instruction (at CUNY, for example, 60 percent of courses system-wide are now taught by part-time adjunct instructors, who have few benefits and little job security); the retrenchment that's allowing many public universities to eliminate degree programs altogether, whether or not their faculty are tenured, under the rubric of financial exigency; the threats to tenure that could remake understandings of academic freedom; the move to hire corporate executives as chancellors and presidents, as more and more colleges and universities adopt business models to remain financially viable; the retraction of state support from public education (so that institutions that were once state-funded, then were state-supported, are in many cases now simply state-located);[7] the court-mandated end of affirmative action in Texas, Florida, and California and other university systems; the widespread tensions over sexual harassment policies and cases on campuses; the speedup caused by new technologies and the ways in which the Internet isolates us from one another, while it appears to bring us closer together; the challenge posed by distance learning to a history of live, community-based education; the antieducation sentiments of many state legislators, who want research faculty to teach more and be paid less, even though arts and humanities professors already earn far less than those in the sciences or than the private sector norm; and finally, the virulent antiarts sentiment inflamed by the conservative attack on public funding for the arts, the implications of which resonate across theater studies, women's studies, and lesbian/gay/queer studies. Issues that seem at first glance to be unique actually connect quite clearly, interlocking with broader social and academic concerns.

Critically addressing the state of the profession, as I do in *Geographies of Learning*, seems timely because of the increasing conservatism of public views on education and knowledge production. In the last ten or so years, conservative media commentary on higher education has moved into an increasingly hostile, aggressive mode.[8] Academics, especially those who teach at public institutions, are more and more under attack and less and less understood as people who labor in institutions whose goal is essentially to produce and distribute varieties of old and new knowledge. American anti-intellectualism and the end of the century's fiscal and ideological conservatism are largely responsible for these ill-begotten attacks. Higher education is an easy target for the Right, because American colleges and universities since the sixties have been stereotyped as hotbeds of radicalism or liberalism. State legislatures and boards of trustees call for more and more "quality control" and productivity assessment, shifting higher education to corporate models of use and efficacy. They present challenges to long-held assumptions about campuses as protectors of tenure, free speech, and a diverse curriculum, and as places of public debate and provocation.

But significantly, conservative narratives of academics' radicalism or laziness are left to stand largely unchallenged. Aside from scattered progressive voices writing most often in university presses, little concerted effort has been launched to counter the Right's and the press's often outrageous claims about how little academics work and how badly they teach and how irrelevant or outlandish is their research. *Geographies of Learning* offers ways to build such a counterdiscourse.

Students and the Ethics of Labor

While universities and colleges cut budgets to stretch their resources, a new generation of undergraduate students in the late nineties and early twenty-first century considers their education less as a path to new knowledge and more as a means to an end. Vocational training more and more delimits educational choice. The *Chronicle of Higher Education*'s survey of 1998's college freshmen indicated that the majority of the new class of students view higher education only as a means to a paycheck that will allow them to enter American consumer culture with the highest possible disposable income.[9] If students aren't encouraged to expand their understanding of history and culture and to develop and explore theories about how they work, but are only motivated to prepare themselves for the capitalist marketplace, what will happen to disciplines built on humanistic knowledge or the arts? If students focus on vocational training, the humanities courses they choose will most likely be canonical and conservative. What becomes of women's studies, and gay and lesbian studies, and critical race studies, and theater and performance studies in such an increasingly pragmatic university and college environment? Who will be the conscience of the university? Who will continue to persuade students that ethics, values, and larger social commitments can also be fostered through education, along with the skills to make a living?

While progressive faculty might persuade undergraduate students to use arts and humanities training to develop critical skills in their understandings of subjectivity, what is a faculty person's responsibility to graduate students, whose training is rightly more invested in professional goals? The demands on these students to professionalize early are growing, as the job market continues to be competitive. Does the curriculum in which Ph.D. students are being trained adequately reflect the needs of the market in which they'll compete? Should graduate training programs pander to the market, even knowing it's impossible to predict what jobs will be available in any given five- or ten-year period? Or should progressive faculty insist on their own beliefs in adequate education, whether it's a core curriculum or a wide range of elective options? Students often ask me if they should tailor their dissertation topics to what they perceive as market demands. I tell them that they absolutely should not, that their dissertation should be a measure of their commitments and values, a demonstration of what they care about in the field and the methods with which they approach its study. But that the question must be asked indicates their level of anxiety and frustration with a shrinking market.

In theater studies, students are required more and more to straddle the theoretical/academic and practical sides of the field. A student who's receiving a Ph.D. and training in theory and history and criticism will still have to be adept enough at teaching acting to persuade a search committee of his or her worth. Despite the divisions between theory and practice in most larger departments in research universities, theater Ph.D.'s are more and more required to be generalists, to be able to do a little bit of everything in a field with multiple components. As a result, it's harder to train specialists in the more esoteric fields of history or theory, since such training takes more time. How can students expect to be good directors or designers or acting teachers, and to write original, publishable dissertations? At the same time, this tight, idiosyncratic market might eventually ameliorate the theory/practice conundrum, as more and more students are required to do both if they anticipate academic employment.

To be considered for jobs, graduate students need to publish articles and eventually books, to present papers at conferences and to network in a professional setting that is itself market-driven. The job market is often at odds with publishing trends. For example, students writing in gay and lesbian studies often find their work contracted at the dissertation stage because of the increasing amount of publishing in the field. But the same students are sometimes less successful securing tenure-track teaching positions because there are very few jobs posted in lesbian/gay/queer studies per se. Since there are very few lesbian/gay/queer programs at colleges and universities around the country, students training in the field also need to maintain a disciplinary allegiance, so that they can increase their pool of potential positions. Likewise, for women's studies, most schools establish programs, rather than departments, which typically means appointing tenure-track faculty jointly with other disciplines, departments that then become their "tenure homes." As I discuss in chapter 6, juggling the demands of two fields means these faculty are doubly (sometimes triply) pressured by their institutional labor. The general job situation for Ph.D.'s in the arts and humanities has erupted into crisis for the MLA, whose graduate student caucus resents the lack of attention paid to their plight by MLA officers. How are faculty responsible for ensuring gainful employment for their students?[10]

Of course, academia has never been a pure place, separate from capitalist, ideological, and political strife. But what concerns me, in *Geographies of Learning*, is the way in which those scholars and teachers who bring to their work progressive political and cultural commitments can navigate in conservative environments. How can we conduct our scholarship and write our research in ways that have wide appeal, outside of market structures that might encourage us to gear our work toward some audiences and not others? How can we bring an activist aspect to our teaching, when boards of trustees and regents intervene more and more in the selection of course materials and in the organization of campus-sponsored conferences? How can we continue to bring progressive values to campuses on which the blanket disbursal of student activities fees has been challenged by right-wing students and conservative national organizations attempting to deny resources to women's centers, multicultural centers, lesbian/gay/queer centers, all because they considered them partisan and politically motivated?

Responding to the Right by Remapping Values

A favorite trashing device of conservatives writing about education is to suggest that the humanities have devolved into so-called victim studies. This misreading is a remnant of the culture wars.[11] Conservatives trash identity politics and identity area studies in the academy by suggesting that these fields are narcissistic, that they allow people to study "themselves" to the exclusion of whole worlds of knowledge. The Left disparages identity studies because it argues that class is most fundamental to progressive struggles for social justice.[12] But in fact, the effort to establish women's studies, lesbian/gay/queer studies, and race and ethnic studies on American campuses has been to enfold the experiences and ideas of once marginalized people more fully into the contours of knowledge. These fields want to knit the knowledge they've produced more completely into a diverse curriculum. Conservatives argue against the separatism (or so-called balkanization) that establishing these fields seems to imply. But as identity area studies have become an established part of university and college curricula, the movement is actually toward (or a return to?) a more liberal humanist environment for education. These fields propose that students research exactly those people who aren't like themselves, with an eye toward commonalities, as well as important political, cultural, and social differences.

Since the success of identity studies in many academic contexts, experience has become a legitimate site of knowledge, although poststructuralist, and "postidentitarian" scholars continue to disavow an undertheorized, more facile reliance on experience as the only source of knowledge. Scholarship has become embodied in people whose lives it reflects and reaches out to move and persuade those whose lives are not necessarily the same. This is not "victim studies." Women's studies and gay and lesbian studies and critical race and ethnic studies offer renderings of cultures that comprise the dominant, that make it textured, varied, and rich, that fragment it productively with resistance and dissent. As scholars of the diaspora argue, no culture is pure or originary, and our nostalgia for simple homelands is always suspect.[13]

By using language like "victim studies," the Right has perverted American culture's image of what happens in progressive classrooms, and in scholarship by radical academics, characterizing it as corrupt, self-serving, undemocratic, un-American. In fact, progressives teaching and writing on college campuses inspire creative oppositional energy by advocating for more and broader participation in the principles of democratic citizenship and by continuing to advance marginalized agendas from positions of relative power and influence. If the academy is necessarily a site of struggle, as new ideas continually compete for place and attention over those that are better ensconced—those deemed "common sense" by previous generations of Americans—then surely oppositional voices must continue to flourish there. The academy is perhaps the one large influential public forum left in American life in which debates can be staged productively, and in which those otherwise disenfranchised from the largest public discourses can find their concerns studied, researched, and examined as worthy and meaningful. As Robin Kelley notes, universities "have historically been places where alternatives to exploitation and oppression have been discussed and imagined in an institutional setting. They have been the sites of historic movements for social change precisely because the ostensible function of the university is to interrogate knowledge, society, and history."[14]

Progressive scholars can help reshape the discussion of values that has been promoted and coopted in insidiously conservative ways by the fundamentalist Right. We can no longer shy away from offering our own systems of belief as alternatives, framed not as nihilist counterarguments, but as full-fledged value structures of our own. For those of us versed in contemporary theory, poststructuralism has revised our understandings of what it means to be agents in specific historical moments. We know much more about the complexities of power and its invidious strategies. But we can't be overcome with cynicism, we can't finally move people through irony. Our passions, our pleasures, the elegance of our worldviews need to be communicated as values to which belief adheres. We need to teach values, to encourage students to make political commitments, informed by global politics, as we train them in skills and knowledge. Teaching values will help reshape how knowledge matters and might allow us to have real effect in contemporary political systems.

I'm not suggesting that we wrest away from the Right its own language. The Millennium March on Washington, cosponsored by the Human Rights Campaign and the Metropolitan Community Church in April 2000, touted a platform that assimilated mainstream values while trying to inflect them with a lesbian and gay sensibility. But a queer march for "faith and family," without significantly revising those values and ideologies, does little for the cause of more radical social reimaginings. The values progressive academics teach are more creative, more inspired, and more motivating of more profound social change. Progressive values might express "faith," for example, outside of organized religious institutions and might describe "family" as several non-monogamous, interracial lesbians and their pets, without the necessity of children *or* marriage to make their kinship legitimate.

Intersecting Worlds of Performance and Pleasure

Since performance in the last decade has become a continual point of contention for conservatives eager to inveigh against homosexuality, feminism, and "multiculturalism," this book addresses the possibilities of theater studies in the academy to offer a community forum for thinking through vexed social, political, and sexual issues. Likewise, in *Geographies of Learning*, I proselytize for theater as an intensely social, still potentially radical site of cultural transformation. As Bonnie Marranca notes, theater is "the only cultural space in which felt speech and concentrated listening and looking is preserved." She goes on, "In this realm one can discover qualities increasingly disappearing from contemporary experience, such as privacy and intimacy and spiritual feeling."[15] I, too, believe in this particular, local, perhaps even utopian promise of theater, in which temporary communities assemble to look at social relations, to be provoked, moved, enraged, made proud by what human beings can do when they're set in relation to one another. Performance offers us a practice that lets us rehearse new social arrangements, in ways that require visceral investments of bodies, of time, of personal and cultural history.

Performer-scholar Anna Deveare Smith exemplifies using theorized, practiced performance toward what she calls "public advocacy." She wants students in her classes "who have been thinking about social issues and would like to try them out, as a way of knowing the issues differently."[16] She describes "collaborative, public advocacy," in which theater students and scholars join with "like-minded" people who "have an interest in learning more about who and what society is and how to speak *for* it and about it."[17] Smith raises the specter of values, when she asks, "What kinds of people do we send into the world in the name of theatre?"[18]

In *Geographies of Learning*, performance links the three interdisciplines under discussion. I use performance in my teaching to (in Dwight Conquergood's words) "privilege particular, participatory, dynamic, intimate, precarious, embodied experience grounded in historical process, contingency, and ideology."[19] Using performance in the classroom helps to disrupt some of the more conventional ways power circulates between professor and student, offering students a chance to try *out* by trying *on* different kinds of experiences and ways of approaching new knowledge. I offer performance here as a tool that might be useful in other progressive classrooms, calling forth as it often does deeper and more meaningful investments from faculty and students alike.

Performance often unleashes the desire that flows just below the surface of the settings in which we work. I believe we are moved through institutional structures like universities because we're motivated by desire—the desire for knowledge, for pleasure, for the intensity of relating that comes from studying and engaging artistic and social and political practices together. Teaching works by transference and countertransference, as students see their teachers as their best selves and aspire to become them, and as teachers find in their students aspects of themselves and their own lives. The intensity of these relationships creates a condition of longing and loss, of need and empathy that can sometimes eroticize a classroom. But eroticizing and sexualizing are quite different things. The complicated discourse of sexual harassment during the last decade has made it difficult for progressive academics to talk about any kind of pleasure in the classroom. While harassment policies protect students from inappropriate and unconscionable sexual advances from professors abusing their power, these policies often create a campus climate in which fear of litigation takes precedent in relationships between professors and their students, in the classroom and outside. These policies, and the litigious social climate, make it difficult to address what I consider the inevitable erotics of the classroom. How can classrooms *not* be infused with desire, when students and their teacher gather to discuss ideas with passion, energy, and the commitment to an ideal future?

I argue here for pleasure as a value that progressive academics might resurrect in their teaching and celebrate more publicly in their scholarly work. Since the Right has portrayed us as lazy, they've made it difficult for us to speak, without embarrassment, of how our lives *are* filled with pleasure, even while we're engaged in hard, long, attenuated work. These conservative myths, flung into popular culture as simple truths about academics, need to be countered with persuasive, nuanced accounts of our pride in our work, and descriptions of how pleasure and labor don't have to be mutually exclusive.

For instance, we could demonstrate, to our students and to our readers and listeners, how we're motivated by the erotics of ideas, by the partialness of knowledge, by the presentness of ourselves in relationship to each other, using performance or any other mode of critical pedagogy. We could use our positions as teachers and scholars to put the body back into thought, to think of pleasures like desire not as a space of absence that language can't lead us to, but as a space of social possibility to which our bodies lead us. If our politics are truly progressive, we have to speak what we know or what we think or what we want to know out into the culture, bringing to bear respect and even love on our own disagreements and generative misunderstandings.[20] We have to remind people that teaching and scholarship offer epistemologies, ways of knowing and understanding, even misunderstanding, that can be productive even if they aren't *re*productive.

Translations and Mediations

In *Geographies of Learning*, I map divisions and dissentions that stall the progress of acute, progressive knowledge production in the interdisciplines of theater and performance studies, women's studies, and lesbian/gay/queer studies. Chapter 2, "Translations: The Critic, the Community, and the Curriculum in Lesbian/Gay/Queer Studies," argues that the internecine sniping between lesbian/gay/queer activists and academics, and between queer performance artists and theater studies critics, can be avoided. I suggest that academics take time to consider the ways in which their ideas can move across public and academic intellectual and political fields, and that activists should recognize that colleges and universities, too, are sites of political struggle.[21] Changing consciousness remains key to political movement, and good teaching inevitably changes consciousness, whether or not an instructor avowedly teaches from an invested political perspective.

Chapter 3, "Theory, Practice, and Activism: Theater Studies and the Polemics of Performance," also argues that all teaching is advocacy and suggests that rather than trying to avoid issues that roil the public sphere, teachers should engage themselves and their students in pressing current debates. I argue that academics in theater and performance studies must see themselves as part of a larger cultural sphere, and use their classrooms and theaters to teach conflicts happening in society at large. For instance, the spate of arts defundings in the mid- to late nineties needs to be placed in the kinds of critical and historical contexts that faculty can provide. And theater professors training students to be artists must prepare them to face a conservative funding climate that will inevitably have impact on their work.

To remain progressive, and to make space for the generation and veneration of new ideas and new identities, academics must continually redraw institutional maps that determine how knowledge is produced. The interdisciplines of performance studies and cultural studies can work toward that end. I argue that in addition to touting their institutional remappings, these newly configured fields must remain attached in intimate ways to the public sphere and its contentions. As academics move into more interdisciplinary work, they can't be seduced into thinking that changing disciplinary borders substitutes for changing social relations.

Chapter 4, "Geographies of Learning: Theater Studies, Performance, and the 'Performative,'" extends this metadisciplinary argument, suggesting that theoretical tropes that abstract "performance" into the now popular "performativity" might profitably reconsider the materiality of theater as a palpable, embodied site of potential social change. Judith Butler's work on gender and performativity, and Eve Sedgwick's on sexuality and speech acts places performance qua performance in something of an ironic position in relation to these theories.[22] On one hand, people who'd never given it a thought suddenly see the potential in performance as a site of resistant political formations. On the other hand, the approaches to theatrical performance that theories of performativity spawned have been fairly promiscuous and dilettantish, rarely grounded in a history of the field and its own theoretical or critical suppositions.

I resist the recent poaching on theater studies, but my intent is not at all to shore up the borders of the field as a separate, singular discipline.[23] My intent, in "Geographies of Learning," is to suggest that scholars must be contextual and historical, rather than simply turning into metaphor a tradition—in this case performance—that comes with very compelling baggage of its own. My intent is to explain the richness and traditions of theater and performance as sites of engagement in their own right. The chapter argues both sides, insisting that theater studies has much to gain from the theoretical nuances of performativity, while scholars in feminist theory and queer theory who employ the trope when describing social relations have much to gain from considering the formal, intentional, ritualized aspects of performance.

Chapter 5, "Queer Theater: Theorizing a Theatrical Vernacular," performs an act of translation of the sort suggested in chapter 2. I argue here that opportunities to speak and lecture afford possibilities for using different kinds of language to communicate common meanings. As an example, I share the keynote I delivered at the queer theater conference organized by CLAGS in New York in 1995, raising questions about what it means to perform ideas for a specific community audience. I follow the keynote here with a critical, ethnographic assessment of the conference, to demonstrate how a critical consciousness can accompany a more vernacular way of engaging. The chapter ends with a discussion of current queer theater and performance, since this is another site at which the theory/practice debates and possibilities for social activism are played out.

Chapter 6, "Performance as Feminist Pedagogy," thinks through the institutionalization of women's studies and its effect on classroom practices. While conservative commentators who've rarely (if ever) set foot inside a feminist classroom spread misunderstandings and misconceptions about their contents and their methods, I find that many of those who consider themselves feminist teachers are actually quite conventional in their goals and strategies. At the same time, their challenge remains bringing radical, nontraditional content to university curricula that are now demanding more and more payoff, vocational training, and commitment to core knowledges.

Because teaching tends to be mystified, people don't really know what happens in feminist classrooms. The mass media is very good at perpetuating myths and rumors about how feminists and "multiculturalists" proselytize, how all they teach is victimization, and how a kind of mushy experiential learning is all that they value. These stories are useful, and the Right propagates them when they decry feminism and critical race and ethnic studies. But it's imperative that progressive educators working in these fields do more to educate people about what they do in their classrooms. What are their goals? What are their methods? What do they want students to do with what they learn? They need to be very clear about how and why they work, and to what ends, in their classrooms.

This is an important time to consider the place of gender and critical race studies in academic institutions. On one hand, identity area studies programs seem to be fairly well established on many campuses (although how well depends on geography, size, and local, city, and institutional politics). On the other hand, they're experiencing a backlash against identity studies. These attacks come from the Right, which despises the "multicultural" or in any way more diverse curriculum as a useless tangent from the "real knowledge" of the Western, Euroamerican "core." But they also come from the Left, from commentators who believe that identity politics has distracted us from the true concerns of the Left, like labor or a critique of capitalism. Scholars such as Todd Gitlin and Richard Rorty now accuse leftist scholars of doing research that's drained energy and time from more pressing national political concerns.[24] As Kelley argues, they "either do not understand or refuse to acknowledge that class is lived through race and gender. . . . The Gitlin . . . group makes the grave error of rendering movements struggling around issues of race, gender, and sexuality as inherently narrow and particularistic. The failure to conceive of these social movements as essential to the emancipation of the whole remains the fundamental stumbling block to building a deep and lasting class-based politics."[25] Those of us who focus on race and ethnicity, gender and sexuality have to guard against complacency and be watchful about the fronts from which the next offensives will arrive. But rather than being defensive or reactive, progressive faculty need to be proactive about describing the rigor of their teaching and their research, and articulate about why the knowledge they produce and teach matters. And obviously, those of us teaching in identity area studies have a large stake in national issues and international concerns; the focus of identity area studies is hardly as narrow and small as its detractors propose.

In the current political climate, it's also very important for scholars, teachers, and practitioners working on issues of race and gender and sexuality to form coalitions. Working together can help clarify that identity area studies, in the twenty-first century's academy, are not coextensive with identity politics; that in fact, much of the work on identity makes of it a much less stable, essentializing project than identity politics once proclaimed. Given downsizing and budget reductions, faculty working in identity area studies have to work together to find and share resources that will help them all survive. Team-teaching courses; writing curricular requirements that include all of their areas; writing grants for major public presentations, from performances to symposia, across identity areas; coalition building on institutional as well as political and intellectual levels can only help them all survive.

Geographies of Learning is in some ways a work of journalism, as it's meant to report on a debate that ranges across many disciplines, although I focus most resolutely here on these three. Much of it addresses knowledge produced and shared at conferences, meetings when the theory/practice debate is often most emotionally and urgently articulated. In gay and lesbian and queer studies, conferences still actively shape the field. New knowledge is offered for the first time at more and more meetings and symposia that often address the first convergence of ideas (the first conference on queer theater is addressed here, for example, as well as the first conference on queer theory and postcolonialism). But unlike mainstream journalism, which purports to be objective, this book is more my own very much invested chronicle, my own polemical argument for how the state of the profession and its relationship to various communities might change.

My own voice here shifts among several ways of speaking, moving from the personal, first-person narrative of my own investments and involvements, to a more critical engagement with theoretical and practical ideas. Using the personal voice has become a contentious issue, especially in recent feminist scholarship. Some critics suggest that the personal devalues scholarship, marking it as confessional and singular, individual and unique, blurring a border between the intellectual and the therapeutic.[26] My intent, here, is not at all to confess or to posit my experiences as a singular truth, but to ground my narrative in specific anecdotes that I think might, in fact, be widely recognizable to other faculty, informative for activists, and compelling for students. Too often, institutional systems make professors anonymous and mysterious, policing the borders between the public and the private. As a professor of theater, women's studies, and lesbian/gay/queer studies, I have always found those borders to be porous for me, as my research and scholarship has drawn deeply on my own passions, beliefs, and commitments. I can't imagine writing a project like this one without sharing my personal investments in the structures of knowledge I'd like to revise.

The two chapters that expand on previously published essays exemplify the range of voice this book employs. Although revised significantly for publication here, chapter 4, "Geographies of Learning," was originally published in *Theatre Journal*, the preeminent peer-reviewed publication in theater studies, as a metadisciplinary inquiry into the state of theater and performance studies and the then nascent use of "performativity." At the other end of the spectrum, chapter 5, "Queer Theater: Theorizing a Theatrical Vernacular," was originally presented as a keynote address and then published in *Modern Drama* with a critical précis of the conference attached. This article has also been extended for publication here. But part of my argument is that an academic's voice should be able to speak and be heard in many ways: in a rigorous critical tone, in a pedagogical tone, in a personal and passionate tone, and in a vernacular tone that speaks into variously constituted communities of listeners. All of those voices are present here. I hope this won't sound like cacophony, as much as it will strike a rather harmonious chord.

At the end of each of the following chapters, I've attached a "road map," a list of ten concrete suggestions for crossing the theory/practice divide. Often, these suggestions focus on performance as an ameliorating device. While I don't mean these suggestions to be prescriptive, I do mean them as evidence of my own sincere desire to be concrete, proactive, and creative in reimagining the many possible combinations of academic, activist, and artistic work.

In *Geographies of Learning*, I'm committed, throughout, to my own preoccupations with contemporary politics, with the possibility of community, and with the potential of the arts in the cultural sphere. I hope I'm persuasive about how much, indeed, they matter.

Translations

The Critic, the Community,

and the Curriculum in Lesbian/

Gay/Queer Studies

Speaking back and forth across different language communities requires a steady awareness of the ways in which ideology often works to make such translations difficult. Edward Said, for example, writes that "culture works very effectively to make invisible and even 'impossible' the actual *affiliations* that exist between the world of ideas and scholarship, on the one hand, and the world of brute politics, corporate and state power, and military force, on the other."[1] In the interest of forwarding lesbian/gay/queer politics in the academic and social spheres, we might work to make those affiliations obvious rather than obscure.

Historian Lisa Duggan makes a distinction among three arenas for lesbian/gay/queer political action that are useful in rethinking academic work as activism. She distinguishes these arenas as "1) the reform politics of liberal and progressive groups, which address social inequities through the courts and legislatures, and work to influence electoral campaigns and referenda through mainstream media; 2) the performative politics of more radical groups, aimed at reshaping the assumptions and categories of political life through cultural production and direct action; and 3) the critical politics of cultural theory and social analysis, circulated through academic writing and journalism."[2]

Duggan's distinctions are useful, but she relegates academics to the final arena of "critical politics." I'd like to suggest that students, scholars, and teachers of lesbian/gay/queer studies really engage in all three arenas: reform, performative, and critical politics. The distinctions drawn between these arenas are often useful fictions that shore up one political sphere's motivations by justifying them against another. For example, it seems that the "community" sometimes sets itself at odds with the "academy" by reifying reform and performative politics as sites of direct action, while sometimes vilifying critical politics and academic practices. In fact, many lesbian/gay/bisexual/trans-gender/queer (lgbtq) scholars and activists frequently cross these designations, working at both sites (and more).

At many CLAGS conferences I've attended over the last seven years, someone inevitably called the center to task for what they consider its academic irrelevance, insularity, and unintelligibility, no matter how "clearly" anyone is speaking. At the "Queer Theater" conference in April 1995, for example, theater critic Don Shewey announced proudly that he didn't think there was a Ph.D. on the panel he was moderating, and everyone in the audience applauded wildly.[3] The "Local to Global: Academics and Activists Think toward a Queer Future" conference in April 1999 was organized explicitly to create a discourse in which academics and activists could presume a common political stand and a common set of issues, approached from different but compatible directions. A series of plenary panels on which people spoke to preassigned and prediscussed questions, carefully moderated, with plenty of time for audience participation and response, did succeed in creating a different kind of discursive atmosphere. But the concerted effort to speak together, in a variety of languages, didn't stop one activist participant from raising the anti-intellectual flag. She remarked that on her own panel, she finally understood everything that was said. Her remark, though, in this context, seemed reductive and ludicrous, as the other activists and academics and participants did feel that tired questions of language usage had not been an issue at this conference.

Another example of the need for translating ideas across communities of different language use occurred at a meeting of scholars and activists called by the National Gay and Lesbian Task Force (NGLTF) in 1996. NGLTF's Policy Institute is one of the few non-university-affiliated queer "think tanks" that tries to bring scholars and their work into direct contact with the movement. The reports sponsored and funded by the task force tend to concentrate on research in the social sciences, studying, for example, gay and lesbian voting patterns and lesbian/gay/queer economic profiles. In November 1996, John D'Emilio, who headed the Policy Institute from June 1995 until April 1997, held a meeting in Washington, D.C., at the task force's annual "Creating Change" conference. "Creating Change" is an enormously popular conference for lgbtq activists, at which numerous plenary sessions, institutes, panels, and workshops are held over a week's span. The conference is generally considered the most important national lesbian/gay/queer movement meeting of the year, and many activists participate or attend. At D'Emilio's meeting, a number of prominent activists and engaged academics were invited to think with him about ways for the Policy Institute to generate useful projects. In a couple hours of intense discussion, a number of productive ideas were raised and amplified.

But the meeting also illustrated some of the theory/practice rifts between academics and activists, because a kind of suspicion seemed to charge the air from both sides. The meeting clarified, for me, the often wildly different contexts in which academics and activists do their work and their relative ignorance of one another's projects. For instance, one of the activists said that what the movement really needs and hasn't yet developed is a coherent theory of sexuality around which to mobilize. Many of the academics present, of course, had devoted their careers to explications of sexuality as an explanatory cultural tool. But it's most likely that by "theory" the activist didn't mean the kind of poststructuralist queer work current in the contemporary academy. The brief remark pointed to the chasm between work conducted in different contexts.

I found the moment personally painful, because it indicated to me the ways in which important academic thinking is generally invisible in the movement with which it wants to be in conversation and from which it so obviously extends. Part of the tension demonstrated at D'Emilio's meeting arises, I think, from the visibility of queer theory as a method prevalent in the humanities, an academic site generally misunderstood by activists as tangential to their concerns. Gay/lesbian/queer academics in the social sciences have been able to demonstrate more directly the importance of their work to the movement.

At the 1997 "Creating Change" conference, CLAGS organized a panel that addressed the potential of queer theory as activism. Although the panel drew a large crowd and inspired a productive conversation, some of the panelists were anxious for days beforehand about the audience's potential hostility, so deeply entrenched are the perceived divisions between academic poststructuralist theory and movement activism. Another CLAGS-sponsored panel at the 1997 conference was devoted to social science research. Another described the nature of the few "think tanks" currently addressing lesbian/gay/queer issues (such as CLAGS, the One Institute at the University of Southern California, the Institute for Gay and Lesbian Strategic Studies at the University of Massachusetts–Amherst, and the Policy Institute). Each of these panels offered useful ways of thinking through the relationship between academics and activists, but only the panel on queer theory inspired a thoroughgoing fear of contestation.

CLAGS returned to the conference in 1998, to present a panel on the ways in which arts defundings nationwide and attacks on freedom of expression on university campuses seemed linked. This panel was well attended, largely because campus issues had been highlighted at the conference after gay college student Matthew Shepard's brutal beating death in Wyoming earlier that year. But I was struck, even at the 1998 conference, by the different ways in which academics and activists approach their subjects. Each of the CLAGS panelists presented fairly formal remarks; a couple even read from papers. At "Creating Change," most ideas are exchanged in participatory workshops and roundtable discussion sessions. Our academic methods, here, seemed out of place and perhaps even condescending, although they weren't meant as such. Thinking more clearly about our audience might have let us revise the terms of our address.

Jeffrey Escoffier has said, "Our emancipation is not possible without a politics of knowledge."[4] A social movement forsakes theory at its own peril. But academics can work harder to translate their theory into various vernacular languages, so that they can share their ideas with people who speak differently through their own, different locations. Queer theory, for example, can be explained fairly easily as a way of considering sexuality as a lens through which to look at culture in general. Queer theory is a concept of sexuality that proposes that sexual identities aren't fixed, but are fluid, changeable, unstable, and often determined by their social context, rather than biological necessity. These ideas can be useful to a movement that wants to expand cultural understandings away from a strict commitment to heterosexual forms of kinship and relating. The challenge is how to develop strategies that allow various languages and sites of engagement to complement, rather than compete, with one another, around lesbian/gay/queer issues framed in the largest possible sense.

Recreating Public Forums: Conferences and Curriculum

In an interview, performance artist Holly Hughes complained, and rightfully so, that "there is a failure of national leadership when we are really embattled, at a time when there should be a natural solidarity because the academy is embattled as well. 'Multiculturalism' is embattled, public education is embattled, 'political correctness' on campus is embattled."[5] Given that political and academic activists should share strategies and information, there are actually very few places for them to address one another's needs and concerns. CLAGS conferences are often marked as only academic, inspiring a peculiar mix of vulnerability and antipathy in some of the activists who attend them, despite the CLAGS' board members' concerted efforts to staff conference panels with people working in both spheres.

Political activist and academic conferences should be crossover sites for lesbian/gay/queer thinkers and writers and artists, but so far, they keep their constituencies mainly distinct. The biannual lesbian/gay/bisexual/transgender conferences that started at ivy league universities on the East Coast in the late eighties and early nineties were potential forums for a kind of public intellectual project sorely lacking in the movement right now. But these ad hoc conferences, the last of which was held in Iowa City at the University of Iowa in 1994, have suffered from a leadership vacuum, and their momentum has been lost. The "OutWrite" conferences in Boston, sponsored by the Bromfield Street Educational Foundation, which publishes the nationally distributed, well-established gay newspaper *Gay Community News*, are well attended by writers and political activists, but not by as many academics. Very few academics regularly attend the "Creating Change" conference. Many academics go to conferences they believe will be useful or interesting to their work, and many deliver papers at conferences to enhance their curriculum vitae, which necessarily or unfortunately makes an appearance at the Modern Language Association's mammoth annual convention more important than attending "Creating Change" or "OutWrite."

But of course, scholars are required to and sometimes supported to attend academic conferences and often can't afford to go to others. Academic institutional structures that offer money to travel to certain conferences and not others, as well as the ways in which academics are awarded tenure and promotion, which make genres of knowledge compete, need to be critiqued and perhaps revised. When academic institutions place as much value on publishing in trade presses as they do on publishing in peer-reviewed journals, perhaps more academics will aspire to be public intellectuals. And when community service becomes a truly important component of tenure and promotion, perhaps more scholars will want to translate their work into local vernaculars and work with activist organizations.

Under the academy's current structure, lesbian/gay/queer scholars might not have time to read Urvashi Vaid, Andrew Sullivan, Gabriel Rotello, Michelangelo Signorile, Sarah Schulman, or other lesbian or gay authors whose books are published by trade presses for public audiences. Given the kinds of knowledge the academy values, reading Judith Butler or Eve Sedgwick and knowing how to quote them will more likely get their dissertations accepted and propel them toward tenure.[6] There's only so much time, energy, and labor, but the choices people make have real consequences, in the very specific contexts in which their scholarship is produced. It takes work to keep up, but the number of fronts on which new knowledge is advancing should invigorate academics and activists, rather than divide them.

Duggan asks, "How can we criticize our infant field of study without engaging in mindless theory bashing and anti-intellectual posturing, or positing a moral universe in which the academy is always bad and the community (whatever that is) is by definition good?"[7] The accusations of privilege often flung at CLAGS, or at the scholars who speak alongside the political activists at their conferences, are often facile. Holly Hughes says that while teaching performance at New York University she's noticed students' tendency to "describe someone as privileged or having a certain kind of power that is tantamount to saying they're unredeemingly 'bad.'" She says, "The misuse of the term 'privilege' [fails] to raise the more important questions, the ones that will move us forward [such as] what do we *do* with our power, our privilege?"[8]

What *do* academics do with their power and their knowledge? How can they demonstrate more persuasively how they use their learning, writing, speaking, and teaching toward activist goals? How can they persuade those who work in other lines of direct action that scholarship and education are also important sites for social change, especially given how endangered public education has become, how significantly access to it is shrinking? If lesbian/gay/queer studies has by now more firmly established itself as an area of academic inquiry, who does it serve and why? What effect has its success wrought, on which subjects? What has it mattered to which lesbian/gay/queer communities? Not enough has been done to establish lesbian/gay/queer programs at the undergraduate level on most campuses, perhaps since curricular reform is a university service or service to the field that doesn't count quite as much toward tenure or promotion as publishing.

Attention to gay and lesbian studies' place in the campus curriculum was highlighted by Larry Kramer's failed attempt in 1997 to endow Yale University with a professorship and a program in the field. Kramer is a well-known gay activist who helped to establish, during the early days of the AIDS crisis, the Gay Men's Health Crisis, now one of the largest and best funded New York–based support service organizations. He was also a founder of ACT-UP (AIDS Coalition to Unleash Power), an important grassroots, confrontational political (what Duggan would call "performative") group that single-handedly called attention to AIDS and HIV and the lack of government interest in funding research into their cure. Kramer is also a successful playwright, whose play *The Normal Heart* was one of the first widely produced dramas about AIDS. As a graduate of Yale, Kramer offered the university a $5 million gift to establish a gay and lesbian studies program on its campus. The provost turned the gift down, suggesting Yale preferred not to balkanize the campus into identity studies areas. Yale's decision to decline a $5 million gift caused the mainstream liberal and the gay and lesbian presses to scramble for facts about the state of gay and lesbian studies in American universities. If nothing else, Kramer's rejected offer called attention to the fact that the field exists, although most reporters filing stories had been completely ignorant about what gay and lesbian studies means and how long it has been struggling to be a part of academic life.

The fact is that there are still very few formally established undergraduate programs in the field. There are no graduate programs explicitly devoted to gay and lesbian studies, although through CLAGS, the CUNY Graduate Center has established an interdisciplinary Ph.D. concentration that lists lgbtq seminars together in its course bulletin. But the sudden media attention brought to Kramer's entanglement with Yale clarified the diverging views that gay and lesbian and queer scholars take on the importance of curricular development and the field's institutionalization. Some scholars insist that creating separate programs is a mistake, pointing to what they consider the "intellectual ghetto" of women's studies to insist that a similar fate shouldn't befall queer studies. Other people point to the proliferation of queer theory and queer perspectives on disciplinary knowledge, and suggest that such diffusion into existing areas of knowledge and established disciplines is a more effective strategy for growing the field.[9]

I understand and acknowledge the limits of identitarian thinking and the potential problems with sectarianism. But because of the pervasive influence of poststructuralist theory, very few identity area studies programs are bastions of essentialism. Most recognize that they need more than ever to build coalitions among themselves to become more powerful institutional forces. But I also believe that without the necessity that colleges and universities demonstrate commitment through the allocation of resources, they will be able to avoid the issue of minority sexuality studies and ride out what their administrators see as a wave of fashion. Without establishing majors or minors, programs or departments, that operate fully sanctioned by curriculum and degree committees and boards of trustees, it's too easy *not* to establish faculty lines and structures that ultimately protect the often junior faculty who teach in lesbian/gay/queer studies. Without dedicated lines in designated programs, too many young scholars in other disciplines are subtly encouraged to wait until they're tenured before they work in gay and lesbian studies. And too many students are encouraged or required to seek their major fields of study elsewhere.[10]

I believe that establishing interdisciplinary degree programs in lesbian/gay/queer studies is necessary at this historical moment, although in chapter 6, I describe my own discontents working in the similar interdisciplinary environment of women's studies. Identity area studies programs are best developed *as* programs, as places that call attention to the intersections of knowledge around a specific content or methodological field. At the same time, the institutional deficits of programs, as opposed to full-fledged departments, mean that faculty workloads increase in order to staff and perpetuate them, and that for students, lesbian/gay/queer studies or other identity area studies are always "minors," appended to another field of knowledge. But perhaps that's the way it should be, since it remains true that jobs, or even future graduate studies, remain discipline-based.

Queer theorist Michael Warner writes, "Lesbian and gay politics . . . is a special challenge to education, because homophobia may be more directly constituted by enforced ignorance than any other sociopolitical problem. Because being queer necessarily involves and is defined by a drama of acknowledgment, a theatre of knowledge and publicization, the institutions that transmit and certify knowledge take on special importance."[11] That is, our efforts to include our diverse experiences into various disciplinary curricula are an urgent matter of survival. The construction of potential identity, of fluid, shifting lesbian/gay/queer subjectivities, must happen at an institutional site that legitimates its existence.

In this moment in history, it's too early not to advocate (or even demonstrate) for lesbian and gay studies as a separate field. Critical race and ethnic studies and women's studies have achieved some success over the last twenty years; with them as a model, it's important to consider what the costs have been of institutionalizing knowledge that began on the street, in the vernacular, and came kicking and screaming into the academy. It's important to continue to develop vernacular knowledge, as institutionalization inevitably changes how gay and lesbian discourse sounds and who is listening. But rejecting the academy as a site to fight for resources and legitimacy and authority overlooks its importance as a place of education and activism. Kramer wanted to give his money to Yale because he was desperately unhappy there as an undergraduate; he thought he was the only gay person on campus and considered suicide. The University of Minnesota received a half-million-dollar bequest in the late nineties for a gay and lesbian student services program, also because the man making the gift had been so miserable as a gay person on its campus. How can lgbtq academics and activists *not* work to change, significantly and profoundly, academic structures of knowledge that continue *not* to name, that continue to exclude the study of the variety and complexity of the lives and histories of sexual minorities?

While curricular reform is often stalled by the vagaries of academic reward systems, publishing has become key to advancing knowledge produced in the field. The commodification of ideas has worked very quickly to position lesbian/gay/queer studies (or more properly, queer theory) as hot property for academic publishers.[12] University presses are more and more market-driven and can't afford to publish traditional scholarly monographs that few will buy. Because queer theory has recently exploded across the disciplines, it seems to have achieved a market niche as distinct as the one that has made queer chic a new force in U.S. capitalism.

But with this quick rise in cultural capital has come a concomitant forgetfulness about recent history, which might exacerbate the perception that academics are removed from activism. As Gayle Rubin says in an interview with Judith Butler, "There now seems to be a certain amnesia about the early work of lesbian and gay studies, as if the field only just started in the early or mid 1980s. This just isn't true. . . . Gay scholarly work was not institutionalized in academia and many of the people who did that work in the 1970s have paid a high price in terms of their academic careers."[13]

The work of reading queer theory and the well-deserved idolization of Judith Butler, Eve Sedgwick, and others, as its stars, have allowed some people in the most recent generation of students and scholars to forget the risky business of gay and lesbian studies in its formative years. Some disregard the still dangerous project of teaching and enrolling in lesbian/gay/queer studies courses in more conservative parts of the United States right now, and too often ignore historical projects or the gay and lesbian theory projects that predate the recent move into queer theorizing. The same forgetting of history plagued feminism, when poststructuralist theory became predominant. Academic knowledge productions have most recently centered on what Duggan calls "critical politics," and text-based work has now become ascendant and most marketable.

The Materiality of Knowledge and Learning

Lesbian critics and theorists such as Sue-Ellen Case, Suzanna Walters, Cathy Cohen, Biddy Martin, and many others have critiqued what they see as queer theory's retreat from the materiality of progressive social politics and its subtle declassing of gender and feminism. In the move toward the appealingly porous boundaries of queer—in a "postidentitarian" moment—the legacy of feminist work on gender is often dismissed as retrograde or old-fashioned. Biddy Martin argues that queer theory "at least implicitly conceives gender in negative terms, in the terms of fixity, miring, or subjection to the indicatively female body, with the consequence that escape from gender, usually in the form of disembodiment and always in the form of gender crossings, becomes the goal and the putative achievement."[14] As sexuality and its mutability take over as the dominant academic theoretical paradigm, gender is approached mostly through cross-identifications, usually with affluent white gay men, which deny the materiality of and appear to reessentialize women's bodies. In other words, according to the terms of queer theory, gender is only interesting when it's crossed, when women take on attributes of masculinity or men take on femininity, and when femininity becomes removed from a real embodiment in actual women. (The recent proliferation of writing on lesbian femmes, however, is a heartening shift in direction here.)

For example, when CLAGS staged a conference in spring 1996 on the differences between vernacular and expert knowledge, one panel concerned transgender issues. But few people on the transgender panel established common cause with nontransgendered or nontranssexual women. In fact, they spoke as though they were just inventing the critique of gender; historical women and feminist analyses weren't considered.[15] While trans crossings and their regendered performances have seemed queer theory's natural allies, why has feminism been discounted? Does this have something to do, perhaps, with the still second-class status of women in American culture? Are women still too uncomfortably close to the real?

Queer theory insists on the mutability of gender and sexuality and takes pleasure in reorienting and revising their costumes. But it often lets students and scholars forget the consequences of gender's reality in other locations and other geographies, and often lets us forget that sexual difference, gender difference, still incites real violence. For example, the *Advocate* reported that on 16 February 1996 "Sharon Clark, 20, of Colorado Springs, Colorado, was sentenced to 90 days in jail and six year's probation for having sex with four female minors. Clark, who dresses like a man, was known to these girls as Sean O'Neill."[16] Pat Califia writes persuasively of O'Neill's pending charges:

> Transgender activists very properly point out that if O'Neill is convicted, the failure to disclose one's genital status could be considered a "criminal deception," and any sex following such a failure to disclose could be chargeable as sexual assault—whether or not it was consensual. Although this possibility is most terrifying for transsexuals, especially those who are closeted or preoperative, it is also an issue for lesbians and gay men who engage in gender play and/or sometimes pass as the opposite gender. . . . It's disturbingly unclear, moreover, whether the mere "act" of looking like a man would be enough to warrant criminal charges, or whether flirting with or seducing heterosexuals would have to take place before the cops stepped in to break it up.[17]

Califia's caution is chilling for everything it could mean to "gender performance" as political activism. As I'll discuss in chapter 4, queer theorists such as Judith Butler have done quite a lot to popularize a notion of gender as a construct that's "performed," rather than revealed from an innate assignment of biology. The trope of performance, or "performativity," as it's described in its more cultural (rather than theatrical) variety, has detached gender into something flexible and changeable, a place of agency and choice, rather than one only of subjection to something that appears "normal" or fixed. How one performs one's gender is delimited by convention, and as Butler points out, there are costs to "doing" your gender "wrong."

O'Neill's case demonstrates the material realities of crossing the borders of gender outside the more protected realm of urban cities saturated with mutable queer visibility. The murder of Brandon Teena, a young transgender person in Nebraska who was brutally raped and killed when he was unmasked as a biological woman who had been dating local girls is another sobering example. O'Neill's and Teena's cases are reminders to be ever vigilant of context, of content, of critical thinking as only one level at which to launch a powerful, political critique of gender's constraints. As sociologist Suzanna Walters writes, "Theories of gender as play and performance need to be intimately and systematically connected with the *power* of gender (really, the power of *male* power) to constrain, control, violate, and configure."[18]

Looking for Alliances and Affiliations

The move away from "gay and lesbian" identity into queer has, according to some scholars, meant leaving experience-based strategies of identity politics, with all their risk of essentialism, for text-based, more disembodied readings of representation. Sue-Ellen Case writes persuasively that "queer's consort, 'performativity,' links 'lesbian' to the tarnished, sweating, laboring, performing body that must be semiotically scrubbed until the 'live' lesbian gives way to the slippery, polished surface of the market manipulation of its sign."[19] In other words, the mutable notion of "queer" considers "lesbian" only a performance, one which is removed of its real materiality to become a chic, desirable appearance for a capitalist marketplace willing to buy an emptied representation of what was once a meaningful identity. Case also reclaims the theoretically discredited notion of "presence" by rewriting lesbian bodies back into time, history, and sociality, saying, "And 'presence'—showing up— at activist disruptions, at live performances, in collective venues, reclaims the 'live'—the body—the visible—looking for lesbians in the political sense."[20] Presence has been discounted by some poststructuralist theory as a metaphysics that implies an unchanging innateness to gender or sexuality. But Case rewrites presence from a political sense, implying that it's the act of having one's real body in a political space that makes the difference to a lesbian/gay/queer movement. Her analysis, then, points out what she sees as the excesses of queer theorizing, and its potential for bracketing a certain kind of political possibility.

Disembodied readings of the lesbian body as only a sign have contributed toward driving a wedge between the political movement and scholars writing poststructuralist queer theory. Queer theory most often approaches topics considered fashionable in the academic arts and humanities marketplace (female-to-male impersonation, marginalized sexual practices, etc.) rather than policy development or legislative issues. Suzanna Walters worries about "the inattention to material social relations" in much queer academic writing.[21] She says, "I would prefer queer theorists spend a bit more time on the mundane figure of the working-class lesbian mother and the horrifying spectacle of the removal of her child than on the endless rhapsodies for drag and dildos."[22] Walters perhaps overstates her case; that is, drag and dildos also have material implications, and Walters is wrong to set these up as a binary choice. Walter also implies that queer cultural practices aren't as important as legal and policy issues. But culture is surely an important site of political struggle. In addition, as many scholars responded to Martha Nussbaum's critique of Judith Butler in the *New Republic*, there's a legislating of the "real" that propels much of the writing by lesbian/gay/queer social scientists against scholars who write in philosophy or the humanities.[23] Writing on cultural representation, on the construction of sexualities through their representation in film, in theater, in performance, on television, in novels, and in other social and cultural texts, can have profound implications for legislative and rights debates.[24]

The many sites at which lesbian/gay/queer/transgender activists and academics work don't have to be mutually exclusive or divisive. Cathy Cohen has argued that coalitions have to be formed around shared relationships to dominant power.[25] Rather than demonizing heterosexuality as the antithesis of queer, she says a gay and lesbian political movement has to theorize heteronormativity as a structural problem in dominant culture. (Heteronormativity is the normalizing of heterosexuality as the only "real," "appropriate" social and sexual relation, which influences public policy and the organization of all social relationships.) Heteronormativity marginalizes so-called welfare mothers, by Cohen's example, in ways similar to how it marginalizes lesbians, by moralizing against the inappropriate display or use of their sexuality.[26] "Welfare mothers" are inappropriate because they have what "normal" heterosexuals consider too many children, and many of their children are born "out of wedlock." Welfare mothers are also racialized in the popular imaginary, so that they typically call to mind African American women, when in fact, statistically, many more single mothers on welfare are white women. Lesbians are inappropriate to "normal" heterosexuals simply because they engage in sexual practices with other women. This theorizing allows lesbians—white and of color—and welfare mothers—white and of color—to build a coalitional politics based on their similar experience of oppressive social structures, rather than on the basis of neatly mirrored, shared identities.

Urvashi Vaid, former executive director of the National Gay and Lesbian Task Force (NGLTF) and now director of its Policy Institute, has likewise written that lesbian and gay politics in the nineties and beyond need to assume a consistently progressive stance. She suggests forming coalitions on the basis of economic and social issues that extend beyond the limits of lesbian and gay identity. She insists that there's nothing inherently radical about being lesbian, gay, or queer, noting that identity politics reach a kind of outer limit when they require a unified movement that embraces the Log Cabin Republicans, gays in the military, and gay marriages, as well as less assimilationist platform planks.[27] How can activists and scholars do their work on welfare and drag, on affirmative action and Oscar Wilde, in sophisticated, politically, and intellectually complicated ways, then speak to one another and enable one another's progress?

The wedge between academics and activists has been hammered deeper by questions of language, driven by a real resentment from those who would hang onto the real as a place that has historical and material effects, against those poststructuralist theorists who insist that the "real" is a figure of speech. What scholars think and write and analyze does have real effects in the social world. (The pope once cited even Judith Butler as transgressive.) Even if there is no language that everyone understands, unreservedly and without mediation, reinstating an interlocutor could be a gesture of rapprochement between political and academic activists. Gayle Rubin says, "There is a common assumption that certain kinds of conceptual analysis . . . provide descriptions or explanations about living individuals or populations, without establishing the relevance or applicability of such analyses to those individuals or groups."[28] Of course, some of Rubin's critique comes from disciplinary suspicions, her own disquietude about text-based work. Anthropologist Esther Newton launches a similar critique, writing, "If the goal is to theorize how representational strategies work, how can intellectuals skip over this ethnographic step to broad abstractions and generalities without being guilty of misleading (and reprehensible) imperialism. . . . Are academic intellectuals only interested in theorizing one another's representations?"[29] In other words, Newton and Rubin suggest that much of the queer theory that makes claims for social behavior has looked at representations, rather than engaging with "the real"—actual lesbians, transgender folk, and so on, in actual communities of social practice.

Part of this dissension is generational and part of it is methodological. Lesbian and gay studies when it first entered the academy was clearly fueled by life experience it hoped to add to the common store of knowledge. Queer theory's text base and its predominance in English departments give it a methodology necessarily different from those of anthropologists, although cultural studies is beginning to borrow from both terrains. And rather than addressing lived experience in ethnographic ways, some queer theory is highly philosophical in its investments; this is in part Butler's influence on the field. But as Said suggests, disregarding humanists as scholars "whose wares are 'soft' and whose expertise is almost by definition marginal" plays into the very kind of power structures that favor politics as "objective" and "real." Said asks, "How can interpretation be interpreted as having a secular, political force in an age determined to deny interpretation anything but a role as mystification?"[30] Redefining the humanities and their methodologies as influential and material might shift the terms of this debate.

Since I work in theater studies, I'm invested in the movement of bodies in space, in the real-time charge of desire between performers and between spectators and the stage. But it's true that my own work about theater and other representational practices has not included talking to the people who create or consume performance and representation, to expand the dialogue about what they could mean. I don't usually interview performers or spectators to develop my critical ideas. And I'm not now advocating a return to "author's intent" or to a purely historiographical/biographical approach to texts or performances. I believe, following Said, that critical interpretation has an important political utility. Critics in feminist and lesbian theater studies, for example, have proposed that plays written in the realist genre are murderous for lesbians. The heterosexist domesticity of the form inevitably requires that the lesbian character—who's typically singular, structurally and emotionally alone—be expelled from the community, usually by suicide or exile. Once such a critical proposition is digested, it allows readers and spectators to see form as intimately connected with content and better prepares them to be critical about representations of themselves and others in all avenues of culture.[31]

But while such textual and generic strategies remain useful, perhaps it's now important for gay and lesbian theater theorists also to engage with actual social subjects (audiences and artists) as part of their research, to broaden the range of social meaning that performances and representations generate in rich and unpredictable ways. Part of the problem is a too strict reliance on disciplinary conventions; a melding of social sciences and humanities research methods might clarify common intents. Such conversations could build affiliations and alliances among critics and theorists, performers and audiences, as they all contribute differently to a common desire for social change. As Said writes persuasively, "[W]e need to think about breaking out of the disciplinary ghettos in which as intellectuals we have been confined, to reopen the blocked social processes ceding objective representation (hence power) of the world to a small coterie of experts and their clients, to consider that the audience for literacy is not a closed circle of . . . professional critics but the community of human beings living in society, and to regard social reality in a secular rather than a mystical mode, despite all the protestations about realism and objectivity."[32]

Lesbian Artists versus Lesbian Critics: Replicating the Theory/Practice Divide

In theater and performance studies, artists deliver against academic critics many of the charges brought against academics by activists in lesbian/gay/queer studies. Artists are positioned here as the ones who do and critics as the ones who build careers by draining creative energy and writing irrelevant theoretical tracts. I remember reading a paper for Kate Davy at the National Educational Theatre conference in New York in 1987. (Davy couldn't be there, so as panel moderator, I read in her place.) The paper was about lesbian performance; Lois Weaver and Peggy Shaw, the two lesbians in the infamous performance trio (with Deb Margolin), Split Britches, were also on the panel. Davy's paper was fairly theoretical, using poststructuralist language that was new even in academic theater discourses at that point. After the paper was read, someone in the audience asked Weaver and Shaw what they thought. The implication of the question wasn't, "What do you think of the *ideas* and how can the three of you engage?" The speaker clearly wanted to know what they thought of the use of *theory*, wanted them to confess whether or not they'd understood. They were positioned as "outside" the critical conversation by a question that already presumed they were excluded. If I recall correctly, Weaver and Shaw looked at each other, at me, and at the audience, and said noncommittally, "It was interesting."

The conversation went on from there. But I remember that moment as one in which the posing of the question established a breach between the performance critic and the performers, set them on opposites sides of a strategy of language usage, rather than pulling them together to examine work with common goals. Thinking about Weaver and Shaw's work (and their work with Margolin) over the last twenty years, I'm struck by how theoretically informed and articulate it has always been. They've partaken of the dialogue with lesbian performance critics that their work helped to start, and they've participated in educating audiences, critics, and practitioners in new performance traditions. The mutuality of the exchange between these performers and lesbian critics has made all of our work better and richer.[33]

On a panel about lesbian criticism and performance at the Association for Theatre in Higher Education (ATHE) conference nearly ten years later (1996), also in New York City, one of the participants accused academic lesbian critics of writing for tenure committees. All academics are certainly, and necessarily, vulnerable to this charge. But many progressive academics do maintain commitments to the political work on which their ideas are based and manage to fulfill their institutional expectations while creating knowledge that's useful to the social movement. Some academics even resist or critique their institutionalization, and it takes work and in some places courage to do so. For the same panel, Babs Davy, of the Five Lesbian Brothers' performance troupe fame, wrote,

> While I can't wrap my mind around much of what is written by lesbian performance critics, I defend their right to write however they want in their noble quest to re-invent language. Resentment builds when performers read about their own work in what is to them unintelligible language that seems more about feminist theory than about what actually happened on stage. . . . The result is ugly stereotypical characterizations of lesbian performance critics as a self-important group more interested in their individual self-promotion than either teaching audiences or influencing artists.[34]

I'd organized and moderated the ATHE panel as a roundtable discussion in which critics and performers could discuss just these issues of language, power, and meaning. I wanted us to think together about ways in which critics and performers all participate in educating audiences to the variety of lesbian identities and their potential to change cultural meanings. I conceived the panel to focus on the pedagogical aspect of performance and criticism, considered as two parts of educating audiences. But for one reason or another, only the critics invited to participate showed up. The performers were either sick, out of town, had performance gigs, or something else. Some of them gave the distinct, if indirect, impression that having a conversation for which they were not getting paid, in an academic setting in which they don't feel comfortable, made the event less than important for them. The implicit point is well taken: do academics consistently attend postshow discussions (the moment of critical engagement that follows selected performances during a run) or join panels at other events to engage with performers? Without getting paid? It's interesting who gets invited into whose "homes" and when, and who's willing to come over and when and why. But for lesbian/gay/queer people, performance and criticism are two sides of a similar project; criticism can't be seen as only predatory or self-justifying.

The Politics of Use Value

As I've described above, those who do reformist or radical political work in the lesbian/gay/queer community sometimes describe those who do critical work in academic locations as sycophants or parasites, plundering the activists' original commitments for the academics' self-aggrandizing ends. Activists often speak about the necessity for academics to give them something they can "use." True, use value is increasingly important in academic work, and efficacy demands that the work have a clear usefulness. And yet arguing a pragmatics for academic work in many ways replicates the argument that critics should engage with performers only at the level of giveback. This implies that artists want good reviews to take to funding agencies to secure a grant, and activists want facts and figures that they can use to counter the latest outrageous claims of the Right. But one could argue that pragmatics are not the point of queer theorizing. Theorizing is in fact about reenvisioning values; it's the utopic moment in lesbian/gay/queer political work, a moment that simply has to be shared more widely for more and various communities to understand its visionary import.

How can academics and activists, and artists and critics, reach one another? How can they reach more people? Describing her entanglement with the media during her long legal battle with the National Endowment for the Arts, Holly Hughes wondered how she might best use her fifteen-second sound bites. If that's all the time we have, what are we going to say? How can academics cultivate representatives who can occasionally, stealthily, speak the language of the majority without compromising the complexity of the critique? How can they build an effective counterdiscourse to the reductive but persuasive rhetoric of the Christian Right? Peggy Phelan once said, in arguing against the Right's attack on the NEA Four that we need to proliferate images and ways to read them.[35] Although academics have done that in the academy to a certain extent, perhaps they've failed to do so more widely in larger arenas of American culture.

Of course, intervening in dominant media systems isn't easy. When CLAGS decided it wanted to represent a counterdiscourse around arts censorship and attempt to be heard in presses like the *New York Times* and other mainstream media outlets, *Village Voice* journalist and Baruch College professor Alisa Solomon schooled the board on the complications of even getting quoted. She stressed that journalists tend to rely on a cabal of sources that can be counted on to give them good quotes. Writing news, she told us, requires boiling down complicated stories to easily digestible, agonist narratives, in which good guys and bad guys battle for supremacy. She said that journalism demands "balance" to appear objective. Given these axioms about newspaper writing, we realized how difficult it is to launch more layered and nuanced, let alone overtly ideological, critiques in venues that can't quite accommodate them. Likewise, in a media workshop organized by the Gay and Lesbian Alliance Against Defamation (GLAAD) in which some CLAGS board members participated, we were told to make our ideas as simple as possible to communicate them effectively.

Although I deplore the "dumbing down" of mainstream media, it's imperative that progressive academics learn how to use it effectively. How can the critical politics and queer theoretical work on representation that flourishes in the academy begin to have a larger effect on the public sphere? Even Urvashi Vaid, in her book *Virtual Equality*, says that "the gay and lesbian movement needs to concentrate far more on culture than on politics as we strive to win deeper acceptance and genuine equality." [36] Many people still have no idea of the variety of ways queer people can look or of various positive, productive ways to read gay and lesbian images once they even recognize them. For instance, there's a rigorous Marxist critique to be made of the commodification of queer images and the insidiousness of a marketplace that trades in them at the expense of political innovation, but I was glad that Ellen Degeneres and her television character came out so publicly in 1997. Not unlike Kramer's rebuff from Yale, the Degeneres event provoked quite a lot of media attention, even if only to white upper-middle-class gay and lesbian lifestyles, rather than to more antiassimilationist politics, social inequality, and continued oppression by heteropatriarchy.

But perhaps instead of trashing the shrewd manipulation of ABC's bottom line by Disney, more academics should have been writing op-ed pieces in newspapers all over the country. We needed to write essays that took advantage of the public fascination with Degeneres's self-outing to call attention to race and class issues within the gay and lesbian community, and to the potential building of coalitions outside of the strict identity groupings on which the mainstream media like to rely. Degeneres and her then girlfriend, Anne Heche, became for a while the darlings of conventional, accommodationist gay and lesbian organizations like the Human Rights Campaign. This choice demands that more progressive lesbians and gay men write op-eds again, to mainstream and queer newspapers, pointing out the limits of celebrity spokespeople who are white, rich, and only recently out as lesbians.

Organizing Public Intellectuals to Reach Academic and Activist Audiences

How might academics juggle the demands of institutional college and university culture, while meeting the challenge of promoting their ideas to a much larger public? Let me cite the challenges faced by CLAGS in this regard. CLAGS began as Martin Duberman's project some ten years ago. As one of the first out gay academic historians, Duberman's work persuaded him of the need for a place to pull together and to publicize the vibrant writing especially in lesbian and gay history that was beginning to appear in community and academic settings. Through five years of grassroots organizing in Duberman's living room in Chelsea, in New York City, CLAGS was established as a center at the Graduate School of the City University of New York and began its institutional life in 1991.

Duberman's success in institutionalizing CLAGS in some ways mirrored the movement of gay and lesbian historical research away from community projects and archives into more secure bureaucratic structures, a move some commentators suggested was necessary for this work to survive.[37] Yet with institutionalization and perhaps a future comes another set of challenges and contradictions. CUNY is the largest urban public institution of higher education in the country, a sprawling bureaucracy, funded by a city council and state legislature that are often hostile to education and to gays and lesbians. The system is currently under attack from its own administration; a conservative board of trustees ran the nefarious former chancellor Ann Reynolds out of town in September 1997, then lambasted its community campuses for (supposedly) not insisting that their students be proficient in English.

To access its budget and to operate its programs, CLAGS works through CUNY bureaucracies that are unwieldy, unpredictable, opaque, and as a result, often paternalistic.[38] CLAGS is one of twenty-four centers at the Graduate School, all of which receive a small budget stipend and are then charged with raising their own funds for programming and operating expenses. CLAGS' position at CUNY, however, marks its institutionalization, its move away from grassroots, community-based political work. But does institutionalizing ensure conservatism? Is CLAGS less radical now because it has a small office and gets its money over the signature of CUNY's budget officer than it was in Marty Duberman's living room? If arrival in institutions, however precarious, is automatically cooptation for a research center, what does this mean for the establishment of lesbian/gay/queer studies programs? Why shouldn't a research center like CLAGS aspire to be a think tank, when so many of the radical Right's intellectual organs have been so influential in promoting conservative thought and public policy?

Potential funders' responses to CLAGS, in comparison to what they see as more grassroots organizations, has been telling, as many are unwilling to support a center that appears to be so institutionally secure. In actuality, CUNY is one of the most precarious public educational institutions in the country, and although CLAGS receives its institutional imprimatur, the center still has to raise 85 percent of its operating and programming budgets independently.[39] But CLAGS' institutional position makes it different from, for example, the Lesbian Herstory Archives, which operates out of a brownstone in Brooklyn, or from other gay and lesbian history projects that remain community-based. But it's important, for lesbian/gay/queer political work to advance on as many fronts as possible, to make "radical" an unstable, context-specific descriptor. If CLAGS remains the only university-based research center in the United States, and there are still very few gay and lesbian studies programs, then doing this kind of work in the academy must continue to be charged with controversy, anxiety, and the potentially positive disruptions that new knowledge brings. Certain vigilance is required about the possibility of cooptation, but it's too early for this work to be dismissed as compromised. In addition, CLAGS struggles to bring grassroots movement values into its institutional setting, working with commitment to make sure that its board of directors is racially and ethnically diverse as well as gender-balanced and that it represents a range of disciplinary and community-based affiliations. Working against institutional values that tend to preserve racism and sexism at their core sets CLAGS off from more conservative lgbtq organizations.

Institutionalization means a confrontation with money, about which political and academic activists are sometimes suspicious. The challenge of reconciling deeply held Marxist principles of social change with savvy capitalist understandings of fundraising is large but necessary, and there are progressive fundraisers who are persuasive that it's imminently possible. Many activists rightly criticize what they see as the corporatization of once grassroots groups like the Washington, D.C.–based gay lobbying group, the Human Rights Campaign (HRC); the Gay and Lesbian Alliance Against Defamation (GLAAD, which has been criticized for taking money from the antigay, politically right-wing Coors Corporation); and the Los Angeles Gay and Lesbian Center, which have successfully raised millions of dollars through membership and corporate fundraising campaigns. Are these groups no longer grassroots? If they reach large audiences, is their ability to attract money from corporate and wealthy (but often politically conservative) individuals a bad thing? Is "grassroots" about where the office is located and where the money comes from, or about how many people these organizations are able to reach? Or is it, ultimately, about their politics—the HRC's endorsement of incumbent Senator Alfonse D'Amato in the fall 1998 New York election lost the organization many progressives' faith, as D'Amato's record on human rights issues was generally atrocious. Or perhaps it's about their leadership— Executive Director Elizabeth Birch's aggressive and arrogant handling of the community disputes over the HRC-cosponsored Millennium March in April 2000 caused antiracist lgbtq activists to be further alienated from HRC's work.[40]

As a CUNY center, CLAGS is encouraged to exchange knowledge in public settings with a broad audience. CLAGS' primary goal is to persuade lesbian/gay/queer communities that knowledge is power, and that education is an important site of activism. At the same time, its mission is to continue pushing at the envelope of knowledge, to develop new theories and new ideas, to continue uncovering forgotten participants in world history, and rereading well-known figures in new ways, all from the perspective that sexuality offers on human knowledge and experience. Surely, such knowledge production will add currency to the social movement as it continues its struggle for civil rights for lesbians and gay people and as it continues to reimagine social relations from a redefined, nonheteronormative perspective.

My three years as executive director of CLAGS taught me a lot about my own position as an activist academic, vis-à-vis a diverse queer community. The microcosm of the board of directors was in itself a place to practice theory and to theorize practice; the various investments present around the table required quite a lot of code switching and a sensitivity to a multitude of issues about which board members cared passionately. Retaining a commitment to feminist, antiracist board practices required diligence and care and a willingness to make mistakes, to be wrong. Running CLAGS also required a sense of humor and an ability to chose which battles were worth fighting in any given moment, when there were always ten or twelve to choose from.

Because of its visibility and its relative strength as a university-based center, CLAGS got called out a lot by scholars and community members invested in how it spent its financial, intellectual, and academic resources. Deciding to do a benefit that would highlight work by certain authors around contentious issues such as safe sex practices spurred calls by other activists and scholars who deplored the opinions and strategies of the authors we intended to present. All we could offer, in that debacle, was equal time and space for alternative points of view. But equal time is actually quite a lot, given that it's not usually available. The board debated long and hard about whether an organization like CLAGS should be partisan, or should, in fact, present public forums on many sides of the many debates through which queer politics progresses. Although most of its board members are progressive, some espoused less liberal views around a number of issues and prompted much discussion about how sectarian our think tank should be.

I was struck, in my years at CLAGS, how some of the most important conversations between activist scholars and activists in the community happened in small group gatherings, when twenty or fewer people gathered to brainstorm a conference or to review grant applications. These roundtable conversations, or these intense, carefully debated fellowship reviews, offered a venue in which people who work in different contexts could approach work to which they were equally committed. The old feminist axiom that process is more important than product seemed to be true time and again, as the planning meetings for conferences were sometimes as (or more) stimulating than the conferences they eventually inspired. I learned quite a lot from listening to people's insights, their disagreements, their arguments, all advanced in a spirit of respect and mutuality.

As CLAGS' executive director, I served as its liaison with the CUNY Graduate Center and as its spokesperson to many of our grant-giving organizations. Seeing how CLAGS' meaning shifted in various contexts always fascinated me and taught me many things about the need for a university-based executive director to be able to speak on multiple levels and be sensitive to context. For instance, at the Graduate Center, while CLAGS was highly regarded by the administration, we stood out as the only queer center of the twenty-four centers represented at CUNY. At meetings of center directors, I felt keenly my own exceptionalism as the only open lesbian and one of the few women at the table, running one of only several explicitly political research centers. The fact that community activists and scholars from other universities and colleges were represented on our board of directors and that they had the power to vote on how we spent our resources was anomalous, given the more top-down, executive director–driven administration of most of the other centers. As a result, I had to carefully explain our structure and the ideology behind our operation to CUNY administrators.

When I met with foundation officers, I needed to explain the ways in which CLAGS remained a politically motivated nonprofit with a real connection to various queer communities. The grants for which we were eligible were surprisingly few, given that our programming crossed social science, arts, and humanities fields and wasn't service-oriented, as are so many lesbian/gay/queer nonprofits. I had to carefully explain how knowledge production is a service to the community and how an academically situated think tank can be quite influential in building policy and perspectives, given the resources to attempt to shape public opinion.

CLAGS also bridged generations of lesbian and gay and queer scholars. While some members of the board wanted to move into higher and higher realms of queer theorizing, others wanted to program conferences and colloquiums that would have applied value to various members of the community. I saw our mission as meeting both of those needs and desires, but creating a variety of programming without antagonizing either side was often challenging. And as one of the first university centers in lesbian and gay studies, CLAGS was often used in proposals by other faculty groups at universities trying to found their own research institutes as an example that their work would move beyond. While CLAGS wanted to retain a cutting-edge position in its intellectual work, it's also committed to increasing voices and centers in the field in a spirit of bipartisanship and collegiality.

Serving as executive director of CLAGS was one of the most challenging positions I've ever held as an academic and provided some of the richest, most gratifying moments of my career. I learned how to translate complicated theoretical issues into compelling, usable practice; how to bring to the same table people who often viewed one another suspiciously and encourage them to respect and admire one another; how to make university resources (even at a public institution with very few) available to community organizations less well off than we were and to form partnerships that would advance common agendas in and outside the academy; and I learned how to be honest and open about my own limitations, politically, administratively, and intellectually while seeing my job as creating an environment in which my colleagues could flourish and engage their best selves. Everyone should take an opportunity to sit in the hot seat of leadership. Learning on the job—especially one in which your role is really about translating ideas and opinions among disparate groups of people—makes for a deeply challenging and inevitably moving experience.

Ten Different Routes toward Addressing Theory and Practice in Lesbian/Gay/Queer Communities

1. Consider the politics of knowledge. Respect and engage the new theoretical vocabularies while taking to care translate them for less specialized audiences. Practice code switching and stay aware of the multiple contexts into which we speak.

2. Work to create, fund, and foster more frequent public forums at which

academics and activists can share common concerns. Use small roundtable discussions without large public audiences to establish trust and common ground. Don't be afraid to ask questions, to simplify, to complicate, to debate.

3. Create lesbian/gay/queer studies programs on campuses and in community centers. Work with local activists and in conjunction with other university identity area studies programs or departments to formalize an interdisciplinary, activist field of knowledge for graduate and undergraduate students and for community people, within the limits of local political constraints and reprisals.

4. Offer and take continuing education programs in lesbian/gay/queer studies. The "Seminars in the City" program begun at CLAGS has been very successful, offering Saturday meetings in a nonuniversity space at which community people come to discuss books addressing various topics (Latino/a literature, transgender issues, etc.) with a scholar interested in leading conversations about the work.

5. Reject single-issue politics or theory. Work to form coalitions and alliances that extend beyond the obvious, in ways that deepen our understandings of oppression and resistance.

6. Publish in university presses and in trade presses. Read academic and popular authors in the field and in the movement, and form book groups with faculty, students, and local activists to discuss their work and its implications.

7. Write op-ed pieces for local and national media outlets. Learn how to speak in fifteen-second sound bites, and offer yourself as a spokesperson on lgbtq issues.

8. Create university- and community-based research centers. Establish and proliferate think tanks with vital ties to both the academy and the movement.

9. Insist that theory is real. Consider how it might offer utopic visions for a queer future.

10. Remember history. Teach it. Learn it. Honor it. Be passionate about your theory and your politics, and communicate that passion widely. Believe in things, and share your beliefs faithfully.

chapter three

Theory, Practice, and Activism:

Theater Studies and the Polemics
of Performance

Theater studies in the academy is a relatively new disci-
pline, one that, in its more practical variety, extended out of speech and communication departments and one that is still, to certain extents, practiced as
an intellectual endeavor in English departments in the United States. The intellectual history of the field, then, is itself fragmented. In English, "drama" is
treated as a genre of literature (and typically a stepchild genre, at that). In
speech and communications departments, theater studies grew out of an attention to the performance of texts. Theater departments, which now com-
bine the intellectual, academic study of the history, literature, theory, and
criticism of theater with studies of its practice (acting, directing, designing,
and playwriting) are still relatively young in many institutional locations. The
many missions and goals of theater departments often foster contention
among differently committed faculty. Their wide range of activities includes
preparing students with intellectual and practical knowledge of the field, as
well as mounting productions that allow students and the local community
to experience live theater, in its contemporary and classical varieties.[1]

The status of these departments on their campuses is also often tenuous,
as many administrators don't understand theater departments' multiple missions and are suspicious of the amount of resources they require for producing their annual seasons of plays in performance. And because "art" is generally measured against national standards (in the case of theater, Broadway,
especially), university theater productions often fail to move administrators
to reward them with funding. Many administrators can't see the pedagogical
aim behind these productions. Some theater faculty, in their own reach toward replications of highbrow artistic success that happens elsewhere, fail to
make a case for the ways in which local productions teach students and audiences how to engage with theater as a more general cultural practice.

If lesbian/gay/queer studies is driven (or riven) by divisions between academics and activists, the field itself, of course, is not hegemonically theory-based. Likewise, in theater studies, while the theory/practice dissension cuts across the entire field, the academic side of theater departments is typically divided into still more fractious debates about how best to deliver historical, critical, theoretical, or literary knowledge in the field. Theater scholars have also fought over the use value of poststructuralist theory. They've suffered a rift between those who champion Euro-American, canonical bodies of knowledge taught and measured through more positivist, objective techniques, and those who believe knowledge is embodied, and who teach and write through politically inflected, identity-based studies, often using poststructuralist methods or postmodernist theory.[2] Because of the historical attention to the body in theater studies, poststructuralist theory here pays clear attention to bodies situated in particular historical and felt ways.

My attempts to mediate among these various binary tensions set me in something of a triangular relationship that's played out still differently here at the site of theater studies. I've advocated for mediation and translation between queer theorists and movement activists through lesbian/gay/queer studies. Here, I'm arguing for mediation between the academic and artistic sides of theater studies departments and between artists and critics, as well as looking for ways to mediate among the various ways of conducting academic scholarship in theater studies. In this chapter, I'll address the curricular debates often staged at conferences around the usefulness of postmodernism and identity studies as compared to more canonical and historical contents and methods. I'll argue that theater departments need to pull together to argue for the urgency of their work in the university and in the culture at large. I'll also demonstrate that theater departments can intervene in social issues by staging (as well as teaching) current conflicts, and use the myriad of arts defundings through the 1990s as examples of a social debate in which theater faculty and students could have taken a stand.

Theater Departments and the Academic Curriculum

Antitheory scholars tend to resent the ways in which poststructuralism created an opening for feminism and ethnic studies and lesbian/gay/queer studies to enter the traditional curriculum and scholarship. These scholars align themselves with those engaging a nostalgic return to core Euro-American values and a unified understanding of which knowledge is the most important knowledge. (The National Association of Scholars or the activists of the American Council of Trustees and Alumni [formerly the National Alumni Forum] have most publicly defended these positions.) These scholars have generally proceeded from a perspective centered on nostalgia for a pure white past. As African American cultural theorist Michael Dyson writes, the desire to return to a unified core curriculum requires a kind of "racial amnesia," "because the goal of unity is the reconciliation of difference and oppositional discourses."[3] Such calls for unity also misrecognize the complexities of the postmodern moment. How knowledge is produced in the academy has been shifted dramatically by computer technology, new media, and the global reach of capitalism and its fetishized commodities. Those who champion core curricula often prefer what they consider more stable, knowable historical moments in which the borders of knowledge could be appropriately drawn.[4]

The current debates within the academic side of theater studies are part of a refusal to acknowledge postmodernity and the new terms and responsibilities it has set for public intellectuals and educators. The borders some theater studies scholars have drawn in the culture wars are built on a suspicion of poststructuralist theory and the new progressive, identity-inflected epistemologies. Cary Nelson and Michael Bérubé suggest that "theory has been deployed as an umbrella term either to justify or to delegitimate the new forms of knowledge and critique generated . . . in the past 25 years; it has also been blamed for demographic changes that have nothing to do with theory."[5]

It has been easy to attack critical theory derived from identity studies, because it's so explicitly connected to larger social movements that force an acknowledgment of changing cultural patterns. The entry of identity area studies into the academy in the late seventies, with women's studies and African American studies, helped change institutional demographics in ways that made it more difficult to consider the academy as an ivory tower, safely cordoned off from the diversifying populations of the United States itself. Referenda in the nineties such as California Propositions 209, which repealed affirmative action, and 187, which limited the human rights of immigrants, were motivated by a desire to ignore, deny, or even reverse the racial and ethnic composition of the country at large.

These sometimes fractious engagements over disciplinary knowledge in theater studies can be recast in several ways. Theater studies scholars might acknowledge that they teach and write in a postmodern context. We might sharpen our thinking about the historical, institutional structures in which we work that shape how knowledge is delivered. And we might actively consider how the changing demographics of the student and faculty populations at the institutions in which we teach frame these debates. If we took these risks, theater scholars from various political persuasions might be able to work together to articulate a vital, coalitional vision for the field. In addition, theater scholars and university-based practitioners might form affiliations with and provide resources for artists. Especially when people considered marginal to the dominant culture create work that's critical of mainstream values, they have fewer and fewer intellectual, artistic, and financial resources through which to develop work. My argument here is that theater production and theater studies are vital contexts for political critique.

Theater Production as a Laboratory for Reimagining Social Relations

Theater studies is in a unique position to experiment with the construction of knowledge and new ways of learning, precisely because many of its departments include production components that can embody the questions of content, context, theory, and history raised by its scholars. Yet there remains something fundamentally divisive in how theater departments are structured, carefully mixing and matching and sometimes blending practice and intellectual work rather than premising both on the other. Theater studies is both an arts discipline and an academic discipline, much like art and art history. Its graduate degrees are often administered from separate schools than are theater studies' undergraduate degrees (for instance, the theater studies Ph.D. is often granted from graduate schools of arts and sciences, while undergraduate degrees come from schools of fine arts). In many especially larger departments at research institutions, scholars work in isolation from practitioners (people who direct, coach the student actors, and design the costumes, sets, and lights). This split between research and practice often draws the fault lines in theater departments in research institutions, as various sets of faculty are positioned against one another in the struggle for resources such as graduate assistantships and other student aid and faculty assistance. On the other hand, small theater departments in liberal arts environments often require their faculty to do everything—to teach literature, history, theory, and criticism classes while directing and designing productions and advising student majors. Faculties in these departments are notoriously overworked and are often required to accomplish tasks for which they're not adequately trained or talented.

I am invested in rethinking the use value of theatrical production in both kinds of theater departments. Typically, large departments grant preprofessional bachelors of fine arts (BFA) degrees along with a host of masters of fine arts (MFA) degrees in everything from playwriting to acting and designing, as well as the academic master's and Ph.D. degrees. They model their production programs on mainstream regional and Broadway theaters. They presume that their students aspire to places in the theater industry and craft their curriculum to offer BFA and MFA students professional training that apes the structure of regional theaters around the country, which in turn, imitate the production practices and success strategies of Broadway theaters. A glance at any issue of *American Theatre,* the trade monthly that reports on trends and issues in regional theaters around the country, indicates that most producing organizations devise seasons that mix a few classics with the most recent Broadway hits and sometimes a musical. These seasons rarely reflect their geographical location, aspiring instead to the homogenous texture of the standard Broadway or off-Broadway New York City fare.

Theater departments, in turn, tend to cobble together similar seasons. Their curricular commitments require perhaps more classics, to train their actors in Shakespearean verse and movement styles, but faculty in university theaters tend to want to try their hand at popular plays. The requirement that box office receipts help cover their costs means that they have to in many cases pander to what they perceive as audience desires. For instance, after the Broadway success of Brian Friel's *Dancing at Lughnasa*—an Irish domestic drama about a mother and her daughters and their alienated brother—numerous regional theaters and university theater programs produced the play. As a result of these repetitions, seasons in colleges and universities across the country suffer from a kind of conformity and use their resources on reproductions, rather than on developing new plays or performances that might speak more directly to their local communities.

Production could come to mean something much more vital in theater departments and the communities in which they're located. Rather than succumb to the marketplace pressures of theater, film, and television for which they're grooming some students, university theaters could take more risks, producing texts that might share with the academic and public communities something new, about theater and about people's contemporary situation in culture. Too often, university theaters fail to use their resources to introduce their faculty and students and others to a new writer, a new performance style, a new issue or identity in the space of their stages. Rather than employing a pedagogical model of theater production and practice, they adopt the market strategies of the industry they seek to emulate. The Broadway productions they replicate are more and more driven by market research, by audience surveys that determine the structure, shape, and narratives of mainstream product.[6] The cultural capital of seeing a Broadway show and reproducing it in a university theater builds intellectual capital in theater departments. But shouldn't university theaters reach higher than that, and try to create performances that reach deeper, intellectually, artistically, and even spiritually?

Of course, many students, lured by the aura of celebrity, desire not to learn a craft, but to apprentice for stardom in film and television, rather than theater. Since theater departments—rather than film, communications, or television departments—still teach acting, students who want to act in visual media take their coursework in stage practices. And surely some of them want to act on the stage. But since theater actors have a harder time achieving celebrity status, given the pervasiveness of film and television and the relatively elite status of theater, many students learn tools they want to apply in mass media.[7]

Theater departments, of course, are hardly free from the market pressures that influence their students. The circulation of academic, cultural, and financial capital drives their teaching and their research and the productions they select for their seasons in one way or another.[8] Departments need majors to survive in academic institutions that are now economically motivated, and they must be responsible in training their students toward some sort of financially viable future. But what kind of future will students training to be actors, for example, have, when Actors Equity, the national American union, still reports that its members are mostly unemployed? Theater majors are already bucking the trend toward professional education by enrolling in degree programs that offer much less secure futures than economics or business majors can boast.

How can faculty more responsibly train theater majors to think of their skills as critical tools, rather than encouraging their fantasies about their future stardom, inspired by an excessive American culture of celebrity? How can faculty persuade students that theater degrees might make them employable later, or that a thoughtful use of their degrees can mean more, personally and politically, especially when they're young, than secure employment prospects? It sounds excessively privileged to suggest that an arts education is more important than a livelihood. But faculty committed to the arts know that they can offer important ways of structuring identity, of seeing the world critically, of thinking about and experimenting with social relations and their potential. Such critical and social thinking should be a vital part of any student's education.

Organizing Knowledge in the Face of Economic Exigencies: Appealing to the Public

The economics of higher education, as I described in chapter 1, needs to be considered when theater scholars think about the place of the field in larger institutional structures. How well are theater departments faring under recent retrenchment and downsizing initiatives? Theater departments, with their productions to budget and facilities to keep up, tend to be expensive, and too often tied to romantic ideas about art production that separate them from the rest of the institution. Can they afford such isolation in this economic climate? Don't they need to integrate their work with other disciplines within the institution, thinking together about the vital importance of performance to culture, as the study of performance, as I describe in chapter 4, cuts across disciplines? What would change if theater departments tried to reach the communities in which their students and faculty live? What would happen if they created multiple kinds of knowledge through theater, rather than considering their programs a delivery system for the "real," "true," "only" knowledge, and for productions of canonical, authorized plays already popular in regional theaters?

A retrenchment plan disguised as a restructuring proposal circulated in the early nineties at CUNY before it was finally shelved. The report suggested that the campus-wide curricula be redesigned so that some system college locations would offer some fields and not others as a way of saving money and resources. Following the report's logic, theater studies, for instance, would be taught at the senior, four-year colleges, such as Hunter, in Manhattan, and Brooklyn College, but not at York College in Queens, or at the Bronx Community College, where historically, the reasoning went, there was little support for theater in any case. Joanne Graham, then chair of the department at Bronx Community College, suggested that such redistrictings institute a class system that presupposes that only the middle class, already situated in cultured urban areas, make use of art as a social practice.[9] The report also, of course, suggested that CUNY campuses in the Bronx and the farther reaches of Brooklyn, Queens, and Staten Island should specialize in technical and vocational studies, rather than liberal arts and humanities, turning cultural presumptions about class stratification into self-fulfilling prophecies.

Although the CUNY plan articulated these pernicious cultural assumptions most explicitly, many university systems work on presuppositions about the elite, highbrow, universal function of the arts in culture. Rather than allowing these to go unchallenged, theater studies faculty might proactively argue for theater as a local practice, one that serves the communities in which it flourishes differentially.[10] Theater departments can't really serve those communities by only teaching a core curriculum and ignoring the social circumstances in which its students live, the histories and different cultural experiences from which they come. Theater faculty might better argue for the value of theater history, theory, criticism, and practice, not just as part of a Western civilization redemption narrative (in which art brings salvation and civilization) but as part of identity practices inflected with postmodern understandings of the productive instability of subjects and communities.

That is, the way we are subjects, or people in the world, is more complex now than ever. Our identities are less coherent; we see ourselves not just through one identity category (immigrant, African American, Jew) but through several simultaneously. As a result, how we identify within communities is also more and more complex. Theater-producing organizations often try to appeal through identity categories to spectators who are actually linked mostly by geography—they live near the theater, or they share a common desire to attend the theater, to see how it might speak to them, inspire them, teach them something about their lives. Who they *are* can't be captured in simple categories. The idea of doing a "black play," as a result, even in a theater with a mixed-race population, is rather ludicrous, as the category is much too simplistic to be useful or interesting.

Some departments have built curriculum and created production projects to challenge traditional understandings of theater as an art. But the theory/practice split that rends the field has allowed many production programs to inculcate romantic notions of artistry that describe the actor, especially, as outside of history, as objective, empirical, inspired not by context but by genius and canonical knowledge. As a result, these departments are often considered naive or irrelevant to the larger intellectual project of the university or college. Theater departments generally haven't done very well at teaching new models for how to be artists at the end of the twentieth century or the beginning of the twenty-first.[11]

Theater scholars and practitioners might revel in what Peggy Phelan calls the nonreproductive capacity of performance, while arguing that its ephemerality is partly what helps it build community.[12] Theater scholar Sandra Richards says that "given the evanescence of theater, and its insistence upon subjectivity as part of its methodological approach, academics from other disciplines all too often view the scholarly validity of drama departments with varying degrees of skepticism; that ambiguity," she goes on, "reproduces itself within departments as a contentious divide between practitioners and scholars, such that each group jostles to privilege its mode of activity, and the insights of one often do not inform those of the other."[13] To counter this unproductive standoff, Richards considers herself as a "critic working in theatre . . . whose directing constitutes a critical praxis addressed to a nonprofessional audience, and whose subsequent writing to an academic audience is partially shaped by those experiences."[14] Such a dialectical movement keeps Richards from foundering in an unproductive debate.

Perhaps in their effort to convince their colleagues and themselves that their place in the academic pantheon is well-won, theater scholars have too often capitulated to scholarly expectations that disembody the work and detach it from the audiences that give performance and critical readings of it their multiply invigorating meanings. Theater scholars willing to engage with poststructuralism have allowed the field to be scientized by theory, while they've not worked very hard to translate that theory into critical praxis, into what Richards calls "the imprint of the vernacular."[15] So while the academics continue to debate their methods, the divide between themselves and their practitioner colleagues continues to increase.

Theater studies hasn't been quite clear enough about the urgency of the field's survival and its ability to share knowledge that matters to a wide social sphere, without which our various cultures would be impoverished on a number of levels. Theater studies might take Richards's challenge to think more clearly about its audience, to see and communicate the wider use value of the productions its departments produce, the knowledge they create, and the theory and practice of the art they venerate. Theater studies faculty can't keep teaching theater as a high art practice, but must see it in connection to diverse communities that use it in different, local ways. If theater scholars and faculty practitioners see themselves as participants in public life, university theaters may be places where key political and social issues are worked out.

Staging the Arguments in Theater Studies

An activist vision of the university, in which various constituencies might cooperate, might come to find a common voice or vision, has long made conservatives fearful, perhaps partly because such an activist intellectual environment would clearly contribute to shaping public life. Carol Stabile, in fact, argues that the debates about political correctness that have long divided college campuses into culture wars were engineered by the Bush administration during the Gulf War as a way to contain campus protests against this conflict and to manufacture consent.[16] Whether or not one agrees with Stabile, the culture wars have succeeded, to a certain extent, in isolating progressive academics by making them appear doctrinaire and ridiculous. Conservative rhetoric about political correctness has made progressives seem against a democratic notion of human community and for the "special interests" that have been disparaged in public culture in recent legislative initiatives against gays and lesbians, against affirmative action, and against welfare.

The world is changing, and rather than be nostalgic for the old days when universality—or radicalism, for that matter—seemed possible in life as well as in art, the terms of scholars' work need to change to connect more directly to a diverse public. Henry Giroux argues that literacy has to be reconceptualized as a critical cultural practice in which students become agents of their own lives by learning to understand the representational practices through which they're often excluded. "This is not merely about who speaks and under what conditions," he writes. "It is about seeing the university as an important site of struggle over regimes of representation and over ownership of the very conditions of knowledge production."[17] Gregory Jay and Gerald Graff, who were active with the progressive advocacy group, Teachers for a Democratic Culture, suggest that rather than trying to resolve them, we should "teach the[se] conflicts. . . . The 'politicized' university . . . would look to turn the campus into . . . a community where empowered citizens argue together about the future of their society, and in so doing help students become active participants in that argument rather than passive spectators."[18]

Even staging arguments in theater studies would make faculty and students more self-conscious of the public, progressive possibilities of theater and performance. Such a staging actually did occur in fall 1996, when the white, Harvard/American Repertory Theatre–based critic Robert Brustein and the African American playwright August Wilson waged their own battle over universal versus particular knowledge, identity politics, and ways of engaging with deeply contentious cultural issues. In the pages of *American Theatre*, Wilson argued that African American plays should not be produced by white theaters, and spoke against color-blind and cross-race casting. Wilson's argument, though persuasive in some respects, was an essentialist and modernist vision of identity politics. But Brustein's universalist, blindly humanist response suggested that art conquers difference. In a later issue of *American Theatre*, Patti Hartigan, a cultural reporter from Boston, suggested that Brustein and Wilson should give their debate over to African American performer/playwright Anna Deavere Smith. Smith, Hartigan suggested, could perform it for them and the theater community, investigating its ideologies and its implications much as she did for Crown Heights and east Los Angeles.[19] Through performance, this debate about the meaning of theater, and how it structures representations of our culture might enter the lives and imaginations of a much larger community.

In fact, in January 1997, Smith moderated a debate between Brustein and Wilson at Town Hall in New York City. Sponsored and organized by Theatre Communications Group, the sold-out event was one of the high points of the season, attracting a more ethnically and generationally diverse audience than typically appears for theater productions in mid-town Manhattan.[20] The evening was contentious, as Brustein and Wilson refused to cede ground to each other's arguments. Despite Smith's mediating presence, the debate framed poles of power in contemporary theater, and still managed to leave out a wide spectrum of work and invested viewpoints. The power dynamics were also disconcerting, as many of the people attending were theater makers in their own right, who were discouraged from speaking publicly into the forum. And although the evening focused on race, both men displayed blind spots when confronted with gender or sexuality issues.

Still, the event was invigorating and moving, and demonstrated how much people care about theater. Why don't theater departments open their theaters to just this sort of debate, about racial issues, gender issues, sexuality issues, about affirmative action, gay/lesbian civil rights, immigration and welfare, or even about the ways in which academic courses and productions create knowledge in theater studies? At the ATHE conference in 1998, the Advocacy Committee organized a plenary session on arts funding called "Showdown on the Arts in San Antonio." The debate was prompted by the City Council's decision (as I'll describe it below) to cut the local arts budget by 15 percent, and to deny funding completely to the Esperanza Peace and Justice Center, one of the city's most progressive performance-producing organizations. The panel framed various sides in the contentious local struggle and extended the questions raised into the national arena. The panelists disagreed vocally, and the audience lined up at microphones in the house to participate in the debate. The event proved one of the most stimulating hours at the conference, and inspired much heated discussion that continued through the meetings.

Why shouldn't theater faculty teach these and other conflicts, so that faculty and students can assume the moral accountability that publicly engaging difficult debate requires? For example, theater faculty might make their decisions about season selection open to faculty, students, and a wide public, who would discuss the kinds of plays that might be produced and why, taking into consideration the new knowledge and aesthetic values they might share and with whom. They might sponsor debates about curriculum with students, faculty, and staff from theater and other departments, which could address how to balance new knowledge with canonical knowledge. They might explain the decisions they make as teachers and administrators about why they teach what and how they do, so that their choices are historicized and contextual.

Teaching the Arts Funding Conflicts

For theater scholars and students, the recent spate of arts defundings provides an obvious conflict to teach. Common themes and their reoccurrence characterize these defundings, and link the three areas of study I'm addressing here. In each case, a performance or theater piece with gay or lesbian or feminist content presented in a public space set off the anxiety and alarm of conservatives. In some cases, a performance that simply displayed the *body* of a gay man or lesbian or woman or person of color or feminist or some combination of these provoked outrage from politicians on the Right. They inveighed against the depravity of the performance, whether or not they'd even seen it, and most never had. They teased out its proximity to and potential harm of the community's children, and then took away or drastically reduced the producing organization's public funding because in their opinion, the performance was a waste of "taxpayer's" money. Lesbian/gay/bisexual/transgender/queer (lgbtq) bodies and bodies of color are once more marginalized by a call to a presumptively heterosexual, white, reproductive family, which is assigned the ideal place of citizenship in American culture.

Arts defundings offer examples of how the Right uses its attacks on theater and performance to squelch public dissent and to marginalize difference. Over the last decade, the arts have been an easy target and a profitable fundraising tactic for the extreme Right. Images of gay and lesbian performers have been as effective for raising money from conservatives as pictures of aborted fetuses waved on picket lines outside clinics. Any performance with gay or lesbian or sexual associations can be damned a priori, with little knowledge of the variety of meanings it might bring to social understandings.

For example, the Esperanza Center for Peace and Justice, an art-producing site that sponsors much Latino/a and gay and lesbian performance work, was denied a large portion of its funding by the San Antonio City Council in fall 1997. A local arm of the Christian Right, in concert with a group of conservative white gay men, engineered the funding cut.[21] The gay and lesbian film festival produced by the organization was held up as justification for the City Council's decision to significantly reduce Esperanza's support.[22] Shortly after Esperanza's defunding, Out North, a gay theater company in Anchorage, Alaska, also lost a substantial portion of its funding. The Anchorage City Council decided that some of its publicity materials were obscene, and they objected to the title of Susan Miller's performance piece *My Left Breast*, which Out North planned to present that year. The piece is a one-woman show about Miller's breast cancer and subsequent mastectomy, but the city council automatically considered the piece, which they hadn't yet seen or even read, pornographic.

The Charlotte (North Carolina) Repertory Theatre also felt these ideological pressures, when they were confronted with laws preventing nudity to keep them from staging Tony Kushner's award-winning play, *Angels in America*, in 1997. The play, which has been widely produced all over the United States and abroad, details the relationships and broad historical context of a man living with AIDS; it includes a few scenes in which as a patient, he is naked under his hospital gown. The resulting uproar in Charlotte persuaded local county legislators to stop funding the arts entirely (although in 1999, the complexion of the council changed and the funding was restored).

In fall 1998, a production of Terrence McNally's play *Corpus Christi* was nearly cancelled because of protests from the New York Catholic League for Decency. McNally's play tells the story of Christ by painting contemporary analogies, and intimates gay relationships among Christ and his apostles. Death threats called in to the theater concerned the Manhattan Theatre Club administrators enough to cancel the production. They reversed their decision only after a national outcry by progressives—artists and activists—accused them of caving in to censorship.

In the most notorious case of conservative censorship of feminist and gay and lesbian cultural expression, the National Endowment for the Arts (NEA) has been the focus of right-wing strategists since the late eighties. First, artist Andres Serrano (creator of the now infamous *Piss Christ*, in which he floated a crucifix in a glass of his urine) and an exhibit of photographs by Robert Mapplethorpe (the late gay photographer famous for his formalist depictions of male nudes and of people engaged in sexual practices) were attacked for obscenity. Then the "NEA Four"—lesbian and gay performance artists Holly Hughes, Tim Miller, and John Fleck, and the sexually explicit feminist performance artist Karen Finley—became targets of ultraconservative sermons about morality and the virtue of taxpayers' funding what a handful of politicians considered indecent art. Fleck, Miller, Hughes, and Finley brought suit against the endowment when then head John Frohnmeyer overturned the decision of the peer review panel and denied their individual NEA grants in 1990. Although they won their suit and the grants were finally reinstated, that event in some ways began the current generation of antiarts sentiment nationwide, as conservative legislators and politicians began to focus on the arts to fan the flames of bigoted religious sectarianism. The shape of federal arts funding has been so distorted by these debates that the NEA has been all but evisccrated as a site that enables diverse work. Most NEA funds now are disbursed as block grants to states in a proportional formula to subvert the possibility that its funds will be used for art that conservatives consider inappropriate. But the new distribution system punishes coastal cities like New York and Los Angeles, where much avant-garde, feminist, and gay and lesbian work has historically been devised and produced. This strategy allows the NEA to abdicate federal responsibility for ensuring that diverse, experimental art has opportunities to develop.

In the aftermath of this debacle, the NEA appended a clause to its grants that required recipients to guarantee, by signing a pledge, that their work wouldn't offend common notions of "decency." In response, the ACLU brought another suit against the government, claiming that the decency clause was unconstitutional and prohibited freedom of expression. In summer 1998, the Supreme Court ruled for the administration in this case, voting to uphold the decency pledge in awarding federal funding to artists. Progressives around the country agree that the effects of this ruling will chill artistic freedom for years to come. Shortly after the Supreme Court decision, in fact, the Whitney Museum cancelled an exhibition/performance by Karen Finley it had planned to mount in fall 1998. Although museum officials insisted the cancellation was for other reasons, its timing made it appear more than coincidental.[23]

Clearly, conservative political forces are behind the argument about decency, which excludes anyone who expresses different values. CLAGS held a roundtable discussion about arts censorship in spring 1998. Scholar and arts activist Douglas Crimp noted that the burgeoning of public funding for art in the 1960s was almost exclusively responsible for the creation of an alternative arts network, much of which was addressed to minority communities and was implicitly critical of dominant values. Public funding freed artists from the constraints of the marketplace and encouraged a diversity of cultural expression. Crimp argued that Reagan-era politicians set out to dismantle the NEA because these policy makers completely understood the radical implications of public art. He remarked that the dismantling of the NEA is a policy decision meant to exclude sexual and racial minorities from a common notion of democracy. Graciela Sanchez, executive director of San Antonio's Esperanza Center, reminded participants at the same roundtable that this debate is as much about race and class as it is about sexuality and gender, since notions of decency stem from hegemonic positions that are typically white and middle-class, as well as heterosexual.[24] Esperanza's defunding, after all, was promoted by a group of white gay men.

Arts funding has become a lightning rod for both conservatives and progressives, and a site of contention regularly reviewed in the media.[25] But very little of the public response to these incidents recasts the discourse about them from a progressive perspective and does the work of explaining, in the public sphere, to large audiences of readers, the operation of ideology and politics at work in each of these examples. Usually, the "victims" of funding cuts—the performers or producers or the museum administrators—are left to speak for themselves, against an array of conservative pundits with national influence. Those under attack are usually ill funded and unable to spend staff and budget resources to respond in a systematic and effective way to the withering attacks against them.

Theater educators and feminist and lesbian/gay/queer teachers and sympathizers need to generate public debate that might shift the very ground on which these funding issues are argued. Teaching the arts-funding debates can encourage students to become arts advocates, as well as informed, open-minded spectators.[26] Students in theater studies need to understand that these issues frame the industry they'd like to enter. Students in lesbian/gay/queer and feminist studies need to understand how the arts are one of many sites at which dominant perspectives on sexuality and gender, race and ethnicity are forcefully asserted. Using university resources (whether theaters, public spaces for debate, or courses in which these issues are profitably addressed), academics can mount a progressive counterdiscourse and help to create more spaces for artists in which alternative work can continue to flourish. Academics at more liberal institutions might collaborate with local theaters and local performers to reinvigorate a counterculture of intellectuals and spectators and critics and artists necessary to support alternative art.[27] Without a vigorous, oppositional counterculture, art becomes homogeneous and hegemonic, commodified and market-driven.

Academics in the arts and humanities ignore the state of arts funding and its relationship to the public sphere at their collective peril. Federal, state, and local decisions about the arts affect the kinds of work theater professors do in their university and college theaters; the kinds of plays and performances and theories they teach in their classrooms; and the kinds of scholarship they publish. Theater studies faculty need to educate themselves on these issues and learn how to be articulate, proactive spokespeople for the vital importance of theater and performance (and education, most fundamentally) to all aspects of American culture. Theater faculty can't avoid talking about recent censorship attempts, or about the dismantling of the NEA, if they're intent on teaching theater students to be artists or critics. Women's studies and queer faculty also need to engage these debates, if they're committed to teaching lesbian/gay/queer and feminist studies as tools of cultural change.

Just as conservative politicians are shutting down cultural diversity by defunding radical artists, those whom Catharine Stimpson recently called "activist trustees" are intervening in faculty governance to shut down diversity of speech on college campuses.[28] While artists are being denied an important aspect of their participation in American democracy, academics are more and more denied their right to freedom of speech, to self-governance, and to a role in shaping the production of knowledge that's autonomous from state and federal interventions.[29]

In spring 1999, faculty at Arizona State University were alarmed when a state legislator objected to a campus performance of the *Vagina Monologues*, a performance by Eve Ensler that encourages women to regard their bodies with delight and dignity, rather than dismay.[30] It's not an accident that campus uproars like the one at Arizona, and local reductions in funding by city and state arts councils, invariably focus on performances that display women's or gay or lesbian bodies, white or of color, with agency, desire, and fullness. Cultural anxiety about gender, race, and sexuality remains fearfully high.

Progressive faculty consciously, proactively teach from a position of social and cultural advocacy for the public sphere and for their disciplines' viability within it.[31] Theater faculty might broaden their perspectives, and think clearly about the audiences for their scholarship, their directing, their teaching as a social force that connects them to history and to the movement of cultural life. To whom are scholars talking? What do they mean to say? What is their vision of public life?

Lawrence Levine historicizes the present academic debate over the curriculum, and although he's not specifically addressing theater studies, his premise applies to my own arguments. Levine recalls that "academic history in the U.S. . . . has not been a long happy voyage in a stable vessel characterized by blissful consensus about which subjects should form the indisputable curriculum. . . . [T]he very curriculum whose alteration so many are lamenting today was . . . adopted at the turn of the century only over the intense and passionate objections of those who saw in its emergence the end of culture and the decline of civilization."[32] Listening now to Lynne Cheney and William Bennett and the conservative scholars of the National Association of Scholars, the anxiety is remarkably the same.

We need to reclaim the terms of the debate, to articulate clearly and passionately how we'll participate in reshaping the curriculum to preserve a dynamic interplay among disciplinary knowledge, postmodern understandings of identity studies, interdisciplinary strategies, and the public sphere that gives all scholarship and teaching meaning. We need to be advocates for the embodiedness of knowledge in a way that acknowledges human particularity while it strives toward a more radical humanism that crosses the borders of knowledge and identity.

A Road Map toward Addressing the Theory/ Practice Split in Theater Studies

1. Respect the ways in which theory, history, and criticism are no longer separate practices in theater studies but overlapping, interconnected subfields with complementary methodologies.

2. Don't be afraid to theorize and historicize practice. Even actors training for the profession should know the history and theory of the work they're learning. Thinking about how performance works doesn't destroy its pleasure and doesn't make an actor (or designer or playwright or director) less creative.

3. Think of theater as pedagogy, in which performers and spectators learn from one another something about their commonalities and differences and how to honor them in their communities.

4. Stage preshow discussions, at which directors and actors, faculty and designers present ideas to spectators that might enhance their viewing experience of the production they're about to see. Put the production in a historical, critical, and/or political context.

5. Invite faculty from other departments and members of the community—other artists and theatergoers—to discuss season selection for university theaters. Program community workshops and talkbacks before and after each production that set out their intellectual and artistic context.

6. Support local artists by inviting them in to speak and by offering them university resources—rehearsal space, theaters, equipment, and student interns. Serve on boards of directors of local theaters, or present artistic work in these theaters that employs faculty and students, allowing them to interact with community colleagues.

7. Use fundraising opportunities to proselytize about the work of your department, to increase both resources and audience base. Give money to local theaters and community-based nonprofit groups.

8. Consider the university both a professional proving ground and a place for countercultural discourse. Sponsor risky performance work that might not be fundable through public sources.

9. Train students to be artists capable of working in a variety of venues, from regional theaters to alternative performance spaces to theater-in-education to community-based companies. Teach them that there are many different ways to be an artist, all of which can be useful and culturally important. Teach them to value their art and aspire to use it toward the largest social good. Offer alternatives to the culture of celebrity. Never tell students they need to diet, fix their teeth, or have plastic surgery.

Theory, Practice, and Activism : 63

10. Teach the conflicts around arts funding, censorship, and "community standards" of decency.

11. Break through the typical self-isolation of theater departments. Interact with other departments and disciplines in the university. Teach continuing education courses; not just acting, but courses on how to be a critical spectator and how to engage the arts as more than idle entertainment.

12. Use performance to stage arguments, to embody knowledge and politics, to open a community to itself and the world in ways that are dangerous, visceral, compelling, and moving.

chapter four

Geographies of Learning:

Theater Studies, Performance,

and the "Performative"

[T]heatrical metaphors are, for reasons that I suspect
do not reflect very favorably on theatre, endemic to our
cultural discourse.
—David Cole, *Acting as Reading*

Theories of the performative—in feminism, gay and lesbian studies, performance studies, and cultural studies—creatively borrow from concepts in theater studies to make their claim for the constructed nature of subjectivity, suggesting that social subjects perform themselves in negotiation with the delimiting cultural conventions of the geography within which they move. But as much as performativity seems to capture the academic imagination, and as much as performance captures the political field,[1] theatrical performances, as located historical sites for interventionist work in social identity constructions, are rarely considered across the disciplines, methods, and politics that borrow its terms.

The proliferation of performative metaphors is prompted in part by feminist poststructuralist vocabulary that refuses a notion of inherent, essentialist ontology, but that suggests instead a constructionist notion of identity as antimetaphysical, emphatically material and historical, constantly refashioning itself in various contexts and configurations of reception. "Performativity" as metaphor is used increasingly to describe the nonessentialized constructions of marginalized identities, like white women and women of color, gays and lesbians, men of color, and various conflicting combinations and intersections of these categories and positionalities. Performativity might be most useful in these cases because marginalized identities are self-consciously alienated from "the real" of subjectivity to begin with. For instance, notions of performativity have been thoroughly integrated into queer theory, as they're particularly useful to the anti-identitarian stand of a methodology that refuses to assign sexuality an innate or stable status.[2]

My desire to see theater studies visited and acknowledged, as part of the proliferation of the performative, rather than raided and discarded, is hampered by theater studies' traditional insistence on privileging the humanist ideology of the aesthetic and by its ubiquitous theory/practice (even mind/body) split. But by borrowing back concepts of performativity, the divided sides of theater departments might find ways not to heal the schism with some transcendent artistic coherence, but to employ complementary languages to do intellectually and culturally committed, moving, embodied, and relevant work.

I want to engage with a reconfiguration of "home" in both a political and a disciplinary sense, attempting to redraw the boundaries of the community in which I conduct my own scholarship and teaching. I'm drawn to Biddy Martin's and Chandra Mohanty's interest in "the configuration of home, identity, and community" in the tension between "being home," "the place where one lives within familiar, safe, protected boundaries," and "not being at home," "a matter of realizing that home was an illusion of coherence and safety based on the exclusion of specific histories of oppression and resistance, the repression of differences even within oneself."[3]

These same tensions pull at my affiliation with theater studies as a "home" for my scholarship and theater practice and as one whose apparent coherence I want to be productively disrupted, by the inclusion of people it has historically excluded and by antihumanist theoretical models. Both inclusions seem antithetical to theater's historically elitist self-consideration as "high art." Yet while theater studies has long traded in a more conventional (white and male) rendering of the form's history, at the same time theater practice has long been considered a haven for the "other," especially for gay men and lesbians who've toiled, mostly unacknowledged, on or behind its stages. It's this tension that has infused the National Endowment for the Arts' debates about decency; when the bodies of "others" come to proclaim theater and performance as a forum for their experience, rather than as simply a place to live safely, hegemonic culture insists on reasserting the elitist, exclusionary status of theater and performance.

Remapping the territory of "home" also resonates with the geographical metaphors that describe, in part, the shifting focus of performance work in American theater, marked by identities and positionalities that refashion theater's spatial boundaries to include "other" ones. These metaphors challenge the centrality of white heterosexual male culture, and of New York City as the apex of theater production and criticism. This newly mapped geography locates specified (rather than humanistically universalized), historically marginalized identities as active participants in the production of theatrical meaning.

I intend to argue here for the retention of theater studies as a disciplinary "home" deeply influenced by interdisciplinary methods, one made less coherent and less safe (even dangerous) by its determined inclusion of other(ed) geographies, other(ed) desires, and bodies othered by what hegemony has refused to allow seen. I would like to sketch a model of exchange between theater and other fields and disciplines, rather than one in which the performative evacuates theater studies.

Some of the locations from which my argument moves and to which it returns are performance studies, a discipline to which theater studies is historically already tied; cultural studies, now institutionally established across disciplines; feminist and gay and lesbian studies and queer theory and critical race studies, which describe identity as performative;[4] and feminist theoretical writing on identification and empathy in performance that uses the power of theatricality to describe and to change the way social identities are performed and received.

Performance as Metaphor

The nonchalance of other disciplines' borrowing of performance metaphors is complemented by some theater scholars' willingness to quit their own territory. Part of the seductiveness of relocating away from home, or of eliding the specific contribution of theater studies from the performative, comes, perhaps, from theater studies' historical borrowings from other fields to theorize itself. For example, feminist theater and performance theory in the mid- to late eighties borrowed from feminist film theory, to form its own methodologies and to describe the very different shape of live performance. But the necessity of looking toward another discipline, even to legitimate the notion of the gaze, seems to mark in that borrowing, something second-class about theater. (Film theorists, of course, borrowed Brecht from us, but it seems as though they think theater studies ended when he died.)

Now that film theory seems to have exhausted its possibilities for ennobling theater studies by analogy, cultural studies is becoming another site of legitimation for theater scholars. Cultural studies' focus on media, popular culture, and the performance of everyday life once again displaces theater practice as a legitimate, different, but related site of inquiry for scholars doing this rich, interdisciplinary work. Performative metaphors get extended into many avenues through cultural studies, but rarely is theatrical performance qua performance a site of such extension. If the practices of everyday life and media textuality appear multiple, contradictory, and open, actual theater performances are too often positioned by other scholars within a humanist aspiration to high art—simple, closed, parsed, "known," and coherent.

For example, in the now classic, defining volume on cultural studies, called simply *Cultural Studies*, none of the forty articles included is about theater, although many look at popular culture forms like music, detective fiction, porn magazines, book clubs, and dancing.[5] These exclusions and absences indicate theater is still marked as "high" art, in an academic moment which, through cultural studies, in particular, is privileging the "low"; the absence of theater examples here also indicates the academic marginality of the field.[6] But such presumptions fail to account for the history and efficacy of American popular entertainments, for one example, as bearers of cultural meanings, even though their effects áre primarily local, rather than "mass."[7] Cultural studies has been quite useful to performance and theater scholars — among them Joseph Roach, Bruce McConachie, Elin Diamond, and Sue-Ellen Case — determined to set out the larger historical and social context for the work they examine; cultural studies scholars might profitably consider the wide application of these proliferating models.[8]

Other area studies, such as women's studies and gay and lesbian studies, have provided sites of interdisciplinary reference for scholars in theater studies, and both fields use theatricality as a conceptual scheme for describing identity. In gay and lesbian studies, for example, sexuality is consistently theorized as performative, but few scholars included in several key anthologies look at the production of sexual identity in actual theater and performance settings where, again, cultural products become sites of negotiation and opposition to dominant meanings. In Diana Fuss's important early anthology *Inside/Out*, none of seventeen articles addresses theater production, although many focus on the representation of sexual practice in film and fiction.[9] The textbook-oriented *Lesbian and Gay Studies Reader* and even *Out in Culture*, an anthology of articles addressing gay/lesbian issues in popular culture, reiterate this omission, with the exception of Case's "Towards a Butch-Femme Aesthetic" in the *Reader*.[10] Theater studies' gaping absence at these foundational sites points to exclusions based, perhaps, on misrecognizing theater production and commentary as anachronistic, humanist relics of artistry rather than as popular sites at which oppositional cultural work is frequently conducted.

The affinities and differences between performance and the performative — as a description of cultural behavior without an innate ontological base — have to be defined to be useful to theater studies. The performative and performance are not the same, if only partly because performance is a genre with its own history, applications, and cultural uses. Janelle Reinelt and Joseph Roach's introduction to their edited volume, *Critical Theory and Performance*, is insightful about the peculiar status of theater studies as a discipline, since performance scholarship, they note, has always crossed institutional disciplinary lines. Yet theater scholarship belongs to a particular tradition,[11] one that Reinelt and Roach recall has had a long history of theoretical speculation, one now bolstered by the interest in critical theory across the academy. "Ironically," Reinelt and Roach write,

> the history of the discipline of theater studies is one of fighting for autonomy from English and Speech departments, insisting on a kind of separation from other areas of study. It was necessary, politically necessary, to claim this distinctiveness, even at the expense of becoming somewhat insular and hermetic—a result that unfortunately became true of many departments of theater. Now, however, it is even more necessary to recognize and insist on the interdependency of a related series of disciplines and also on the role of performance in the production of culture in its widest sense.[12]

My own commitment to studying performance under the rubric of theater studies comes from a keen awareness of the second-class status so many departments maintain in their institutions, and only partly because they've chosen to seal themselves hermetically from interdisciplinarity. Institutions too often reductively equate theater studies with the most undertheorized theater practice, and sometimes their assumptions prove true. Caught up still in romantic notions of artistry as unthought, as unmediated by choice and work and modes of production, academic theater practice often aspires to imitate "real theater" that happens elsewhere, replicating the high-art, elite centers of production that cultural critics are simultaneously challenging. Preprofessional BFA and MFA programs often virulently insist on unexamined discourses of high-art elitism, as they prepare students to enter what is described monolithically as "the profession." And as Joe Roach has suggested, even the architecture of theater buildings tends to separate our departments from the rest of the campus, removing theater to sometimes isolated locations with ample parking and room to build shops, fly lofts, and large auditoriums.[13]

Theater's notorious anti-intellectualism, which is perpetuated in the academy and in the popular press alike, is also part of what vexes the status of the field. Along with the humanist fetishizing of the artist practiced by some—although not all—university theater production areas, the model of consumption brought to bear by uninformed reviewers for popular presses, and the paucity of culturally committed theater and performance criticism in the trade press, contributes to a perception of the theater profession and the academic departments that feed it as star-breeding, ego-stroking sycophants for the entertainment industry. "Entertainment" is a vital part of the cultural landscape, but theater studies needs to think about the meanings that it generates, along with critic/theorist/practitioners in film, television, and other media studies.[14] In the academy, theater studies faculty could choose the luxury of striving to be "scholar/artists," a position that public culture disallows and that public resources too often can't enable. But public discourse is so entrenched in the debilitating separation of thought and action in the arts, it has been very difficult to change the academy to understand the potential in the conjunction (rather than separation) of intellectual work and creativity.

Part of my argument for theater studies comes from an optimistic reading of its new maturity, from a sense that practitioners and theorists alike are questioning these old ideological assumptions. Such questions are shaped partly by an engagement with critical theory across disciplines, which has shaken the positivist foundation of the field, started to meld the historic dichotomy of theory and practice, and begun to critique the cultural and historical implications of theater as high art or as popular culture.[15] Yet ironically, it's critical theory itself that has legitimated the performative and lured people in theater studies away from home. Rather than enriching theater studies, some scholars sometimes leave it behind for other newly charted, interdisciplinary territory. Why should theatrical performance seem old-fashioned and naive when theater scholars use new critical theory?

As Reinelt and Roach insist, "In a way, theory gives theatre back again to the body politic," since it allows performance to "be articulated in terms of politics: representation, ideology, hegemony, resistance."[16] The issues become where people look for knowledge (epistemology); how they get there (methodology); and what they do with it (the enactment of performance practices). How can theater be a tool to move the body politic to theorize its diverse identity? How can theater engage the body politic to negotiate with its own cultural locations? How can academic theater studies manifest its pedagogical and political alignments?

Academic Modes of Production

In the last twenty or so years, the objectivity and empiricism of traditional theater departments have been challenged mostly on the basis of identity politics. Feminism's application to theater, in particular, has ensured that universal "man" can no longer be presumed as the subject of any performance, contemporary or historical. This ideological adjustment has had enormous impact on the field. Critical race studies have likewise had a large impact, so that racial and ethnic categories, too, cannot be ignored responsibly, or located purely in instances of cultural impersonation like minstrelsy and blackface that absented people of color as subjects even while they derided them as objects of an imperialist white gaze.[17] Margaret Wilkerson, in an article that stresses the changing demography of American theater, reminds theater scholars that they will have to continue to rethink the Eurocentric history of their theory and practice if theater programs are to succeed into the twenty-first century. Wilkerson says, "Theatre provides an opportunity for a community to come together and reflect on itself. . . . It is not only the mirror through which a society can reflect upon itself—it also helps to shape the perceptions of that culture through the power of its imagining."[18] Wilkerson's aspiration for theater requires that it look—along with the scholars who teach it—elsewhere than the Eurocentric canon for knowledge.

James Hatch offers a similar reminder of the continuing importance of criticizing racial exclusions based on identity categories in the contents and methods of theater studies. Hatch excoriates theater programs for continuing to overlook African influences in theater history and African American work in contemporary theater. He suggests, "The roots of the problem are woven inextricably into America's social history and perpetuated by graduate programs in theater departments. This continuing apartheid in an era when our scholars show increasing sophistication in national and multiethnic theater history is unfair to students—and dishonest."[19]

Hatch's argument might profitably haunt interdisciplinary strategies propelling theater scholarship. Hatch and Wilkerson propose using knowledge gained from identity area studies to infuse theater studies' practice and methods with difference. Wilkerson says, "We can no longer teach or even study theatre as we have in the past. Those of us in theatre production programs will find ourselves increasingly marginalized or isolated in our institutions if we do not include in very fundamental ways the new population (students of color and others) constituting our student bodies. . . . The pathbreaking scholarship in [other] fields is revolutionizing the ways in which we see ourselves and the places where we look for knowledge."[20]

University theaters, for example, can be used for radical interventionist work, despite their location in academic institutions that sometimes militate against such thinking, by offering a forum for embodying and enacting new communities of performers and spectators, by actualizing the potential of well-meaning political buttons that two-dimensionally purport to "celebrate diversity." University theaters are spaces that might productively be given over to theories and practices of performance in all its aspects, and studies of identity in all its complex intersectional variety, rather than protected as museums to house imitations of canonical white masterpieces. Yet such moves remain surprisingly difficult. At the 1998 ATHE conference, on a panel addressing (once again) race and gender in the profession and in theater departments, panelists and participants bemoaned the continuing lack of opportunities on their campuses for production work that includes attention to minoritarian experience.[21]

While these identity politics have been brought to bear primarily on theater as written and performed texts, they also occasion a revision of the materially productive aspects of theater programs. Design and technology areas, prodded into newly sophisticated systems for producing visual effects and artistry, aren't exempt from the challenges of realigning their commitments to a differently mapped geography of theater production. Opening up the categories of theater worker—designer, technician, actor, director, and so on—to include those whose identities have historically defined them within the hegemonic American tradition as decorative spectacle (white women) or exoticized other or servant (men and women of color), might reorient theater's material production. Actor training, needless to say, is most often marked by assumptions of whiteness and maleness as the standard from which white women and men and women of color are trained to perform. But visual sign systems that audiences see embodied in performance are built on prior production labor (by actors, designers, directors, and technicians, among other theater workers) that are also ideologically marked. Additionally, the simple fact that theater departments around the country, and the national professional organizations that advocate for them, remain racially and ethnically homogenous means that the field still needs to consider the politics of identity, even as its theorists argue against identity politics or against identity altogether as a perspective from which to engage representation.

As Roach reiterates, after Raymond Williams, "The convergence of material productions with signifying systems inheres in the fundamental nature of theatrical performance."[22] Because of such a productive convergence, theatrical performance offers a special site, one that slows the spin of postmodernist and poststructuralist relativity. Theatrical performance also offers a temporary and usefully ephemeral site at which to think through various important questions. For instance, questions of the signifying body that determine how we read what bodies mean, by considering them as "signs" of meaning, are readily available by looking at actors' gestures and their relationships to one another in the physical space of the stage. Questions of how bodies in space exemplify social relations can be studied in the embodiment of texts as performance, and a director's choices to position actors around a set. Performance demonstrates the ways in which any reading is always multiple and illustrates the undecidability of visual as well as textual meanings. Performance allows an investigation of the materiality of the corporeal, the presence of bodies that require direct and present engagement. Such questions can still be brought to bear in the temporary communities that theater producing and theatergoing construct. Theater scholars might productively borrow the language of science to explain their goals and methods. As Wilkerson has remarked, research universities understand the workings of "laboratories." Theater studies might use the analogy, even while it discards its positivist trappings.[23]

Performance Studies, Cultural Studies

At a time when new journal initiatives [in the human sciences] have been flee-
ing from identification with disciplines, Cultural Anthropology . . . *nonethe-*
less has recognized the importance of siting critique and exploration of other pos-
sibilities within the frame of given disciplinary traditions. Initiatives within
disciplines are as important as those that apparently float free in self-styled in-
terdisciplinary space.
— George Marcus, *Rereading Cultural Anthropology*

Several years ago, at the ATHE conference, a major debate surrounded the relationship between theater studies and its interdisciplinary cohort, performance studies.[24] While theater studies traces its genealogy through speech departments that once focused on the oral interpretation of literature, as well as English departments that focus on dramatic literature, performance studies has also branched off from several different genres of academic study. One prevalent form of performance studies incurs an equal debt to the performance of texts in speech departments, while another grounds itself in methods and theory borrowed from literary criticism, folklore, social science, and the study of popular culture and performance in everyday life. The Department of Performance Studies at New York University has perhaps been the primary proponent of this latter, interdisciplinary, social sciences–based branch of the field, and Richard Schechner, an experimental theater director working actively since the sixties, and a long-standing faculty member at NYU's Performance Studies, historically has been one of its preeminent spokespeople. At this particular ATHE conference, and in a "Comment" that he published in the journal *TDR* shortly after, Schechner argued that professional theater training programs sell "snake-oil" to students and that they should be dismantled so that theater can return to the humanities (and social sciences) through performance studies, in all its cultural variety.[25] Essentially, he was arguing that so-called professional theater training programs, or any program that purports to prepare young students for a theater industry in which they can hardly make a living, is offering a corrupt sense of possibility and training toward a future that doesn't exist. Schechner's comments, and a slowly building consensus among some scholars in the organization that theater studies could well be amplified by a broader attention to performance in more of its variety, led to various public debates about the relationship between the two fields.

I was a graduate student at New York University when it had just converted its Graduate Drama Department into the Department of Performance Studies. I had returned to graduate school because I wanted a supportive intellectual context in which to think about feminist theater criticism. I had an activist artistic agenda that the feminist political community in which I then lived in Boston wouldn't support, so I tried the academy. As I learned more about performance studies, it appeared that although I hardly knew what I was getting into, I'd made the right choice.

In Performance Studies, I'd landed in a program that was proud of its resistance to traditional modes of knowledge that wanted to give students the tools to produce knowledge differently, through popular culture studies, interculturalism, and folklore. Performance Studies was unconventional enough to enable feminism to carve out a niche there. The notion of performance could accommodate the marginalized productions of women's theater. It offered methods through which to account for women creating texts of their bodies and their lives, whether as mimes in front of Greek theaters or in upper-middle-class salons. A performance paradigm helped analyze these women's rejection of public architecture, which was in any case out of their reach, to create new meanings in private spaces in which they wielded some power. As performance studies scholar Dwight Conquergood notes, "Particularly for poor and marginalized people denied access to middle-class 'public' forums, cultural performance becomes the venue for 'public discussion' of vital issues central to their communities, as well as an arena for gaining visibility and staging their identity."[26] Performance not only broadened what I could study, but helped me understand how feminism could profit from thinking through performance as an embodied relationship to history and to power. The notion of performance could let me find Dick Hebdige's book *Subculture: The Meanings of Style* and use it to theorize about lesbian erotics and style as a performance of resistance.[27] I charted my own itinerary through my own desires and, through performance studies, helped establish for myself an embodied relationship to poststructuralist theory, which was just beginning to be applied in feminism.

When I confronted a class of students as a first-time teacher in the School of Drama at the University of Washington, I had to explain my training in performance studies and entice students to go with me as we revised the frame of reference through which to look at theater. My performance studies training let me persuade them that the plays we read extended well outside the classroom, that they were artifacts of culture (what James Clifford calls "survivals") that needed to be engaged, studied, and contested to figure out what they might tell us about how we live, but more importantly, how we might live.[28]

As I describe later in chapter 6, I encouraged students to stage cross-gendered versions of scenes from the canon in my play analysis class. We delighted in the fact that gender was a performative practice (although we didn't have that language then) that was part of our performances. Feminism brought me to an embodied approach to learning for which performance offered a strategy. Using performance in the classroom became a different epistemology, a way of knowing not just our selves, but the world. Performance studies refused to privilege the text, and connected theater and performance as what Schechner calls "restored behavior."[29] These ideas invigorated my interventions into a more traditional theater studies curriculum, and the classroom became a new site of my feminist activism around gender and representation.

I need an expanded notion of performance to challenge the conventions of theater training that jealously guard the theory/practice split that hobbles our field. I also need a politicized performance paradigm to generate ways of looking at theater that aren't gilded with the rhetoric of highbrow culture, and what Lawrence Levine calls its missionary attitude toward saving or guarding itself against an "uncivilized" public.[30] I wanted to help find rationales for theater studies and performance in the academy and in culture that aren't about how they rescue people from degeneracy, but that articulate clearly and forcefully how they offer tools for cultural intervention, ways of engaging and thinking about social relations as we know them and as they could be.

When I later chaired the Department of Theatre and Drama at the University of Wisconsin–Madison, bemused administrators tolerated my impassioned explanations of our work in theater studies, but never appeared to take our department seriously. Our productions seemed pale imitations of work they hoped to see in New York, the real center of what they understood as theater.[31] Our scholarship seemed odd in its interdisciplinarity; I recall the dean of Graduate Studies, as I was trying to impress upon him the connections theater studies has made with a number of different fields, asking why we needed to work in a theater department, then? As Marvin Carlson has written, we have to be able to "say clearly what distinguishes theatre history from [other histories]," or the "university administrators, legislators, or funding agencies . . . may . . . begin to wonder why our activity cannot be as easily taken care of by one or several of these other disciplines."[32] The total quality management (TQM) philosophy of academic management might make interdisciplinarity desirable for all the wrong reasons.

At the Ph.D. Program at the CUNY Graduate Center, on the other hand, I was impressed that, this being New York, people presumed they knew what it was we did in the Theatre Program. They still couldn't quite grasp that ours was a solely academic study of theater and turned to us for cheap entertainments occasionally. Carlson, my colleague at CUNY, was irate during the student demonstrations against the budget cuts some years ago when he was asked if the program could put together some sketches, or something dramatic, that might be effective on the streets.[33]

I had mixed responses to this request. On the one hand, I agreed with Carlson that we have to educate our institutional colleagues against the notion that our labor is simply available to throw together skits. On the other hand, following more of a performance studies itinerary through this anecdote, I do think it would have been interesting to encourage our students and faculty to work with the protesters to integrate performance into their activist strategies. For the Theatre Program to be perceived in this new way would require a different kind of institutional educating. How can we offer what we know to student demonstrators and striking workers, to people without large public forums to share what they know, through performance? How can we offer performance as a tool that can be embraced and harnessed toward exactly that kind of public educational process, a process of difficult social change? Implicit here is a rationale for theater and performance that extends well beyond the academy.

Theater Studies in the Disciplines

Many graduate students in theater and performance studies are compelled toward interdisciplinary mappings that might finally leave them isolated in the more established disciplines in which they're hired, if they've worked hard enough and are lucky enough to find jobs at all. Many theater scholars find positions in English departments, in which their hybrid scholarship is often precarious among more traditional text-based studies. Phil Auslander points out that "the consequence of [the] diaspora of performance scholars . . . is the intellectual isolation of the individual scholar."[34] How can we forge common cause and community around disciplinary practices that remain exclusionary, that are enticed by the presumptive faddishness of performance and performativity but might use it and discard it just as they have other academic fashions?

Schechner's argument for performance studies seemed to promise a progressive aspect that would look everywhere for knowledge. In a review essay on performance studies, published in *Theatre Journal* in the mid-eighties, Phillip Zarrilli says, "Schechner's view is all-encompassing. . . . [His] scheme is grandly conceived in the most challenging mode of the Western liberal, humanist tradition—the entire world is before him as he charts his 'performance' map."[35] In Zarrilli's description of Schechner's vision, performance studies' methods appear so avant-garde and radical they presuppose an inclusion of the politically marginalized through a naturally democratic progress.

But the rhetoric of progress in which Schechner trades when he encourages us away from theater into performance studies, makes a gesture that's suspiciously imperialist. As Bruce McConachie notes appropriately, "Traditional American theatre and drama scholars have tended to accept uncritically the notion that individualism, democracy, and progress characterized the 'American way' and that the American theatre has embodied and reflected these attributes."[36] Progressing away from old, entrenched disciplinary thinking toward interdisciplinary thought isn't, in itself, a politically progressive move adequate to ensure the inclusion of more contents or methods.[37] Leaving theater architecture to study the world as a stage doesn't guarantee that all geographies will receive comparable attention. Schechner's promise of liberation through performance studies, and contemporary theory's promiscuous citation of the performative, will prove appropriative unless they're securely linked not just to new ways of seeing, but to new places and multiple identities.[38]

Feminist writer Ellen Rooney makes a similar argument about the necessity for clarifying the politics of cultural studies as it, too, achieves academic legitimation. Cultural studies has been configured in United States academic institutions with a large debt to its British progenitors. The field is clearly marked by an investigation into what John Fiske calls the "definition of culture as a constant site of struggle between those with and those without power,"[39] but Rooney argues that there's a danger, in its institutionalization as an area of study, that this political inflection will be recuperated and erased.

Rooney suggests that the problem with the American version of the field is that its institutional situation "does not yet allow us to name any particular political movement (outside the university) as 'properly' affiliated with cultural studies."[40] She insists on asking what this political investment might be and how the field revises the production of knowledge. "The student of cultural studies is a cultural worker," Rooney writes, and "students and critics [should] have the theoretical tools to see their own work simultaneously as a tactic of resistance *and* an exercise of power, a process of exposing the concealed investments of disciplinary systems and deliberately re-organizing the pursuit of knowledge as such."[41] Otherwise, Rooney argues, cultural studies will become just another discipline.[42]

The questions Rooney brings to cultural studies might be profitably posed to performance studies. Performance studies, as richly interdisciplinary and intercultural as it now seems, must establish a political alliance, an interested position in the circulation of power through cultural meanings, to avoid becoming just another major. A politically aligned performance studies could invigorate theater studies without eviscerating it. Perhaps the most distinctive contribution of performance studies is to expand even further the scope of the textual object, opening its purview into folklore and festivals, rituals and rites, stories and sports, all across many cultures, rather than leaving the text ensconced in the Eurocentric markings of traditional theater history.[43] In its folkloric and intercultural variety, performance studies frees its performers and ethnographers from the constraints of canonical texts and institutional architecture, but its commitments and questions are similar to those posed in theater. Whose stories get told, to whom, and how? What are the modes of production and contexts of reception for cultural performance?

These are questions that theater studies has always asked, posing them primarily to the playwright, who tells, and to the actor, who is supposed to erase the epistemological question just as it's posed, to eradicate the seed of doubt about a story's truth status by laminating him- or herself so thoroughly to the experiences of the character that the audience never questions their conjuncture in his or her body. All these conjunctures are now, of course, unsettled and questioned, which is part of the current invigoration of theater studies as a site of theory and practice.[44]

Performance studies also dislodges theater studies' historical inquiry from the constraints of architectural location,[45] examining new, intersecting axes of texts and spaces. Locations at which texts and spaces meet mark off places to which people come to experience, critique, engage with, and produce cultural representations. Performance studies widens the range of locations, and suggests that all of culture is in some ways performative. How can we (or should we?) articulate the specificity of theater as something performative, yet unique among it, as an activity marked by traveling across or within geographies to be with people in other, often "othered," spaces, looking, inten-

tionally, pleasurably, meaningfully? How can the liveness of theater performance reveal performativity? Theater studies offers, literally, a place to investigate some of the questions posed only metaphorically elsewhere.[46]

Cultural performances—intentionally performative moments—are
slightly different from a Goffmanesque view of performance in everyday life.
Zarrilli quotes John MacAloon, who says cultural performances are "occasions in which as a culture or society we reflect upon and define ourselves,
dramatize our collective myths and history, present ourselves with alternatives, and eventually change in some ways while remaining the same in others."[47] MacAloon's definition of performance echoes Wilkerson's definition of
theater, both as sites at which a culture reflects on the structure of its relationships and their possibilities.

The inquiries and productions of theater studies (in its redefinition) and
performance studies, at base, are linked by a commitment to studying the
construction of social relations around ideological belief systems that organize experience through cultural representation and regulation. They assume
that, in Fiske's definition, "culture is a process of making meanings that people actively participate in; it is not a set of preformed meanings handed
down to and imposed upon the people."[48] Zarrilli suggests that "in view of
this more comprehensive notion of performance, the narrower foci of traditional theater studies—history/historiography, aesthetics, literary theme,
etc.—become important specific strands in the nexus of cultural metacom-
mentaries."[49] My own gentle amendment would be that rather than subsum-
ing theater studies in the metacomments of performance in a hierarchical
way, a dialectical movement might be established that reconfigures both
fields.

For example, Zarrilli stresses process in the performance model, and its
importance to both anthropologists and theater theorists and practitioners.
He quotes Victor Turner's and other social scientists' admiration for theater
people's "laboratory of performative experiments normally inaccessible to
field anthropologists, who can look and stare but seldom change or experiment with the cultural performances they encounter."[50] This interventionist,
experimental possibility can distinguish theater studies from other fields
studying performativity.[51] If theater studies is the postmodern, interdisciplinary aspect of the older, disciplinarily bound theater, it can raise questions
about the imperialist gesture of performance as ethnography. The reconceptualized field can skeptically draw out the partialities of stories as truth, demystify the coincidence of actor and text, and fill its spaces with complex
identities that anchor its commitments to a politics of anticanonical, antiracist inclusion.

Practicing Performance in Production

Theater studies' distinct contribution across disciplines can be a place to experiment with the production of cultural meanings, on bodies willing to try a range of different significations for spectators willing to read them. At UW–Madison, for example, the productions I directed were all experiments within this framework. *A Midsummer Night's Dream*, which I directed with Phillip Zarrilli, experimented with environmental theater and drag performance, shifting the text to examine closely the regulatory systems of gender and sexuality it upsets and finally upholds. Through references to gay and lesbian culture, to Madonna and Alan Jackson, Sylvester and Gloria Gaynor, and other icons of gay and straight pop culture, we made the forest and the court destabilized places of play, in which gender was more of a mask, and sexuality a continuum of options. Our production was a celebration of performance, even while it offered a critical look at gender performativity and argued for rearranged and reimagined social relationships.

In *Etta Jenks*, Marlane Meyers's play about pornography, we created a Brechtian learning environment, surrounding the original text with commentary challenging its narrow view of women's relationship to sex work by interrupting the text with irony and skepticism. We cross-gender cast here, too, to disrupt easy assumptions about gender and pornography and held a number of discussions that encouraged people to address the issues we raised. *Etta* was far from a traditional evening in the theater, and some spectators were too alienated aesthetically to appreciate it intellectually. Many younger students, taking the department's "Introduction to Theater" course, resented that the production refused to tell them how to think about its meanings, and that it left so many of its ambiguous references open to numerous interpretations. But at least the production was a radical experiment in the university theater context.

When I directed Wendy Wasserstein's comedy *The Heidi Chronicles* for the summer theater season, I was challenged to deconstruct a popular play that I found intensely antifeminist while still bringing in box office receipts (since the University Theater at UW needed to make money in the summer to support the mainstage schedule during the year). It was difficult to intervene in Wasserstein's play; her conservative view of feminism is tightly structured and nearly unbreakable, ideologically. But through a few bold choices (mostly in costume and set design but also in acting), we managed to signal a quarrel with some of the text's most excessive statements about the status of white middle-class women. For example, we designed exceedingly large presents for the baby shower scene, so large the women staggered under their weight. We dressed the women in the scene in parodic versions of maternity clothes, and padded the pregnant women as though they were having sextuplets. In the final scene, when Heidi sentimentally rocks and sings to her new baby, we used a baby doll to obviously signify the child, which the actor spun around her head in the play's final moment. Working resistantly with comedy was a real challenge, and taught my students and me much about the insidiousness of genre and structure.

My last production at Madison, Sophie Treadwell's *Machinal*, attempted to simply honor and fulfill the promises of the text, which tells the story of a young woman oppressed by social structures of family and the law, who marries her overbearing boss and finally murders him to free herself to pursue what she's found is a truer passion with a young drifter. The play's expressionistic style was most challenging here, and as a director, I'm not sure I completely achieved the manic, perspectival view of the Young Woman's crushing constraints. But we worked long and hard on the acting challenges, discussing how to portray the Young Woman as strong, even as she fails before the social discourses that finally conspire to execute her. We also theorized how to move audiences, how emotion can be harnessed not just to make people feel, but to move them emotionally and socially to some sort of understanding or maybe even action.[52]

Unlike for example, English departments, which focus primarily on texts, theater studies requires an acknowledgment of the physical use of space in theater buildings and other performance sites.[53] And theater departments are typically attached to spaces, to proscenium and/or "black box" theaters, to rehearsal rooms and design/technology shops in which students physicalize their studies through practice. Theater studies becomes a material location, organized by technologies of design and embodiment (through artisanry and actor training), a pedagogically inflected field of play at which culture is liminal or liminoid and available for intervention. Theater studies—as a discipline and as a geography, tied to the academy but resonating far outside of it—can offer this potential.

Feminist and Gay and Lesbian Studies: Translating Performative Theory Back into Theater Studies

Poststructuralist feminist and gay and lesbian theories that employ social constructionist models have found performativity rich metaphorical currency. For example, the metaphor is useful for materialist feminists, who argue that gender and sexuality are not innate psychological attributes, but clearly constructed performances that take place on the surface of the body.

These performances—or "stylized repetition[s] of acts," as Judith Butler has so persuasively argued[54]—occur continually in culture in ways that only appear natural, through their inculcation in dominant discourses of family, education, and the law.

Much feminist work on gender as performance in theater studies[55] can be traced to Teresa de Lauretis's influential essay "The Technology of Gender" (1987), in which she argued several points usefully applied to feminist performance theory: "(1) Gender is (a) representation. . . . (2) The representation of gender *is* its construction. . . . (3) The construction of gender goes on as busily today as it did in earlier times. . . . (4) [T]he construction of gender is also affected by its deconstruction."[56] The notion of gender as a representation, taught, resisted, and negotiated through cultural representational systems became enormously useful as a strategy for feminists in film and concurrently, in theater and performance studies. It offers historical places to investigate the operation of gender as only representation, as only constructed and created through the cultural and historical moments that needed it to work. "Gender as representation" resonated fruitfully with feminist theater scholars' inquiry into the representation of gender, changing the terms of the study within the same object and subject of analysis.

Butler's work extends this strategy into theorizing gender as a solely performative act, a surface enactment on the body of culturally and historically specific discourses that require how gender is to be "done." Butler argues that these repeated, stylized, corporeal acts work to create the subject as object of discourse, rather than expressing an essential gender identity waiting for its articulation in discourse.

The body, Butler argues, is not "passively scripted with cultural codes, as if it were a lifeless recipient of wholly pregiven cultural relations."[57] Consciously extending the theatrical metaphor, she notes, "Just as a script may be enacted in various ways, and just as the play requires both text and interpretation, so the gendered body acts its part in a culturally restricted corporeal space and enacts interpretations within the confines of already existing directives."[58] The metaphor of a body staged, directed by cultural imperatives, figures the social as a theater.

Theater scholars and practitioners might put Butler's provocative performative metaphor to use in theater spaces, in which the intentional performance of gender acts might be examined, disrupted, and reconfigured. Performers and directors might ask together, Where does gender begin in a gesture? Can there be a gesture not already marked by a gender performance? How can the actor employ Brechtian methods to enact Butler's theories in performance? How can audiences be encouraged to read and critique performances of gender?[59] These are only some of the questions that might be posed and studied when performative theory is translated back into theater studies.

Butler argues that gender is always performed under situations of historical duress, with harsh punishments for "those who fail to do their gender right."[60] Ideology asserts overt pressure to maintain the coincidence of biology and gendered appearance, so that a transvestite, in Butler's example, might be at great physical risk performing his or her resistant appearance on the street.[61] Butler suggests such a noncoincident performance is authorized, and therefore made safe, by the not-real structure of theater, but I wonder if the cultural danger of an illegitimate gender performance might not be usefully employed for theatrical representation as well. On the street, as Butler would have it, noncoincident gender appearance versus what is perceived as gender reality creates a great deal of cultural anxiety.[62] How can theater become an equally dangerous site of anxious incongruity, of profitable, discomfiting looking, a place in which the work of stylized repetitions is made palpably clear?[63] In the context of theater, what might "dangerous" mean? The theatrical frame doesn't have to render transgression safe.

People in dominant middle-class U.S. culture go to the theater to be reassured, in matters of gender, that what they see is what they are, what they see is who they love, that nature provides and structures privilege and power into the cultural arrangements through which they profit. Maria Irene Fornes has said, "We get narcissistic pleasure in reviewing what we know. We go to theater to see ourselves on stage. We lose interest in that which is unlike us."[64] How dangerous and useful might theater be if it showed, with gestic insistence, that we are not even like us, that we are not the self-same individuals theater has reassured us we appear to be?

If theater is engaged in deconstructive epistemology, questioning how we know what we think we know, and who we think we are, its representational apparatus can be pressed into service. We can use it in specific contexts to study and play with, for example, performances of sexual identities, to make subcultural codes widely legible, to resist the inculcations of heterosexuality performed as congruent with "correct" gender acts. Diana Fuss points out the useful distinction between inquiries into sexual identity as epistemology versus sexual identity as performative, saying, "Questions of epistemology ('how do we know?') enjoy a privileged status in theorizations of gay and lesbian identity. . . . [T]he very insistence of the epistemological frame of reference in theories of homosexuality may suggest that we cannot know, surely or definitively. Sexual identity may be less a function of knowledge than performance, or, in Foucauldian terms, less a matter of final discovery than perpetual reinvention."[65] Theatrical representation is a place of "perpetual reinvention," wired by the danger of performing against the rules. This is a space in which theater practice—spectators and performers coming to a place to show and to look and to think through the danger together—regains its efficacy. The laboratory of theater offers a site for working through some of the gender troubles that would be too dangerous, in different ways, on the street. For example, certain resistant ways of performing gender, received through the critical apparatus of performance, might incite thought about the strictures of normalizing gender roles. On the street in certain parts of the country, these same performances might incite violence. Yet at the same time, staging these performances even in a theater can be bold enough to stimulate anxiety along with thought, which might upset spectators even as it challenges them to rethink commonsensical ideas.

Perhaps the danger in the theater is ideological and even emotional. Although some poststructuralist critics have recently engaged with emotion as discourse, much postmodernist performance criticism remains cynical about its power, which it often relegates to an old-fashioned humanist plane, since emotion seems to emanate from a body that is always deeper than its surface. But I'm persuaded, along with Ed Cohen, that emotion is vital to motivate political change, be it righteous racial or gender anger, or an ameliorative notion of "affection," which Cohen says "becomes one of a number of impelling forces that move us to realign, interrupt, or alter our trajectories, challenging us to join with, observe, deny, ignore, or resist the movements that are coalescing within and around us." Cohen cites the importance of "understanding 'who we are' not as a standing still but as a moving, as a speaking to and a being spoken to, as a being touched by and as a touching."[66] I still believe this can happen in the theater, that people destabilized by difference can speak and be spoken to, be touched by and touch. Theater can be a mobile unit in a journey across new geographies, a place that doesn't center the discourse in white male hegemony, but a space that can be filled and moved, by and to the margins, perpetually decentered as it explores various identity configurations of production and reception. University theater, in particular, has the potential to teach spectators how to be moved by difference, to encourage them to experience emotion not as acquiescent, but as passionate, and motivating toward social change.

On Identification: Moving (the) Metaphor(s)

The widespread belief in the possibility of understanding has committed us, however unwittingly, to a concomitant narrative of betrayal, disappointment, and

rage. . . . It is perhaps past time that we begin to attempt to see the inevitability of misunderstanding as generative and hopeful, as opportunities for conversation . . . rather than as a betrayal of a promise.
—Peggy Phelan, *Unmarked*

In the academic and activist proliferation of theatrical and performative metaphors, it occurs to me that rather than seeing theater theory and practice metamorphose away from a material site of study and embodiment, other metaphors might realign and restructure the objects and subjects of inquiry in the field.[67] Theater studies needs different metaphors to challenge from where and how people see in theater, how they can hear at least partially, without theatrical speech devolving into empty confession, how theater can disclose new knowledge without voyeurism, how theater can be an ethnography, while avoiding the imperialist gesture of the anthropologist's gaze.[68]

Some of the metaphors that have been used in earlier moments in contemporary feminist theory now seem prescient about the notion of what's come to be called "performativity," as well as evoking the potential for reimagining the ways in which we perceive the production/reception exchange in theater. For example, Chicana essayist and theorist Gloria Anzaldúa uses the metaphor of masking, a trope historically used by women of color and white women to describe the frictions and pleasures of dual-identity discourses. In her introduction to her edited anthology, *Making Face, Making Soul*, Anzaldúa points out the performative nature of identity productions, which rely on context for their various articulations. She writes that "the face is the surface of the body that is the most noticeably inscribed by social structures. . . . We are 'written' all over, . . . carved and tattooed with the sharp needles of experience."[69]

Anzaldúa is very precise about the material inscription of discourses on bodies, and the potential for Chicanas to "construct [their] identity" by grasping the agency of making faces.[70] She employs an explicitly performative metaphor to theorize identity and political community. The mask is her strategy for articulating multiple, conflicting identities, embodied by women of color crisscrossed by the needles of gender, race and ethnicity, class and sexuality experience. Multiple masking, or screwing one's face into variations of "false ones," is often used as a social survival strategy. Along with the urgency of activist race and gender performance "on the street," such masking resonates with resistant acting strategies in theater practice that broaches the productive danger of incongruent identity performances.

If the masked face, or the agency of making faces, offers a metaphoric possibility to the performer, Anzaldúa's reception metaphor offers a position for the spectator. At the other side of the production/reception paradigm that frames her writing, Anzaldúa notes, "I am acutely conscious of the politics of address. . . . Contrary to the norm, [this book] does not address itself *primarily* to whites, but invites them to 'listen in' to women-of-color talking to one another and, in some instances, to and against white people."[71] How can audiences be trained to "listen in," to retool our expectations of how and what we hear in the theater? How can "listening in" model a rejection of voyeuristic, appropriative identifications?[72] How can audiences, as Fornes asked ruefully, be persuaded to look at those unlike them?

White feminist Iris Marion Young's metaphors of geography and location also offer a useful way to situate theater as a site for this work. Young works with a utopic notion of the city as a place to enact a politics of difference, replacing idealistic notions of community with "our positive experience of city life to form a vision of the good society."[73] She writes, "City life is the 'being-together' of strangers. Strangers encounter one another, either face to face or through media, often remaining strangers and yet acknowledging their contiguity in living and the contributions each makes to the others. In such encountering people are not internally related, . . . and do not understand one another from within their own perspective. They are externally related, they experience each other as other, different, from different groups, histories, professions, cultures, which they do not understand."[74] In this lack of understanding, however, Young finds pleasure, respect, and aesthetic inexhaustibility, which defines the "unoppressive city" as "openness to unassimilated otherness."[75] Her description of this urban geography models the most hopeful experiences of being among an audience at a theater, in which performance texts move multiple identities out from under, between worlds, onto new grounds, and out front, for audiences who actively, productively misunderstand, as Phelan would have it, their racial, sexual, and ethnic difference.[76]

Another metaphor used in the late eighties to propose a bridging of differences within and among women could be useful in building audiences to inhabit theaters in the unoppressive city, and it also has a performative value: Argentinian feminist philosopher Maria Lugones's metaphor, which she calls "world traveling," implies an identification or empathy fundamental to certain kinds of actor training and the conventions of spectator response. Lugones reworks these concepts in reference to the politics of difference within feminism. She believes that part of the "failure of love" between women of color and white women includes "the failure to identify with another woman, the failure to see oneself in other women who are quite different from oneself."[77] Constructing a metaphoric ontology, she suggests that "travelling to each other's 'worlds' enables us to *be* through *loving* each other."[78] Such traveling both requires and extends the positionalities and locations from which our work begins.

Lugones insists on the necessity of identification and its material contexts. "A 'world,'" she says, "has to be presently inhabited by flesh and blood people."[79] She allows for a nonstable definition of what a "world" might be, but ties it insistently to bodies in relation, touching and being touched, moving across social and bodily geographies together. Traveling, then, is the "shift from being one person to being a different person."[80] Lugones says that the "playful attitude" brought to this travel allows a flexibility, a way to be in each world creatively, not passively.[81]

"World-traveling," as much as Lugones insists on its embodiment, remains a metaphor for a psychological identification, one in which consciousness shifts through imagination. The imperialist, touristic implications of traveling to other, exotic locales, is displaced by Lugones's insistence that a loving desire to empathize, to know differently, prompts a shift in consciousness, in which psychic space is profoundly, profitably unsettled. Lugones offers the possibility of consciousness shifting to imagine worlds lived differently.

The more material aspects of her ideas echo productively with other feminist theorizing on identification, which also critiques a well-meant, humanist erasure of difference on the path toward understanding. As Young says, "Political theorists and activists should distrust this desire for reciprocal recognition and identification with others . . . because it denies difference in the concrete sense of making it difficult for people to respect those with whom they do not identify. I suggest that the desire for mutual understanding and reciprocity underlying the ideal of community is similar to the desire for identification that underlies racial and ethnic chauvinism."[82] Identification, as feminists working on the limitations of theatrical realism have persuasively shown, promotes a chauvinistic likeness as the basis for gathering knowledge and experiencing emotion.

But feminist critiques also need to account for the political effects of emotion that is compelled on the basis of identification. Especially spectators still marginalized by identity categories need the motivation of identification to confirm a drive toward social change. And current critiques of identity politics have unsettled the totalizing quality of old identifications, pointing out that the categories from which and to which one identifies are never as stable and coherent as they seem. For example, how might identifying with a gender category lead people to explore the mutuality and difference of race and sexuality categories? How do people identify with multiple categories in performance? Where is the inclusive gesture of identification to be made?

Elin Diamond suggests that a continual process of serial identifications becomes part of a subject's psychic and social history in a manner ultimately fragmenting and destabilizing. She proposes that "the borders of identity, the wholeness and consistency of identity, is transgressed by every act of identification."[83] Identification is predicated at least in part on desire, which Lugones, from her less psychoanalytic orientation, calls "love." Diamond says, "We are continually taking in objects we desire, continually identifying with or imitating these objects, and *continually being transformed by them.*"[84] Traveling a world of desire and identification breaks the humanist borders of the self, rather than assimilating otherness to it to form coherency. As Diamond says, "The humanist notion of identity as . . . unique, unified, coherent, and consistent—is belied precisely by the temporality, the specific historicity of the identification process."[85] Joining Lugones's with Diamond's more historically and materially located processes of identification provides new uses for metaphors of identification, a trope and a strategy with which theater studies must, at least because of its history, continue to engage.

Unstable, historical identification can operate by "loving" otherness and refusing to assimilate it to the sameness of the self, when bodies and their differences are dangerously present. Anna Deavere Smith's performance piece *Fires in the Mirror*, which chronicles responses to the racial strife in Crown Heights in New York between African Americans and Hasidic Jews, could be an example of Lugones's notion of world traveling and of Young's critique of identification based on understanding. Smith interviewed people from the divided Brooklyn community and performed their responses to the event in their words, on her body. Thulani Davis, who dramaturged for Smith, said the diverse, conflicting viewpoints about the events in Crown Heights "come through Anna" in her performance, and "we have to listen."[86]

This strategy enacts Anzaldúa's challenge to pay attention, to listen, to decide how to act on the basis of information that I, for instance, might not understand, listening to the African American or Hasidic residents of Crown Heights. This is not a gesture toward deferring to some exalted state of pure understanding, but as Young might suggest, acting on respect for things you might never understand. Smith implies that the language we use to address diversity is inadequate, that the humanist understanding of difference has become worn and needs to be retreaded. She says that "understanding isn't necessarily going to bridge differences."[87] Phelan, too, reworks the bridge metaphor through misunderstanding: *"It is in the attempt to walk (and live) on the rackety bridge between self and other—and not the attempt to arrive at one side or another—that we discover real hope.* That walk is our always suspended performance—in the classroom, in the political field, in relation to one another and to ourselves."[88]

It seems significant, too, that Smith, who takes the language of others and embodies it, refashions it into another discourse, should make this claim against the efficacy of understanding as a political (and by analogy, performative) metaphor. Smith illustrates the potential of embodying, even imaginatively, what it might mean to be in a body that you don't recognize or with which you don't at all identify. Spectators, perhaps, attempting to identify with Smith's impersonations in a traditional, liberal way, are thwarted by the layers of difference and division that don't meld, but insist on their separateness, their insistently unassimilated otherness, and their constructedness in her own discourse.[89] Smith's piece also exemplifies a strategy in cultural studies of talking to "real people," rather than simply theorizing the constructed subject as interpolated into the text—people struggling with their stories and how they're told, struggling over how cultural meanings are made, how they're seen, and how their identities are constructed and negotiated. Multiple identities are engaged through a wildly revised but still theatrical form in *Fires in the Mirror.*[90]

Likewise, in a more recent performance piece, *House Arrest,* Smith preserves her method of capturing people's speech and gestures to evoke their politics, their beliefs, their values. Impersonating with interpretive skill people from President Clinton to Studs Terkel and an African American woman imprisoned for allowing her child to be beaten and die, Smith puts into play an array of human actors, relating to one another metaphorically through their embodiment in her skin. Whether they agree or debate, they become part of a fabric of human community that Smith brings for analysis to the theater.

Danny Hoch, another performer whose cross-racial, cross-ethnic impersonations present a progressive political effect, demonstrates Diamond's insistence on identification as history and desire. Hoch builds his characters in more depth than Smith, illustrating not simply how they serve an ideological function but how they dream and interact with the environment that forms them, through which they persevere and sometimes triumph. Hoch's vocal and physical techniques provide the rhythm and texture of race and ethnicity, as he embodies Dominicans, Latinos, Jews, and African Americans, among other kinds of people from the neighborhood in which he grew up. As a white man, he envoices through empathy and his own desire to know, even if he can't be, different people.

Politically committed theater makers and cultural critics can get larger audiences to "listen in" to one another, to imaginatively embody "unassimilated otherness." People need new words to speak to one another, words that describe their similarities and their differences in much more complicated ways, words that will allow them to account for the inevitability that what they say will only partially be heard. Theater studies and theater practice can provide places where instead of looking between performers and spectators and assuming sameness, people can learn to look at difference in a way that doesn't require that it become them or that they become it. They can look, fully, at who's there (or who appears to be there), using and surpassing metaphors of performativity.

Although the enactment of these metaphors and practices might prove challenging, scholars need them to read across identity differences. Contemporary antihumanist critiques launched by poststructuralist theorists have usefully questioned theater's capacity to generate an untheorized "communitas," but theater remains a site to which people travel to view and/or experience something together. Because of this persistent potential to engage with the social in physically, materially embodied circumstances, looking at theater (studies) continues as a vital, important research agenda.[91]

A Road Map through Different Geographies of Learning

1. Use interdisciplinarity to reinvigorate and expand disciplines, without erasing the disciplinary histories and methods it melds. Encourage students and scholars to cross disciplinary borders, but to respect the terms and debates of the fields from which they borrow.

2. Use theater and live performance, as well as theories of performativity, to study the social performance of gender, race and ethnicity, class, sexuality, ability, nationality, and other ways of being in culture.

3. Exploit the liveness of theater as a material place to which to bring academics, artists, and activists together to look in complicated ways at the topics of the day and at history, and to imagine a radically altered future. Build theater laboratories that prove nothing, but that experiment with everything.

4. Reject the missionary, evangelical posture of theater as civil redemption or salvation, and refocus on performance as cultural intervention shared in pleasure and fun.

5. Use the emotion theater inspires to move people to political action, to desire reconfigured social relations, to want to interact intimately with a local and a global community.

6. Produce dangerous theater, and use theater as a place to test dangerous

ideas. Produce theater that rouses people to leave their seats, to respond physically and vocally to the performance. Build a generation of spectators who care as much about theater as those who fought in the Astor Place riots in the nineteenth century.

7. Consider theater a site of world traveling and world building. Discard the romantic notion that full understanding is available through artistic expression, but create theater that doesn't shy from productive misunderstandings.

8. Use theater and performance to experiment with theoretical ideas that seem abstract in print, but that become alive and persuasive when embodied in a classroom or on a stage.

9. Seek alliances within and outside your discipline, with theorists and practitioners. Cross intradepartmental borders, while striving for the possibilities of interdisciplinarity.

10. Practice love as a value in academic work, in activism, and in artistry. Use it to spur feelings, emotion, movement. Allow yourself to be touched by people's research and by their art and by their beliefs, and make it your goal to touch people with your own.

chapter five

Queer Theater

Theorizing a Theatrical Vernacular

While I've argued elsewhere in *Geographies of Learning* that scholars should write for wider audiences, speaking is also a way to expand a constituency and to make a case for the relevance of research. Giving papers at conferences and lectures at various universities offers a way to share research in progress and to test out ideas, but it also provides opportunities for different kinds of engagement than publishing books and articles in scholarly journals. Since papers and lectures require interlocutors, they demand both performance and performativity. A good lecturer performs his or her talk, aware of how the words sound, what the accompanying gestures emphasize, and how well the audience is following. A good lecture is also performative: it's a speech act that *does* something.

As I proposed about presenting research in chapter 2, giving public lectures demands code switching, an ability to speak in more than one vocabulary depending on one's context and listeners. Because of its immediacy, and the presence of listeners, speaking demands adjusting to new and different locations. Speaking offers a chance to *form* an interpretive community, rather than presuming that one preexists a lecturer's visit. In his article "Opponents, Audiences, Constituencies, and Community," Edward Said says, "Is it the inevitable conclusion to the formation of an interpretive community that its constituency, its specialized language, and its concerns tend to get tighter, more airtight, more self-enclosed as its own self-confirming authority acquires more power, the solid status of orthodoxy, and a stable constituency?"[1] Although such closed communities are sometimes a consequence of academic systems of power building, I don't think that their formation is inevitable. Traveling regularly outside of such self-enclosed spaces reminds me of the need to translate and reorient my ideas so that more people can join the community I'd like my own interpretations to inspire.

Lecturing is enormously pleasurable for me as an activist academic. The stakes are always high, regardless of where I'm speaking—at the MLA, at ATHE, at "Creating Change," at CLAGS, at colleges and universities around the country. But once over the nervousness, my performance of my ideas helps me connect to my audience. Because in another life, I, too, was a performer, I'm very conscious of the rhythm and structure of my talks as well as the quality of my own delivery. I worry about pacing; I rehearse at least once by myself and once in front of someone else; and I listen for clarity and coherence. I want to be easy to hear and compelling enough to engage.

I look forward to discussions afterward, in which I'm challenged to explain, amplify, and extend my ideas. Speaking extemporaneously is a creative project for me, one full of faith. I feel nearly rabbinical in those moments, not because I enjoy or want the authority of theology, but because those are moments in which I articulate my deepest beliefs and my most utopian desires. They are also moments in which I feel the bond of community, even with relative strangers. I've been invited to their locale, whether it be a college or university or community center, and I feel keenly my opportunity to exchange gifts—mine of ideas and questions, theirs of hospitality and inquiry. I see this very much as direct action, community organizing, and alliance building.

In 1995, CLAGS presented the first theater conference on gay and lesbian theater, called "Queer Theatre, A Conference with Performances."[2] The keynote I gave at that conference was, for me, an act of translation, a chance to speak to a public audience as an academic critic about queer performance work. But I was deeply anxious about being asked to open the conference. I had worked with the organizing committee to help determine its themes and focus; I knew we wanted it to speak to artists and audiences of queer theater as well as to academic critics who document and theoretically analyze the work. I worried that since my credentials are mostly academic, I wouldn't be properly heard. I wanted to speak as a critic, but also as a spectator of queer theater who has taken great pleasure in and been profoundly shaped by the performers whose work I've seen evolve over the last twenty years. So I set out to write a keynote that might capture my emotional as well as my intellectual and academic commitments.

After twenty-five years or more of creating queer theater in the United States (depending, as I explain in the keynote, on where you start this history), the Queer Theatre Conference was the first national meeting devoted to this work.[3] I served with many people on the organizing committee, attending chaotic but creative meetings at which we would debate how to best spend a short three days. In that context, I met artists and critics whose work I'd seen or read. I wanted to honor the conference committee and their choice of me to keynote by choosing the right words to start off our public week.

I repeat the keynote here as I delivered it that day in April 1995, because it stands, in the context of *Geographies of Learning*, as an example of an activist academic speaking into a public community. [4] The keynote remains a partial artifact of my performance that day; how I sounded, my gestures, my expressions, my timing are irrecoverable. My performance—the only one I've ever given of this lecture, only on that day—was site-specific and ephemeral. But the record of my speech stands here, I hope, as an illustration of the kinds of translations it might be useful for an erstwhile academic critic to make, in yet another geography of learning.

After reiterating the keynote here, I'll offer my own analysis of the rest of the conference, becoming the ethnographer, the participant-observer who lives in the community and is part of what she observes. Reasserting my critical/journalistic perspective allows me to record something of the conference proceedings from the perspective of an invested audience member. My field notes, of course, are bound by the politics of location. The performances to which I refer are mostly New York–based or –bred, although because of the survival structures of queer arts, and the growth of a national community of spectators and consumers of queer work, many of the performers I mention have presented across the country and even internationally. The national gay press—magazines such as the *Advocate* and *Out*—regularly review performance work first presented in New York City. In many ways, new distribution outlets for performance and for its criticism are creating a national queer culture.

After my record of the conference, I'll continue in this critical vein to think about the politics of queer theater in the twenty-first century. Queer theater is one place where all my work—as a scholar and activist, critic and director—comes together. As I argued in chapter 4, it's important to me to give my own interdisciplinary field its due, while I argue for the influence of performance across disciplines and communities.

The Conference Keynote: Speaking from and with a Community

If "queer" means anything at all, especially as an adjective for theater, it means multiplicity. It can't be anything as stable or coherent as agreement over what we're about here. And that's good. Yet at the same time, the insistent antihegemonic pose of "queer" can also be a ruse for not taking responsibility for the vagaries of a movement, a style, a life. I'd like to retain the sense that queerness has no leader, no authority, really, but insert my own sense of responsibility into what I see as my community, of listeners and of readers: gays, lesbians, queers, and "theater people" in all senses of that rich,

evocative phrase—practitioners, theorists, critics, academics, devoted spectators, and more. My intent here is to frame some issues, ask some questions,
share some of my own musings about the state of queer and gay and lesbian
theater and performance as it's practiced, consumed, and discussed in New
York City in April 1995.

I describe myself and my work, these days, as lesbian and feminist and
sometimes queer. I say that I am a theater and performance critic who also
teaches in state and city university systems. I offer these however provisional
identity categories because they work for me now, as a way of locating my
perspective on the questions that frame my thinking about gay/lesbian/queer
theater and performance, which come from at least two directions: One, I've
watched lesbian and gay and queer studies become visible or even fashionable in the academy.[5] Two, for the last twenty or more years, as a critic and a
very enthusiastic spectator, I've watched gay and lesbian and queer theater
build its own history and future, its own vocabulary and multiple audiences.
My position within this always shifting description of my location and my
work is not, I'm sure, unique to me in theater studies. But I do think it will
be interesting and important as this field grows to see how we put our various perspectives, locations, and identities, however provisional or suspect or
indeterminate we might desire them to be, into conversation around the
questions raised by the practice, production, study, and proliferation of
something we're now calling "queer theater."

If I were going to frame the story of the rise of gay and lesbian and queer
studies, and gay and lesbian and queer performance and criticism, I would
dissemble a bit, and insist that there are many ways to organize such a narrative. I would resist chronology. I wouldn't want to install a progress narrative
in which gay and lesbian theater and performance is closeted, then comes
out, then gets avant-garde, then looks queerly, then goes Vegas, or something. One thing that interests me in this field is that many modes of gay and
lesbian and queer theater production continue to exist side by side, in New
York and across American geography. Our history, too, resides next to our
present. So, for instance, the realism and popularity of *Love! Valour! Compassion!* might be the contemporary inheritor of *Boys in the Band*, in terms of
form and genre, and the ways in which the larger culture adopted these representations as an index to certain kinds of gay male experience, within their
particular moments in history.[6]

But while the media and audiences—gay and mainstream—debate Terrence McNally's play as representative of a theater style or a lifestyle, other
modes of queer and gay and lesbian production happen simultaneously, and
belie the apparent centrality of the Broadway stage or the identities, histories,

and experiences that *Love! Valour! Compassion!* encompasses. While the men in *Love! Valour! Compassion!* exchange rings and repartee about Broadway musicals or modern dance performances and offer their bodies to one another and to the audience as aestheticized love objects, Tim Miller could be downtown at P.S. 122, demonstrating that the rich history of our theater happens variously and simultaneously. Miller would be performing his personal/political/historical narratives, and offering *his* body as a referent for a collective reading of the events the last fifteen years have wrought.[7] Miller's theater style and publicly performed lifestyle, his analysis of the political as something that writes him, as well as something he writes, seems to form itself in a different galaxy than McNally's. And yet not really.[8] Differences, multiplicities, gaps, contradictions, desires, sexualities—that is, the stuff of queerness—arch like a gay rainbow from 42nd Street to First Avenue—if that's not too unifying or idealistic an image. Let's leave it as an image that shimmers for a moment, then disappears. Or let's call it an image of unity into which holes are poked, perhaps, by the lesbian theater workers who somehow remain on the streets below the rainbow, agitating.

But not just on the streets: the WOW Cafe's series of lesbian performances, now close to twenty years old, continues in the East Village. And Dixon Place, on the Bowery, offers a regular bill of performance work by queers, lesbians, and others.[9] The situation of queer theater produced by lesbians mirrors the typical situation of the lesbian bars that historically have organized our communities: geographically marginalized, in neighborhoods colorful, eclectic, and maybe just a little scary to walk to by yourself at night, if the culture still reads you as a woman on the street. This compared to the easy access to 42nd Street, to Broadway, to subscription houses like Manhattan Theatre Club that are somehow centered in their touristy neighborhoods, just as gay male bars tend to be centered in their communities. Money makes access easy. And access, to queer theater, and not just for queers, is key here. The situation of lesbian theater practice and production in the United States continues to suffer from the sexism that afflicts work by most women trying to make their way in theater.[10]

Lesbian and gay and queer theater, then, happens across geographies, accessible only variously and particularly, although those terms, too, change with history. The audiences at WOW are now very different from what they were when the Cafe started on East 11th Street, and their difference is a good thing. New audiences at WOW implies that the history of theater and performance with which we're engaged isn't static, isn't even predictable, can't claim us all in some monolithic description of our past, present, or future. The fact that the Queer Theatre conference happened at and was sponsored by theater-producing organizations like the New York Shakespeare Festival and the New York Theatre Workshop is enormously important. Whether you read this placement as a subversion of dominant cultural production or an affirmation of how queer these spaces already are, the conference's discussions and performances have been located in the places where they come from, where they move toward, and/or with which they're in dialogue, simply because of the structure of theater production in New York and in the United States.[11]

I don't think we can really say that lesbian/gay/queer performance and theater work has progressed formally (or politically) in some linear fashion. But we can perhaps productively say that different forms and contents and contexts of queer theater production and reception coexist, and that they're differently useful to different audiences in different locations, whether they're straight, gay, lesbian, queer, of color, of money, of ability, all of these at once, and more, many more. What would it mean, in fact, if queer production and consumption weren't ontologically queer at all, but simply a position of art practice or reading that anyone so inclined or so desiring could assume?

Alexander Doty, in his book *Making Things Perfectly Queer*, describes such a strategy for engaging with popular culture, of which we might consider theater, our theater, a part.[12] Queerness becomes a place to which people can travel, to find pleasure, and knowledge, and maybe (or maybe not) power. Anyone in the audience of *Belle Reprieve*, for example, might experience a queer pleasure, because the performance structures its references to popular and high cultural icons—burlesque, vaudeville, drag, Tennessee Williams—as insistently queered, as only meaningful through the queer, postmodern appropriations of a performance group that's queered itself through its own affiliations across gender, sexual practices, class, access to production.[13] The melding of Peggy Shaw and Lois Weaver and Bloolips into the cast of *Belle Reprieve* perhaps represents the hopeful, coalitional politics that queer theater might set as a standard for the larger activist movement.

We have a history, and a couple of articulated examples, and more examples that we hold in our collective memories of theater work that might or might not fit under the banner we're waving of "queer." Is queer more radical than gay or lesbian? Can we say that gay and lesbian theater in the sixties, for instance, was more or less radical than queer theater and performance in the nineties? Or than performance in the nineties that still calls itself lesbian or gay? What kind of yardstick are we using to judge radical or political, and why is this an important standard to bring to theater (if you agree that it is)? Is all gay and lesbian and queer theater political because of its identity politics, its insistence on visibility (or its more covert generation of meanings that subvert dominant systems)? Or, in the age of queer, is this theater polit-ical because it proliferates meanings not necessarily linked to identity politics or visibility, but tied more squarely to sexual practices and gender rebellion and social performances of the mutability of race and ethnic categories? Is sexuality enough of a category here, when we know, now, through theory and experience, that sexuality never stands alone?[14] Is sexuality all we mean by queer anyway? What tools are we all using to critique or to make plays and performances we see and create, according to what presumption of po-litical effectiveness?

Is it desirable to look at history as a progress narrative, always assuming that now is better, even if we're wistful and nostalgic for an unrecoverable past? Or is it more important to give history and local contexts their due and assume that while New York generates "queer" as a new category of activism and performance, people in smaller, more isolated communities are still risk-ing maybe even their lives by producing a lesbian play like *Last Summer at Bluefish Cove*?[15] With the new hegemony of queer as an identity, "gay" and "lesbian" have been made essential, ontological, fixed spaces and have been thrown into apparent disrepute by contemporary queer theorizing. What happens to gay and lesbian drama now? Does it get "queered"? At several panels of this conference, panels proposed to "queer the canon," or "queer Shakespeare," but can we or should we queer our more recent past? Can we queer feminism, from which lesbian theater derived much of its initial en-ergy? Should we?

Queerness has come to encompass numerous strategies, all of which carry the charge of multiplicity, openness, contradiction, contention, the slipperi-ness of sexual practice seeping into discourse, into fashion, into style and pol-itics and theater. Queer skids on the slipperiness of its investments, its identi-ties, its human composition, the multifacetedness of its interventions in culture. To be queer is not who you are, it's what you do, it's your relation to dominant power, and your relation to marginality, as a place of empower-ment. "Queer" opens spaces for people who embrace all manner of sexual practices and identities, which gives old-fashioned gays and lesbians a lot more company on the political front lines, as well as in capital consumption, and, of course, in bed. That's the beauty and the flaw of "queer," depending on how you look at it.

I'm insistently using the words "gay" and "lesbian" along with "queer" in relation to theater to remind us of history, to remind us of differential power, to remind us that however fluidly we might practice and perform our identi-ties, regulatory systems tend to fix them and to legislate against them, through juridical, medical, and educational discourses in which the theater we make and write about must intervene. And gay and lesbian theater has a hard-fought history, as a genre, as a renegade style of wresting the power of representation from dominant voices, of insisting on our right to imagine ourselves, to take pleasure from displaying and receiving one another's bodies through the representational frame. I hope that as our scholarship and practice progresses, we'll celebrate the achievements of gay and lesbian theater and performance, along with the queer version, so that we can remember our history.

In the framing narrative I would tell, were I telling the story of gay/lesbian/queer theater's situation in culture, I would insist on the importance of history for all of us, regardless of how we define our selves or our sexual practices, regardless of whether or not we believe there is anything there, on the stage or in our homes, to define. This, of course, comes now, in an age of poststructuralist theorizing and postmodern style that privileges surfaces, and their transformations, their subversions, perhaps, over depth, soul, spirit—sometimes, at least. Joan Nestle remains my guide here, always my inspiration. In *A Restricted Country*, she writes, "[F]or gay people, history is a place where the body carries its own story. . . . If we are the people who call down history from its heights in marble assembly halls, if we put desire into history, if we document how a collective erotic imagination questions and modifies monolithic societal structures like gender, if we change the notion of woman as self-chosen victim by our public stances and private styles, then surely no apologies are due. Being a sexual people is our gift to the world."[16] Being a sexual people is our gift to the theater, as well, where in our own representations, in our revisions of the relation between performer and spectator and among audiences, in our rewritings of the relation between art and culture, we insist on the importance of desire as history, desire as future, on our import as bearers and shapers of different, necessary cultural meanings, through the presence of our desire. Our theater is our historiography; it encompasses our past, present, and future; our practice writes our history, in sedimented forms that converge in our cultural productions. Theater is our cultural memory.[17]

Desire is our legacy to theater and, probably, theater's past and its future. I hope we'll indulge ourselves, in our scholarship, in describing the pleasure we take in queer performance, because on some level, our pleasure is our resistance. I hope together, we'll chart the thrill of being in audiences charged with overt erotics, of consuming and writing about and making performances that are enormously seductive on multiple levels, from the aggressive presentation of queer bodies to the embodiment of texts that are smart and wry and irreverent, back to bodies, dressed or not in unpredictable, incongruent ways in the accoutrements of gendered raced classed eroticized culture, switching codes for one another and for us.

I hope we share the pleasure of going to WOW with other lesbians and with straight women and with men of all stripes, and being so proud on some level of the different pleasures we could offer in this space. I hope we share the pleasure of seeing Alina Troyano's Carmelita Tropicana develop as a character and as a performer who gives so much to our communities; of seeing Holly Hughes grow from a manic, barely controlled bombshell in *The Lady Dick* at WOW to the mistress of queer language, the performer who can wrap her tongue around discourse and queer it by drenching it with juices (and I don't just mean saliva); of seeing Peggy and Lois sing "I Like to Be in America" in Yiddish with Deb in *Upwardly Mobile Home* and seeing them deconstruct marriage in *Anniversary Waltz*, and perhaps their own relationship in *Lust and Comfort*.[18]

If Roberta Sklar and Sondra Segal, Jane Chambers, Karen Malpede, Martin Crowley, and Terrence McNally offered me a new ancestry, one different (and yet strangely similar) to the Jewish one I brought with me to New York, packed in my baggage, I feel like I grew up with Carmelita Tropicana, and Holly Hughes, and Peggy Shaw and Lois Weaver and Deb Margolin, and Lisa Kron Babs Davy Mo Angelos Domique Dibbell Peg Healy separately and as the Five Lesbian Brothers, whose name alone, when I describe their work in places removed from the downtown New York context, inspires gasps of wonder and either dismay or delight. I did grow up, watching their work, learning new genre conventions and how to queer the old ones, thinking about the radical potential in the expression of lesbian desire in these out-of-the-way spaces. I'm noticing, now, that we're all getting older; I see it on our faces. This persuades me that as critics and practitioners, as theorists and producers, we have to teach ourselves how to incorporate our past with our present.

At the organizing meetings for the Queer Theatre conference, we seemed continually excited about work that looked forward, but unsure how to approach work from even the recent past. Likewise, "downtown," "off-center," "marginal," or, more positively described, "community-oriented work for constituent audiences" captured our imaginations and our commitments, and we weren't quite sure what to do with work that we could determine more "successful" in predictably traditional, mainstream terms. Does a play or performance lose a queer credential when you can buy a ticket for it in Duffy Square on the TKTS line? I don't think it does. I think in fact it can't, but something about the presumed outlaw status of "queer" made us stumble over the question of "midtown" success at our planning meetings.

I think what we came up against in our contentious, productive discussions was what Kobena Mercer describes as "the burden of representation" placed on marginalized work that seems to gain access to wider audiences or distribution systems.[19] Mercer suggests that we consider gay, lesbian, queer representations as speaking *from* community or identity positions, rather than speaking *for* them.[20] This might help us navigate the roiling waters of political responsibility and accountability when we think about queer theater: an understanding that dominant media burdens queer producers with speaking *for*, and that those of us who locate ourselves in relation to queerness in one way or another might read queer productions as speaking *from* multiple, always partial places within constantly changing definitions of queer community.

We might think about what we use our theater for, how it provokes us to investments of fantasy and desire, how it employs what Cindy Patton calls a "sexual vernacular" or how it might use several, to speak differently into the specific, local communities with which it would affiliate.[21] I recall reading Patton's description in *How Do I Look?* of a group of queer activists carefully watching a porn film to decide questions of representational efficacy around condom use.[22] How might queer theater inspire the same kind of close looking, not necessarily to find an unmediated relationship to the real, not necessarily to secure a too direct link between cause and effect, but because performance and theatrical representation had become an intervention in matters of life and death? Richard Schechner once made a distinction between theater and ritual that hinged on need. Participants *need ritual* to sustain them, he suggested, but theater *needs audiences* to sustain it.[23] How might *queer* theater become a kind of social ritual that *audiences* need for sustenance?

Finally, we work at many different sites. We write and make theater and performances for an activist movement; to offer pleasure to our communities; and to circulate our cultural practices, our art, widely through various social geographies. We write about performance in academic journals and the popular press. Queer theater and performance has been buffeted and bolstered by academic criticism, by academic residencies, by critics and performers very clear about how we mutually support and need one another.[24] Queer theater has been brought to wide attention by gay and lesbian and queer cultural critics in the wildly proliferating gay press, and in established presses like the *Village Voice* and even the *New York Times*, as well as in weeklies and dailies in large urban areas around the country. Gay/lesbian/queer journalism has engaged critically with our performance work and has insisted that others look closely at the new forms, styles, meanings, pleasures we're producing in the theater.

There are many questions to pose, many disagreements to have, many re-membrances to be made for those who have died and can no longer mark their own contributions to our theater history, and much pride to be shared in the fact that we've arrived at this historical moment at all. We can't rest on our laurels, even if we're surprised to find that we've accumulated any. We have to push forward into the future and backward into the past, knowing all we know and wanting to know more as we work under the risk of erasure, of vilification, of further political and artistic disenfranchisement as the spaces that produce our work watch their finances become more and more precari-ous. The inhospitable political climate under which we're working is the one under which gay and lesbian and queer work has always been produced. It shouldn't seem worse now, but somehow, it does.

To counter the political machinery of the Right, we should transmit our knowledge. We should form sexual and theatrical apprenticeships, to teach one another and others what we know and what we don't. We should trans-form consciousness with our theaters and our performances, offering our multiple representations of desire up for what Doty calls "sexually trans-mutable" responses.[25] Our theater can bridge theory and activism by offering a sexual vernacular for speaking desire in performance, and invite the world to partake with us in the politics of our pleasure.[26]

Participant Observations: Conference Field Notes

The 1995 "Queer Theatre" conference proved a rich and varied three days of performances and panels. In many ways, the conference lived up to the promise of queerness in the multiplicity of its presentations, performances, and topics and in the fragmentation of its overall trajectory. My one regret, as a conference participant, planner, and observer, was that much of that prom-ising multiplicity devolved into predictable binaries: men/women, theory/ practice, academic/artist. Despite the potential of "queer," most discussions seemed unable to hold these terms suspended in a coalitional relationship, without stretching them across a more competitive or comparative pole. For example, David Savran moderated a panel of playwrights (two men and three women, three people of color, two white) that illustrated the often awkward, too too solid gender politics of the queer movement. Nicky Silvers and Chay Yew sat to one side of the gender divide with Savran, while Joan Schenkar, Maria Irene Fornes, and Janis Astor del Valle anchored the other. As each took their turn answering Savran's thoughtful questions, the sides became more ideological, taking shape as though a schoolyard brawl was about to be staged. Silvers and Yew laughed and whispered when the women talked, and

Silvers began each of his comments with a parody of something one of the women before him had volunteered. Schenkar's and Fornes's faces expressed their displeasure with Silvers's camping, and their remarks took care to distinguish themselves from this category "queer," especially if Silvers's antics were exemplary of its style.

Other instances of gender tension extrapolated to the uneasy alliances that queer requires among people with very different histories, ideologies, and political and aesthetic investments. On a panel about the "Out Aesthetic," moderated by Don Shewey, Ana Maria Simo distinguished her work from feminist theater and from gay theater, whose patriarch at the conference was the late Charles Ludlam and his Ridiculous Theatre. Simo began Medusa's Revenge, one of the first lesbian theaters in the country. On the panel, she related that she recruited women from bars to perform in what she considered her community-based theater, and noted that the women of color and working-class women with whom she worked in the early seventies felt little affinity with feminists or gay men. She also admitted that she hates the phrase "queer aesthetic," as she finds it "detrimental to lesbians and non-whites" because it homogenizes and erases differences. The generational and aesthetic and political differences performed by and significant to many of the panelists foregrounded the complexities of coalition politics under the rubric of "queer."

While the tensions on the playwriting and the "out aesthetic" panels illustrated the gender and generational politics that sometimes charged the proceedings, these panels also set up a vocabulary with which to speak about theater arts that I found irritating at several moments throughout the conference. I was disgruntled by what I perceived as some (certainly not all) of the artists' unwillingness to think analytically about their work or even to prepare to talk about what they do in an engaging, challenging way. Some artists' undertheorized remarks seemed disappointing from people who, as gays or lesbians, must have thought more deeply about the conditions that allow or obstruct their work. It surprises me that queer artists hold themselves hostage to the same mystifications about process that stall discussions about most artistic practices in American culture.

Yet at the same time, I noticed that in many panels, moderators and spectators seemed to want the artist to be the only one doing the investigative work. The onus always seemed to be on the artist to have all the answers to the questions posed. If we're really committed to community building, we have to ask what all of us can do. How can we persuade spectators that we, too, need to contribute to this work, by thinking about how we use and participate in queer theater as collaborators, as makers of queer meanings and queer theater markets? How might spectators understand their complicity in the process of production that keeps most lesbian/gay/queer theater marginalized, unknown, and unaccessible? Queer spectating is an artistic practice, as well as a deeply ideological one. If spectators marked their investment, instead of hanging on to a misplaced sense of innocence, queer audiences could become quite activist.

The romantic vocabulary about art practice held itself suspiciously removed from a more critical rhetoric at the conference, which perpetuated the theory/practice split that feminists in theater production and theater studies have worked for years to deconstruct, and echoed the perennial academic/artist divide. Queer theater can't afford to be antiacademic or antiintellectual. Those of us who teach help develop new audiences for queer theater and teach them our history. We also write about practice and offer places for residencies that foster creative work. But most of all, our theater needs ideas and theory to sustain and enrich it, and we forget this to our collective detriment.

If we're going to take Mercer's challenge to share the burden of representation, we need a larger arsenal of information, of strategies, of knowledge within which to contextualize and advance our work. Surprisingly little connection was made throughout the conference among the remarks of practitioners, theorists, and critics. When artists field questions, they tend to respond from individualist perspectives, rather than historical or collective ones. When academics delve into history or theory, they could more often make connections that resonate for contemporary artists, since those resonances are easily available. This problem is endemic, of course, to all conferences or meetings that bring together artists and critics;[27] not enough time is spent developing a common set of issues with which to address larger cultural forces, rather than directing our frustrations or contentions against one another. We need to work with one another, instead of against or singlemindedly parallel to one another.

Throughout the conference, many panelists shared their coming-out stories, redemption narratives in which going to the movies or the theater had enabled their lesbian/gay/queer lives and inspired their work in theater. I found these stories moving and affirming, as one after another, panelists related going to films and reading them queerly, or finding their way to the Ridiculous Theatre or the WOW Cafe, becoming one of the troupe, and finding their lives profoundly changed. But I was surprised that these were the conference's dominant narrative trope. The coming-out story, after all, is a structuring fiction of gay and lesbian experience, but not so much of the queer perspective, which tends to use "out" as an insistent, sudden, in-your-face verb, deleting any of the tentative apologia of process implied by the "coming." The occasional clashes of old-style rhetoric with the presumptions of new-style queer made for one of the many interesting tensions at the conference, marking the generations that had gathered by the way they positioned themselves around "queer," its history, and their own experience.

The conference offered something for everyone, and there were many kinds of everyone.[28] I found many moving and provoking moments in the three intense days of speaking, listening, and watching performances, and as one of the organizers, was very glad for what the conference accomplished. But I regretted that each constituency seemed to get what they came for independently, that there was no one panel or discussion at which all the issues about which we cared seemed to intersect with, or challenge, or touch one another deeply or profitably. Despite the promise, perhaps, of the coalitional concept of queer, we remained, I think, two hundred or more gay men and lesbians and others, some of whom perceive themselves as thinking, some as doing, some as consuming. For queer theater to really flourish, perhaps we need a community that thoughtfully, passionately, and responsibly goes about engaging in all three.

Ruminations on Queer Pleasure and Performance in the Twenty-First Century

Queer theater and performance remain embodied places in which we can think through our personal, public, and political relationships in ways that call forth our distinct pleasures; that exemplify our divergent values; and that demonstrate the usefulness of staging visions of radically revised social relations. Yet at the beginning of the twenty-first century, queer theater seems entangled in the snare of capitalism and its discontents in ways that challenge the promise of what I continue to see as its radical critique. After many years of working in subcultural spaces for little or no money, queer performers want more for themselves: higher earnings, larger audiences, book deals, and other media ventures. But once the work enters these markets, it competes as a commodity that of necessity fashions itself to the structures of supply and demand. I no longer prize notions of authenticity that require work to remain subaltern to retain its transgressiveness. But I do think that maintaining an active and creative political and artistic subculture is necessary to create performance work that remains truly "cutting edge," formally and politically.

I became interested in gay and lesbian theater shortly after I came out in college in 1977. I had been a theater major, a theater person in general, and when I started doing feminist and lesbian activism, I was concerned to find these political ideologies reflected or addressed in performance. But lesbian and feminist theater in the late seventies and early eighties was very marginalized. You had to know where to look for it; it often wasn't advertised, except in small community settings. In many ways, you had to be already part of the community it addressed to find it, and once you became part of the audience, the presumption was that you would enjoy the show.

I saw a lot of feminist and lesbian (at that point, they were often interchangeable) performance in Boston and later in New York, when I moved there to go to graduate school in 1981. Much of it was terrible; it was political and ideological more than aesthetic or even theatrically interesting. Much of it set didacticism above form; or the forms it used over the conventional ones it eschewed were influenced by cultural feminist or lesbian separatist notions of female/feminine aesthetics and ritual. I didn't like this stuff at all—I found it hegemonic in its own way. I hated being told to close my eyes, to chant, to touch the stranger next to me during a performance. I felt the work forced me to presume a place in a community of agreement, with which I often had arguments. So while I'd looked hard to join my politics with theater, at lesbian and feminist performances I mostly felt like the nonbeliever at a seance.

The story of the WOW Cafe has been told and retold, but it deserves its somewhat hallowed place in the history of gay/lesbian/queer performance mostly because it was one of the first community theaters to break this lesbian-feminist ideological and formal mold. While WOW was a collective, and committed to inclusive working principles, it held to an "anything goes" aesthetic policy that encouraged work that was much more daring formally and much less reverent politically. While other lesbian performance cleaved to essentialist notions of feminine aesthetics to answer traditional theater conventions, the work at WOW reclaimed just those conventions, deconstructing them and opening them to radical reinterpretation. Rather than eschewing popular culture, performers and writers at WOW delighted in queering it, so that everything from detective fiction to forties radio shows were ripe for satire and sexualizing.

In its early years, audiences at WOW were primarily lesbian. WOW was very much a community center, a place where lesbians came to meet other lesbians, to mingle, to form a cohesive social life. Performers acted their hearts out for people they knew. While the need for authenticity and essential femininity were jettisoned, reception practices at WOW were still grounded by lesbians performing for one another, in ribald, sexualized ways, in a space where they could presume that their intentions could be safely interpreted by like-minded spectators. Performers used butch/femme codes and artifacts, simulated sex on stage, played men, and wore male or female drag. But they could presume their audiences knew they weren't trying, for example, to *be* men, but that they were parodying the strictures of dominant culture's assignments of gender and sexual practices.

Of course, WOW was just as marginalized, community-based, and hegemonic as I've accused lesbian-feminist theaters in the seventies of being. Any theater asserts its belief system as right and true and most appropriate. I'm sure much of the lesbian-feminist performance that made me cringe moved many other women and affirmed their politics. I found those affirmations at WOW. Being in WOW's audience, in those early years, was exhilarating. Lesbians who weren't particularly interested in the antipornography rap; who were interested in sexual practices; who were politicized, but irreverent as well as radical, had very few places to see their experiences or their likenesses captured in representation. Going to WOW and reveling in sexualized humor, in the erotics of performance, in a scene infused with cheap beer, cigarette smoke, and theatrical as well as social daring, provided a kind of validation and legitimation that was unavailable elsewhere in culture. As Robin Kelley notes about African American culture, it's wrong to simply read expressive forms as mirroring social circumstances, when they also display aesthetics and style that reveal deep community pleasure.[29] Creating and attending performances at WOW was political in part because it was so pleasurable. WOW was a fun and sexy place for radical performance that created a politically activist spirit of adventure. Theory and practice dated and had intercourse there. Gender deconstruction and parody and everything else Judith Butler ever wrote were achieved with great orgasms of inventive, hilarious performance.

The pleasure of attending performance at WOW was perhaps its most activist aspect. As Michael Bronski argues in *The Pleasure Principle*, heterosexuals fear gay and lesbian sexuality because it's based in the pursuit of pleasure rather than reproduction.[30] Since performance itself is inherently nonreproductive, as Peggy Phelan has argued so eloquently, the combination of performance and queer sexuality at WOW created a place in which pleasure was intensely present and insistently present-tense, transgressive in its refusal to reproduce anything but the insane, satirical fun of the moment.[31] I'm sure there were other community-oriented spaces in cities around the country that offered similar pleasures. But its placement in lower Manhattan gained WOW notoriety. WOW stills serves as the best example of a theater that produced both politics and pleasure, a theater of fun, erotics, and daring, that valued the lives of queer people for their difference and their potential.

The WOW Cafe spawned some of the most important figures in gay and lesbian performance history: Split Britches, including Peggy Shaw, Lois

Weaver, and Deb Margolin, each of whom has gone on to do solo work; Reno; Holly Hughes; The Five Lesbian Brothers; Carmelita Tropicana; Babs Davy; Lisa Kron; and many others. Many of these performers, rather than thinking of their work avocationally, began to make their livings from performance, and wanted to widen their audiences and their potential income sources. Some performers moved to venues like P.S. 122, a major space for performance art in lower Manhattan, and even to the Public Theatre under George Wolfe's artistic direction. But WOW has retained its relative anonymity and status as a community site. The collective still refuses to apply for grants, always supports its work on box office, and operates out of the same almost condemned building that has housed it for nearly twenty years.

As lesbian work left a strictly lesbian audience base, all sorts of troubling questions were raised about authenticity, about politics, about ideology. In an infamous, mostly damaging published debate between Holly Hughes and Sue-Ellen Case, Case argued against the transfer of lesbian work into the heterosexual mainstream, and Hughes accused Case of being the Ayatollah Khomeini of lesbian performance criticism.[32] This early nineties argument represented the field's growing pains. Academic critics tried to hang on to lesbian performance's transgressiveness by insisting that it preserve its marginality, while performers, many of whom had by then been working for ten or fifteen years, understandably wanted more attention, more notice, and more money. Many of these performers still scratch out their livings, working for the door at still off-beat, poorly funded performance spaces, supporting themselves from university engagement to university engagement. Why shouldn't they want larger, more lucrative venues in which to work?

Academic critics writing about subcultural work often take great pleasure (and accrue a modicum of professional value) by writing about "outlawed" performance work in subcultural spaces. For some critics, maintaining radical academic credentials seems to require finding the most offbeat, the most potentially offensive, the most outrageous performances about which to write. Continually scoping out the fringes is important, since queer work still flourishes there. But a new generation of queer performance scholarship now addresses work across a spectrum of access, formal and political radicality, and geography, from Broadway to the Bowery, from the East Coast to the Midwest, from the South to California.[33] More specific studies of performance by queers of color scan a different range, in which queer work speaks concertedly to Latino/a or Asian American or African American producers and spectators.[34] This work redresses the whiteness of the work at WOW and other notorious queer performance spaces.

In the early nineties, the tension between radicalism and accommodation (loosely put) was very much about modes of production and reception. I think many critics wanted to hold on to the exceptionalism of lesbian performance, wanted to own it and be legitimated by it in the same way we always had, claim it for its difference, its outlaw status, the validation it offered our lives and our ideas. At this point, questions of authenticity have been troubled theoretically and politically. Few critics want to argue for an essentialism in lesbian performance, or that only lesbian audiences can truly "get" lesbian performance. But what interests me is the way the work has grown and moved and flourished (and where it hasn't), and what its higher profile has meant to its politics and its aesthetics. If you're not an outlaw anymore, what part do you play in pushing progressive activist values?

How we can ameliorate this tension? How can we keep creating a community of outlaws, who offer different kinds of identifications and validations, and foster creative work that stands a chance of growing and flourishing in spaces that can support it financially and distribute it to wider audiences? Academics who value radical, activist performance work can help by resisting narrow definitions of alternative performance. We need to look at work that appears at WOW and on Home Box Office (HBO) for its potential to imagine a different social configuration, for the pleasure it offers a wide range of spectators and audiences variously contextualized. No one wants to ghettoize queer theater and performance work. But many of us want to honor the counterculture in which so much of it began and which continues to inspire creative and critical careers. This, again, is a place where theory and practice, academics and activists, artists and critics need to talk about effective artistic and critical strategies and to think through how changing audiences provide new forums for work that's about the promotion of queer pleasure and queer values.

The cultural context of queer theater and performance and its reception is very different in the early twenty-first century than it was in 1980, when WOW began, especially if we expand the boundaries of what we think of as performance to include film and television and even the music industry. Broadway musicals currently address gay and lesbian life; cable television specials narrate stories of lesbians through the last forty years; nationally known lesbian and gay recording, film, and television stars speak at national political rallies; and lesbian/gay/queer political activism makes the front pages of national newspapers.

For instance, whatever one thinks of its politics, *Rent*, the late Jonathan Larson's revision of *La Bohème*, is still sold out on Broadway, several years after it opened. A progressive political critique of the musical is easy to launch. Larson portrays downwardly mobile middle-class young people acting out a bohemian life and generally equates privileged kids opting to be poor artists with homeless people who perhaps haven't chosen their lives on the streets. The gay male African American/Latino couple has HIV/AIDS, and one dies a tragic death onstage. The interracial lesbian couple fights constantly, and their relationship appears tenuous and shallow. The heterosexual couple, on the other hand, are the tragic hero and heroine of Larson's reimagining; the heterosexual woman with AIDS even comes back to life at *Rent*'s end. Underneath the celebration of queer and boho culture, the values of heterosexual America prevail.

David Román argues in *Acts of Intervention* that however politically suspect *Rent* is, and however caught up in its own commodification of "lifestyle" instead of politics, it represents a rarely seen vision of community that remains potent in an age when individuality is touted as everything necessary to success.[35] I, too, was moved by *Rent* each of the two or three times I saw it, despite my utter suspicion of the politics it endorses. Although I couldn't quite identify with its characters, the fact of their queerness was implicitly validating and made me feel somehow visible, watching the show. The score compelled me emotionally; I tapped my feet, I bought the cast album, and I still sing along when it plays. As a spectator, I admit that I sometimes lower my critical threshold because I so much *want* to be addressed, I so *want* to have fun. As a critic, I find *Rent*'s values and its commodification appalling. I believe *Rent*'s book demeans performance art as trite and ineffectual, offers no coherent politic about homelessness or HIV/AIDS, or about the difficulty of creating alternative art, and fails to truly imagine relationships outside of a coupled, traditionally gendered norm, whether queer or not.

Author and queer activist Sarah Schulman, in *Stagestruck*, argues that *Rent* has ripped her off (literally, since she says Larson stole the plot from her novel, *People in Trouble*, and figuratively, by misrepresenting her own experience as a lesbian denizen of the Lower East Side where the musical takes place).[36] This raises once again the question of authenticity. Schulman can't see what she knows is true in *Rent*. But is representation ever true? If it offers redemption and community, does authenticity matter anymore? Why has *Rent* meant so much to young audiences, spectators who waited for hours in line outside the theater for cheap tickets? Was their desire just about cultural capital? Or did *Rent* strike a chord in young people looking for something to believe in, however trite or accommodationist those of us with more sophisticated, progressive politics might find its message? I'm interested in what people *do* with cultural productions like *Rent*, in how they become widely useful. *Rent* opens questions not just of queer audiences, but of a diverse audience looking at work that imagines queer lives.

Television also presents many more queer representations for mainstream audiences in the late nineties and the turn of the century than it did in the seventies and eighties. For example, in spring 2000, HBO presented the second installment of *If These Walls Could Talk*. The first installment looked at changing attitudes toward abortion by narrating stories of women who inhabited the same house in several different decades. The second installment used the same structure to tell three stories about lesbian relationships from the sixties to the present. Two of the most famous white upper-class lesbians in the United States, Anne Heche and Ellen Degeneres, produced the program. Again, a progessive critique of *If These Walls* is obvious, especially of the third segment, in which Degeneres and Sharon Stone play a very wealthy white lesbian couple trying to have a child. This segment prides accommodationist family values and erases the complicated financial and emotional investments required to build nontraditional families. But one of the most notable things about the second and third segments of *If These Walls* was their frankness about lesbian sexual practice. However authentic or not its representations of lesbian sex, at least the program presented sexuality as a key and valid aspect of lesbian lives over the last half-century. Too often, mainstream representations shy away from imagining queer sexual relationships, while heterosexual sex gets more and more explicit, even on television. That this production didn't shun sexual activity but presented it as fundamental to queer lives was perhaps its most radical action.

Also at the end of the century, Hilary Swank won an Academy Award as Best Actress for playing a transsexual, Brandon Teena, in *Boys Don't Cry*, a remarkably empathetic and direct film about nonconformist sexual and gender practices. The film narrates Teena's attempt to pass as a man in rural Nebraska, where he falls in with a group of working-class white toughs who finally rape and kill him when his biological sex is revealed. Unfortunately, the gender-nonconformist's murder at the end of the film repeats the pattern of representations in which sexual outcasts must be exiled from the social or meet tragic deaths. But the film is clear-sighted about the violence brought to gender nonconformity and quite moving as it relates Teena's successful sexual experiences with women. Swank's utterly convincing and compelling performance made her Oscar well deserved. While cameras at the Academy Awards ceremony cut to Swank's husband, Chad Lowe, to affirm her heterosexuality (as her low-cut, flattering gown affirmed her femininity), she used her speech to honor Teena's life and to argue for sexual and gender difference. I found this moment extremely affirming, just as I found the film wrenching and identified with Teena in many complicated ways.

But what does it mean to queer theater that multiple queer identifications and representations are now more and more available outside of the marginalized, subcultural spaces to which we used to travel, hoping to experience them? What does it mean that most of these mainstream representations are still almost entirely of white and middle- or upper-class people? What does it mean that in addition to subcultural, local theater, off-Broadway, Broadway, and mainstream film and television now include gay and lesbian characters as a matter of course?[37] Does it make attending theater less important as a community practice? Is queer theater, as I proposed in my keynote, no longer a ritual that queer audiences need to sustain them?

Because of a successful American economy, the slow but steady gains of the gay and lesbian movement for civil rights and equality, and, in some places, a rejection of the radical Right's vilification of homosexuality, attitudes toward queer lives in the United States are shifting and becoming more open. We're also in the middle of a gay and particularly lesbian baby boom, in which the recreation of family (through commitment ceremonies or marriages and/or bearing or adopting children) is becoming a major political rallying cry of the mainstream movement. Vermont passed legislation in April 2000 that legitimates gay and lesbian civil unions that look much like marriage. The same month, the Human Rights Campaign—the politically conservative, largest gay/lesbian lobbying group in the country—cosponsored the Millennium March on Washington, the major theme of which was faith and family. At least half a million people attended.

Although from many perspectives, these gains in visibility and political status are positive and laudable, they assimilate lesbians and gay men into dominant culture, rather than dramatically changing its terms. The mainstream gay and lesbian movement, as Michael Warner and Michael Bronski both argue, erases queer countercultures. For queer people with different politics, marriage, or serving in the military, or achieving tax breaks through partnerships is not as important as a wholesale reenvisioning of values and an embrace of wider visions of social justice.[38] These mainstream achievements do nothing to form alliances with other oppressed groups and focus on issues that matter most forcefully for white middle-class lesbians and gay men. Warner, in his provocative and compelling book, *The Trouble with Normal*, argues that mainstream gay and lesbian politics sold out the promise of a more transgressive, sexual queer public culture by aping heterosexual values and giving up the real difference of queerness.

Certainly the Millennium March's emphasis on faith and family is a good example of such accommodations. What do we give up when queer people parade as normal, when normal is defined so conventionally? Not surprisingly, the participants in and speakers at the march were almost uniformly white. Activists of color who did advance more coalitional platform planks, who did analyze the larger politics of oppression, were given mostly late slots in which to speak at the six-hour rally at the Capitol following the march. Conventional values do little to allow us to think about sexuality, race, and gender together, rather than as separate and bounded aspects of identity, or to advocate for the ways in which oppression is widespread and common outside of strict identity categories.

I realize my own contradictions here. First, I'm arguing that queer performers should be encouraged in their assimilation into mainstream culture. And I do believe they deserve visible success that will make their daily lives more comfortable. At the same time, I'm criticizing the HRC and the mainstream lesbian and gay movement's efforts to assimilate because I find their values regressive.

But what interests me about queer theater, and what's always captured my attention as a lesbian performance critic, is how performance can do more than assimilate othered identities into the cultural mainstream, even when it's presented outside of subcultural spaces. I believe that through the immediacy of performance, through the exchange between spectator and performer in a live community environment, we can transgress hegemonic cultural norms, and present even utopian ideas about a completely revised social sphere. I'm interested in how performance can offer alternative imaginaries, ways of viewing the world that free us from the constraints of the present, that allow us to imagine something different, something other, a broader notion of freedom and justice than becomes available through commodified, sanctioned forms of popular entertainment. To even glimpse such a utopia, I think we have to learn to live with a certain number of contradictions.

I'll end these more recent ruminations by returning to one of the questions I posed in my keynote in 1995. What *is* queer theater in the twenty-first century? Who can see it? Understand it? Receive it in the way that it's meant or use it toward some other progressive or pleasurable end? I haven't been to a performance at WOW in many years. I keep up with queer performance when I visit New York City, where I see Holly Hughes and Tim Miller and Carmelita Tropicana and other performers, mostly presenting their work at P.S. 122 or Dixon Place. Or I see them when they tour around the country, performing at off-beat art spaces like the Off Center or the Vortex in Austin, or Theatre Project in Baltimore, or the Woolly Mammoth in Washington, D.C. I wish regional theaters would book their work, so they could increase their fees and attract even larger audiences of even more conventional people, whose worlds might be profitably—even surprisingly, pleasurably— overturned by their work.[39]

Hughes is now touring to funkier, community- and art-based producing sites. Her most recent performance, *Preaching to the Perverted*—whose title riffs, of course, on the old accusation that queer theater and performance "preaches to the converted"—recounts the ten years she spent dealing with the fallout from the NEA debacle of the nineties. In her elegant, activist reading of the court battles and the cultural war that brewed over her performances, Hughes brings an incisive political critique. She once again risks her own body, offering for examination under a harsh public glare what were also private experiences of vilification, attack, and censure.

Miller is now touring his piece *Glory Box*, which addresses the problems of international couples prevented from staying together by immigration laws that don't legally acknowledge gay and lesbian relationships. His work, too, retains a personal and political investment that blurs the borders between public and private. Carmelita Tropicana, in her performances *Milk of Amnesia* and *Chicas 2000* and in her book, *I, Carmelita Tropicana*, continues to image national and ethnic differences across gender and sexuality, experimenting with gender drag in the context of Cuban American politics of home, nation, longing.[40] Deb Margolin tours *O Wholly Night*, a piece that examines Jewishness and art. Brian Freeman, formerly of Pomo Afro Homos, tours a performance based on civil rights activist Bayard Rustin's life and work.

These performers work solo, in forms that are narrative and expository as well as theatrical. Queer performance artists seem to have abandoned the raucous, larger-cast productions for which WOW or the Ridiculous Theatre (for that matter) first became renowned. Carmelita's work is still parodic, and Peggy Shaw and Lois Weaver are still working together and with other actors, as well as performing solo. But it's as if as we age, the exploration of a life or a moment or a memory, captured in embodied, theatricalized narrative, is more vital than deconstructing television. All of these artists offer a set of revised values. They give queer communities things to believe in, to continuing fight for, utopian places of possibility still worth desiring. Their work has deepened in the last five years, becoming aesthetically and politically more sophisticated, combining art and activism, personal and political, pleasure and pain in ways that are now distinctly queer. But they continue to be captured on a fairly small cultural radar screen, unless they're being used by politicians to prove queer people's depravity. And this is where their danger lies.

At a talk I gave recently at the University of Maryland, someone told me that when she saw Hughes's performance in Baltimore, she overheard someone in the audience complain that the NEA debates were old and "over" and that Hughes shouldn't dredge them up again.[41] The NEA debacle might be history, but Hughes continues to live it. When she tours, Hughes still gets death threats, and some producers admit that they're still just not brave enough to produce her work. Pickets and demonstrations and violence attend Miller's appearances around the country. These outcries are personally damaging for the artists who continue to weather them, but they also indicate that while capitalism makes it possible for certain gay and lesbian representations to enter the mainstream, the true force of queer difference is kept far from its gates. We mustn't forget how threatening lesbian/gay/queer bodies remain to the social imaginary, especially when they don't look like Ellen Degeneres, Anne Heche, or Sharon Stone, or travel in elite, monied white circles. When queer bodies look like Matthew Shepard and Brandon Teena and James Byrd and travel the bars and backroads of rural America, they inspire terror and put themselves in danger. Performance stands as an emblem of that fear and as a safer place to study that danger.

A Road Map with Which to Explore and Engage Queer Theater

1. Produce and consume queer theater that practices the politics of pleasure. Revel in the pleasure of queer performance as a progressive value in itself. Support subcultural performance spaces that offer sexy, fun, life-affirming alternatives to reductive mainstream representations of lesbians/gays/queers.

2. See gay and lesbian films and enjoy gay characters on television (with a certain level of cynicism), but create and consume theater as something vital and necessary, fundamental to shaping the future and archiving the past of queer communities.

3. Experience subcultural and mainstream works with an eye toward their utopian possibilities. Use theater and performance to reimagine social relations as more just and equitable.

4. Train audiences to engage passionately with thoughtful artists who speak clearly and intelligently about their work as process and product.

5. Cultivate a generation of critics who believe in queer theater's effectiveness in the largest cultural contexts, who both support queer work and advocate for it in mainstream venues.

6. Work against gender, race, and class barriers. White male queer artists who find a modicum of success should feel responsible for advocating for queer work by white lesbians and queer people of color, so that the variety of lgbtq work can reach larger audiences.

7. Encourage lgbtq theater-makers (actors, directors, designers, producers, agents, etc.) who work in mainstream venues to come out publicly. Role models still matter, and it's enormously legitimizing to know, for example,

that Tony Award–winning actor Cherry Jones and Pulitzer Prize–winning playwright Paula Vogel are out lesbians.

8. Give money to queer theater-makers. Remember that theaters are non-profit organizations that need your contributions to enhance and sustain their efforts to enrich people's lives and to help them produce queer performance artists, as well as plays.

9. Encourage queer theorists and practitioners to respect one another's language and practices, while we find ways to stage more productive public and private dialogues that will enhance the work and its reception.

10. Honor our history in work by feminist lesbian and gay and radical artists of color. Scholars and critics must continually remind audiences and practitioners of the roots of contemporary work, so that we can build a shared legacy. Queer theater people need to transmit what they know across generations.

chapter six
Performance as Feminist Pedagogy

If conservatives unfurl their banners against queer performance art, determined to keep it from "infecting" their worldview, they are now starting to rail against progressive college and university teachers, whom they see as corrupting their impressionable youth. Conservatives fear what they perceive as a teacher's freedom in the classroom to introduce her own politics and values rather than canonical ones. Recent moves by state legislators and boards of trustees to more closely regulate classroom conduct and material stem from the same concerns that propel the censorship of alternative art. The radical Right wants to reclaim education as a bastion of its own truths, its own values, and its own methods, and increasingly finds more intrusive ways to achieve its goals.

This chapter addresses the complicated daily life of a feminist teacher working in an institutional environment fraught with such debates about curriculum and teaching style. How can radical teachers respond to the intrusions of the Right into our course contents and methods? How can we better publicize what we do in our classrooms, to provide a counterdiscourse to the Right's faulty, demeaning portraits of our work? How can we explain the tensions and rewards of working as a feminist teacher in higher education in the twenty-first century? Trying to answer these questions requires strategizing on a daily basis, sometimes within communities of supportive colleagues, sometimes alone, in the classroom, in front of students. These attempts to address locally issues that dominate the national scene can be exhausting and frustrating, as well as rewarding. Knowing how to build alliances, and knowing where to find support systems, are crucial for progressive faculty trying to maintain an activist stance on nontraditional curriculum and teaching methods.

This chapter also addresses how feminist faculty establish sometimes surprising affiliations, prompted by a search for intellectual and institutional "homes" that traditional departments often don't provide. After all, we spend much of our time at our universities laboring and building relationships. Questions of affiliation, comfort, contention, and support are tangible and real. Similarly, for students, questions of where they find institutional "homes" are pressing, especially for women's studies majors who expect women's studies programs to present a less impersonal front than many other departments. I found that my own need for a "home" in women's studies wasn't met, and that likewise, I disappointed my students' desire for me to make them a safe harbor in my classroom. The desire to find a home in an institutional setting, for faculty and students, is always compromised by politics, ideology, and power.

I also want this chapter to serve as a pragmatic illustration of common classroom challenges that I tend to meet by using performance. I describe feminist teaching in women's studies and in theater studies, but I hope my examples will be helpful to any teacher interested in using performance in the classroom to embody knowledge. My aim here is to counter conservative derogations of progressive teaching, but also to offer my own pedagogical strategies. Teachers are translators, just as I've suggested scholars and speakers should consider themselves. Teachers speak to an audience, try to build communities and constituencies, and often employ all the qualities of performance that make good theater. Teaching represents performance in everyday life, while at the same time, a classroom can be a highly theatrical place in a more conventional sense.

Because teaching is one of the most intimate activities in my life, I'll rely on personal anecdote for examples as well as engaging other writers whose preoccupations resonate with mine. I'll describe my courses here as specifically as possible, to illustrate how knowledge, skills, and ideas are communicated in (my) feminist, progressive classroom(s). I'll end with my own rules of thumb (or "ten commandments," although they're hardly biblical) for effective progressive teaching.

The Privatized Classroom

Teaching is an important aspect of the historical transmission of knowledge across eras and generations and a way to preserve an alternative cultural heritage. Yet despite the large amount of attention most academics give to their courses, college and university teaching for the most part is privatized. Faculty only see one another teach under situations of duress, when they're being evaluated or assessing their colleagues for tenure, promotion, or now, increasingly, posttenure review.

During my term as chair at University of Wisconsin–Madison, I visited classes taught by my theater colleagues, with an eye toward evaluating them for merit raises, promotion, and tenure. I was struck, that year, by how varied their methods were, how they each brought different commitments and ways of enacting them to the subjects for which our department had given them stewardship. I learned important things about styles of teaching, of delivering content, and of connecting with students from those observations. At CUNY, since the faculty was tenured and their raises determined by a union contract, the only time I observed people teach was during job interviews. A position for which we searched in 1998 required each candidate to teach a section of the same undergraduate theater history course, which offered a good opportunity to notice differences in styles, approaches, personalities, and methods around vaguely similar material. Sitting in on those three candidates' course meetings was a surprisingly moving experience, since finally, there's something very vulnerable, intimate, and personal about standing in front of a room full of students, trying to impart meaningful ideas. The experience was also quite useful, as it let me and the rest of the search committee compare these candidates' strategies against our own, and decide what our students might need to be able to learn effectively.

Most departments offer few occasions to engage more collegially with the very thing that occupies much of its faculty's time. Likewise, very few graduate students are taught to teach as a matter of course during their long years of apprenticeship in the academy. Most learn to teach by watching others, but opportunities in which teachers and students can discuss their strategies and their successes and failures are relatively few.[1] At some conferences, people share teaching strategies, describing in detail their syllabi and their in-class operations. Graduate student teachers and junior faculty seem especially eager to compare classroom notes, to develop new ideas and to borrow from their colleagues. But it strikes me how rarely the profession itself addresses, in a systematic way, issues about good teaching.

Pedagogy also is a site at which to work through questions of social and institutional power, yet relatively little attention is given to how the presumptively radical ideas many faculty bring to their scholarship are presented in their everyday practices as teachers. Whether they work in public or private colleges or universities, the current political climate requires more and more that faculty explain their teaching strategies in the classroom, as well as in their research and scholarship. Legislators continually press for accountability measures at public institutions, and groups such as the American Council for Trustees and Alumni aggressively intrude into the choice and supervision of the curriculum of private institutions.

Such offensives require that those of us who bring a progressive perspective to our work justify our methods and strategies outside of the small enclaves in which our choices naturally make sense. We need not bow to conservative calls for impossible quantitative outcomes assessments, but we should publicize more widely the stuff that comprises our teaching. The aggressive attacks on women's studies, critical race and ethnic studies, and gay and lesbian studies, published so eagerly by prurient mass media, are readily persuasive. No counterdiscourse regularly offers examples of how faculty teaching in these areas consider their scholarship, or how they argue for its esoteric necessity, or how they bring it rigorously to their classrooms.[2] Progressive faculty need to produce more specific and frequent, local and national examples of how their teaching in the classroom and their research and publications is knowledge that matters, widely and resoundingly.

I consider myself a "progressive" teacher for a number of reasons. First, I believe that teaching is activism, that changing students' consciousness is important to contesting social and cultural structures that perpetuate gender, race and ethnic, class, and sexual inequities. I believe that teaching students how ideology works, whether in women's studies, gay and lesbian studies, or theater studies, allows them to engage critically with the various discourses they encounter and by which they are shaped. Rather than imparting great bodies of knowledge to my students, my goal is to offer them critical skills with which they can approach any topic and to give them research abilities that will let them find any kind of knowledge they might need. Those of us who teach in multiple disciplines face the challenge of teaching a number of vocabularies at once, to students who are often unschooled (or differently or partially schooled) in all of them.[3] Progressive instructors often teach new knowledge in new ways, and our own commitments push us to teach them well, so that our classrooms become activist sites at which consciousness regularly changes.

Any description of teaching remains incomplete without examining the institutional context in which it takes place. And it's impossible to address teaching without considering the national and local contexts that set its conditions. Decreasing legislative and popular support for public education; "white flight"; Pell grant reductions; the race bias of SAT and GRE tests; school voucher debates in public elementary and high schools, which are also more and more driven to fight for resources based on standardized testing; the establishment of Teach for America; faculty unionization; the history of women's studies; the growth of feminist methods across the disciplines; the concomitant rise of critical race theory and ethnic studies; the persistent struggle of gay and lesbian studies to found itself in colleges and universities; labor struggles by graduate students, clerical staff, and maintenance workers; the rollback of affirmative action—all these struggles provide the backdrop against which progressive faculty teach. Contextualizing the knowledge students learn is an important gesture toward helping them understand the history of their own education.

For example, women's studies students at the University of Wisconsin–Madison, where I taught from 1988 to 1994, were often blithely unaware of the history of their field or of the program in which they took their majors or minors. Students now registering for gay and lesbian studies or queer theory courses also need to understand the activist history that makes such courses possible in some institutions and their egregious absence in others. Understanding the impulse behind social identity area studies programs that now appear fully institutionalized on some campuses allows students and faculty to remain attached to the fractious history of these fields and to think critically about the costs and benefits of their increasing institutionalization.[4] Understanding the ways in which educational patterns have shifted over the years in American education is also crucial to historicizing the so-called culture wars, and other battles fought over the appropriateness of certain curricular contents and certain advocacy-based teaching styles.[5] To ground my own observations about teaching, permit me a tangent into my own educational history, which will illuminate how my own classroom work is influenced by the contexts in which I've learned and worked.

Feminism in Context: From Outlaw to Institution

I never intended to be a teacher, or an academic, for that matter. I entered a graduate program in performance studies at New York University because I wanted to be a better feminist writer. I'd written film and theater criticism for a women's newspaper in Boston called *Sojourner* but found that I lacked a community with which to discuss ethical and political issues confronting a critic of feminist performance and representation. My choice to pursue further training was motivated by political commitments to a clear feminist critique. I chose a graduate program that promised to train me in critical writing, but I didn't consider, when I applied, how I would pursue my feminist interests in this new academic context.

When I first arrived at the Department of Performance Studies at NYU, I thought I was the only feminist around. Starting graduate school in 1981, the feminist critical community I yearned to establish was nascent in the academy, at best. I felt alienated from some of the more conservative ideas I was being taught, and from the male students who inevitably held forth, unchecked, in our seminars. Some time passed before I found other women in the department willing to express feminist commitments. Nationally, the story was similar. I attended conferences about "women" in the early eighties, and worried that I'd be the only feminist, and often, I was. Going to conferences about "feminism" in the mid-eighties, I worried that I'd be the only lesbian (I never was). Women of color and lesbians of color during that period must have felt their singularity even more keenly. Eventually, in my graduate program, five or six women formed a feminist support group, which led us to found *Women and Performance Journal* in 1982 and to agitate for courses on women and feminism and theater.[6] Many years later, the department hired Peggy Phelan, its first tenure-track faculty person with an expertise in feminist theory and performance.

In the late seventies and early eighties, women students and faculty created the field of women's studies and feminist theory through their own determination, courage, and labor. Women faculty who already had tenure-track jobs risked their promotions to begin articulating a feminist critique. Women students without jobs risked being sidelined, hobbled by a lack of directors for their dissertations, an implicit censure of their work, or banishment to the poverty of perpetual adjunctships because their work had no institutional foothold or was outright rejected by their disciplines. I had to chart my own way through feminist studies because my department offered no coursework in the field. In 1982, I taught myself feminist theory outside of class. If there was a women's studies program at NYU at the time, I never discovered it. The faculty person I first approached to advise my dissertation on feminism and theater spectatorship turned me down because it was feminist and "political"; he refused to mentor me, even though I'd worked closely with him in other capacities throughout my graduate career. Luckily, Phelan was hired soon after on a permanent line, and she agreed to take on my project, even though we'd never worked together before.

Like many women of my generation, I was never formally trained in feminism or in women's studies. I also wasn't trained to teach, since my financial support at NYU required me to work as an editor on the department's journals rather than as a teaching assistant in a classroom. Still, when I took my first teaching position in 1987, substituting for a colleague on sabbatical, I immediately realized how closely teaching resembled performance, and how much I loved the dynamic of speaking with and engaging my audience of students. I was never trained to be a feminist pedagogue. But I wanted to incorporate my feminism with teaching. I wanted my classroom to be different from the mostly totalitarian ones I'd experienced as a student.

Although I'd never anticipated such a plan, I went on the academic job market that year. By the time I was hired as an assistant professor in theater at the University of Wisconsin–Madison in 1988, feminism had successfully integrated its methods, contents, and theories into a number of institutionally sanctioned departments across the country and had established separate programs, majors, or minors on many campuses. When I arrived at UW, I eagerly sought a place for myself in the Women's Studies Program because I assumed it would be a haven for my feminist scholarship and a supportive place for me as a feminist and as a lesbian. The liberal history of UW–Madison enabled Women's Studies' early establishment and its eventual institutionalization there; the program is one of the oldest in the country. By the late eighties and early nineties, the program was well respected and highly considered on the UW campus. Such approbation hastened the program's shift from outsider status to insider, as more and more women groomed in women's studies moved into positions in the university's higher administration. These women facilitated a proliferation of feminist discourse throughout the institution, as women's issues moved closer to the center of larger institutional and disciplinary concerns.

I was invited to join the program and soon moved to a joint appointment between Women's Studies and Theatre and Drama. Teaching courses in contemporary feminist theory and in lesbian culture for the program, and sitting on most of its administrative committees, I learned quite a lot about the evolving status of the field. I heard stories of the UW program's "mothers," and their hard work in the seventies to establish courses and find office space from which to serve students and coordinate faculty efforts. The activist history they informally related grounded my understanding of the program's importance and its place at UW–Madison and in women's studies nationally. The "elders" of the program taught me some of the program's history; some of it, I participated in making; most of it, I passed on to my students, determined for them to understand the context of their study.

By the early nineties, the program's history, while mythologized, was already very different from its present. The institutionalization of the field over the intervening years of the program's existence had brought new challenges and complications. Even to me, who not long before didn't know women's studies existed as a subdiscipline, it was clear that grassroots activism around gender and feminism in the academy, at least at Madison, was already on the wane.[7] During my six years with the program, its most contentious meetings were held over whether or not students and so-called community people should continue to sit on program governance committees. Many women's studies faculty felt strongly that the program should more closely conform to the governance policies of existing departments. People were coming up for tenure with joint appointments in women's studies and other disciplines and would be reviewed for promotion by the executive committee of the Women's Studies Program. Only faculty, the argument went, should be permitted to review these personnel decisions. The discussions over this change in practice were acrimonious, as many faculty, students, and community women felt that a different policy would decrease the program's commitment to local and institutional activism.

I was ambivalent about the proposed change. On one hand, it seemed inappropriate to me that people without certain credentials should vote on people's tenure and promotions. On the other hand, maintaining a lived commitment to an activist, local community seemed vital to women's studies's goals and commitments. Mostly, I regretted that many larger issues about activism and institutionalization went unaddressed as we focused on the micro level. The change did, in fact, go through, and the Women's Studies Program committees were restructured to align with those of other programs and departments. A woman was hired on a renewable staff line through Continuing Education to serve as the community liaison, and although she regularly gave detailed reports at program meetings on her numerous activities, her work outside the institution somehow seemed marginalized, implicitly less valuable.

I had expected to feel more secure as a feminist in the Women's Studies Program than I would in my home department, but ironically, the reverse proved true. The Department of Theatre and Drama into which I was hired fostered my intellectual and political growth in unexpected ways. The self-styled women's studies students at UW–Madison at the time seemed terribly dogmatic and rigid in their expectations about what feminism meant and how it should be taught; I was often ill at ease with their prescriptive, presumptuous behavior and ideas. The theater students seemed more open to ideas; I suppose I preferred their romanticism about art to the women's studies students newly suspicious attitude to the history of "male-dominated" intellectual thought. The Women's Studies Program seemed very hierarchical; being an untenured junior faculty person mattered at Women's Studies meetings. In Theatre, I quickly became a respected, reasoned voice at department meetings; at Women's Studies meetings, I was quiet, intimidated by the vehemence and authority of many of my senior colleagues. It seemed as though I couldn't know the history they had lived, and without it, my opinions mattered less. In Theatre, I quickly became fully enfranchised; Women's Studies seemed a elite club in which only seniority counted. In Theatre, I was one of several lesbian or gay faculty; while I expected to find lesbians in Women's Studies, there were surprisingly few. And the program was thoughtlessly heterosexist. The few lesbians involved did much of the labor, while many of the married women left meetings early to retrieve their children from day care (this, of course, was before the lesbian baby boom; I'm sure everyone has children to attend to now).

I was lucky to join a progressive theater faculty, one with leftist roots and a commitment to thinking through cultural difference as an important factor in theater production, reception, and study. I appreciated how theater studies centered my teaching and my scholarship, while I engaged it in a deeply critical feminist analysis. My affiliation with Theatre over Women's Studies was in any case more emotional and intellectual than institutional; that is, I continued to attend Women's Studies meetings, events, and discussions, but never felt "at home" in the same way in the program. And theater studies, I have to say, was something of a curiosity in a Women's Studies Program that despite its commitment to interdisciplinarity, tended to value the knowledges of disciplines such as English, history, the languages, social sciences, and hard sciences over "the arts." Too many times, one particular senior professor in Women's Studies publicly dismissed my own home discipline. My scholarship in performance theory (before the popularity of performativity) and my preference for poststructuralist thinking somewhat alienated me from some faculty in the program's core.

I don't mean to malign the Women's Studies Program as I found it at Madison. Eventually, I began to feel more secure there, and some of the senior and junior faculty became close friends and supportive colleagues. Women's Studies, along with Theatre, participated in my tenure, and my committee was very supportive of my case. My surprise, though, was how much more comfortable I felt in Theatre. I don't mean to offer anything but a partial history of my own involvement with women's studies as a field, as a way of charting certain contentions around its institutionalization. The things that concerned me about women's studies at Madison are issues the field brings with it, rather than idiosyncratic, personal ones. The politics of labor; an activist history in a land-grant institution committed to democracy, which had been overshadowed by institutionalization; complacency with power that reinforced conventional status divisions around rank and disciplines—the way these problems played out might not have been happily attended to, but that they existed wasn't particular to UW–Madison.

I know there are many women of my generation in the academy for whom women's studies provided a lifeline, offering community and solidarity for feminist work disparaged or even despised in their home disciplines. In some ways, because of the field's success at UW–Madison, many feminist faculty were comfortable and secure in their position as academics, and didn't need the emotional and experiential support that women's studies once provided.[8] The project of women's studies remained important, but the program's goals seemed less activist than institutional.

Renegades Still

This institutionalization of feminism in the late eighties and nineties on many university campuses meant a move away from the singularity I knew as a young graduate student, a move from frustrating isolation, to the empowerment of community, and to the power of position in academic systems.[9] Despite my personal surprise at my somewhat ambivalent relationship to the program at UW, I continue to believe very strongly in the importance and impact of women's studies as a field. As I've argued earlier about lgbtq studies, separate programs require institutional acknowledgment and fiscal support, which is a good thing. Ironically, some scholars believe that women's studies—as an institutionalized discipline—has lost its edge, and some later-generation queer theorists impugn its motives and methods. The critique of the historical whiteness of women's studies has allowed an unfortunate general disparagement of its intellectual and institutional contributions.[10] And as essays in Dana Heller's collection, *Cross Purposes*, make eloquently clear, the ascendency of queer theory has made both "feminist" and "lesbian" politically degraded positions in some academic taxonomies.[11] I prize my work in gay and lesbian studies, but, as I detailed in chapter 2, I am concerned about and suspicious of the tendency in queer theory to dismiss feminist work on gender as old-fashioned and outmoded. I applaud scholars such as Sue-Ellen Case, Biddy Martin, and Teresa de Lauretis, who have taken the risky position of reminding current theorists of political and institutional history.[12]

For many of us who trained ourselves in the sixties, seventies, or early eighties, feminism's renegade beginnings will always influence how we perceive it, even as we watch it settling into a more domesticated academic routine. As Joan Scott notes, "We have lost, or seen diminished, the master narrative of progress that informed the social movements of the 1960s and 70s."[13] This loss fundamentally changes the relationship of feminism in the academy to a sense of struggle in the public sphere. And the fact remains that although some scholars feel feminism is "over," faculty and students' freedom to take courses and do research in women's studies still isn't guaranteed on many campuses.[14] Any reading of the field has to be couched in careful understandings of the politics of location. In smaller colleges in smaller cities around the country, in religiously affiliated institutions, in states without more liberal educational traditions, in large state institutions determined to cut what deeply conservative boards of trustees see as "irrelevant" programs, doing women's studies or engaging in feminist pedagogy or research is seditious.

For example, in fall 1997, at SUNY–New Paltz (a branch of the State University of New York), a conservative trustee of the SUNY system brought the media's attention to a conference on women's sexuality. Trustee Candace de Russy attended a session on lesbian s/m practices, and another on sex toys and deemed both beyond the bounds of academic propriety. She encouraged the SUNY board of trustees to censure the New Paltz president for allowing the conference to take place and established a fact-finding team to investigate whether the conference was appropriate for students. Vitae of the people who organized the conference and syllabi for courses in women's studies were collected and examined. As a result of this witch-hunt, the New Paltz president was put on probation. A report by the university-appointed fact-finding committee that deemed the conference academically appropriate was rejected by the board of trustees. They declared that the faculty governance system that exonerated the president and supported the conference was faulty and should be reconsidered.[15] The New Paltz president kept his job and was later honored by the American Association of University Professors for his stand on freedom of speech on his campus. But the New Paltz example serves as a troubling reminder of how powerful trustees can be in reordering campus curriculum and in threatening the job security of progressive faculty. No matter how much women's studies seems to be firmly institutionalized, the current wave of conservative, activist trustees, especially at public universities, will no doubt target gender (along with sexuality, race, and ethnicity) for attacks on what they consider superfluous, politically oriented knowledge. Their effort is to consolidate resources, limit spending on campuses, and return to a pristine Western core curriculum.

While conservative challenges continue and strengthen, progressive scholars need to work together against them. Our challenge is to form intellectual and institutional partnerships as new fields and modes of thinking (and being) catch fire and capture imaginations. It's important for scholars working in fields that really do complement one another to continually make arguments for the ways in which women's studies, critical race studies, lgbtq studies, and now, disability and other identity area studies, interlock and need common resources. Such coalitional work will be key to our common survival in leaner, meaner academic institutions.

Affiliations, Coalitions, and Labor

Questions of affiliation press at faculty from all sides and presume loyalty and commitment to various fields within our interdisciplinary work. Some of us name our scholarship "performance studies" or "feminist studies" or "queer theory"; others retain "theater studies" or "women's studies" or "gay and lesbian studies." The names matter to the extent that they determine which numbers our courses receive in the official bulletin each semester, which professional conferences we attend, what journals we read, and with which presses we publish. What we call our work and our disciplinary allegiances determine the jobs for which we're perceived to be eligible and the funding opportunities we're able to unearth and seek. In other words, much remains invested in the nomenclature of disciplinary distinctions, and, as I argued in chapter 4, how we move from one to the other matters quite a lot. The conventional organization of disciplines and the knowledge they produce are very much contested, no longer just by feminism or identity studies per se, but by new traditions of radical intellectual inquiry that bring with them their own critique. Disciplinary boundaries shift continually, over fields that bear geographical or national or methodological affinities, as well as those based on identity. Yet while such intellectual regroupings make for exciting scholarship and teaching, on their face, institutions are still very much organized according to traditional disciplinary structures.

As a result, disciplinary affiliations are very meaningful locally, because they determine labor. Leora Auslander's description of her work with the Center for Gender Studies at the University of Chicago is worth quoting at length because it's so familiar for those of us with multiple academic commitments:

> Our two greatest institutional challenges . . . are assuring faculty energy and financial support for the Center. All of our faculty owe primary allegiance and time to their home departments, and we have limited power to influence renewals, tenure decisions, and promotions. Most of the work done for the Center is invisible and, when noticed, sometimes (understandably) resented by departmental colleagues. In addition, recognition within the University and reputation in the academic world are still heavily based on disciplinary achievement. As the numbers of interdisciplinary programs grow, faculty feel increasingly stretched. This is an almost universal and, in a sense, not very interesting problem, but it is one with enormous consequences for the health and survival of this and other programs like it.[16]

The problem also has consequences for the health and survival of faculty. For instance, as an assistant professor jointly appointed in Women's Studies and Theatre and Drama at UW–Madison, I attended two sets of faculty meetings (sometimes three or four or more each month for each program and department) and performed double the amount of service. At the CUNY Graduate Center, and by then a full professor, I was appointed in Theatre, English, and Women's Studies, and was the executive director of the Center for Lesbian and Gay Studies. Most of my time was taken up with long committee meetings and professional commitments. My labor was expected, and the demand for my physical presence was very high.

Current departmentalized structures mean that people with cross-disciplinary (and typically activist) affiliations also advise double or triple the number of students and generally act as role models for students who are themselves marginalized by identity positions or who crave a more socially responsible educational experience. Typically, these overworked faculty are people of color, lesbians, and women and especially those whose identities cross these categories, who are already disenfranchised by the culture at large, and now find themselves working overtime to combat academic structures that marginalize them once again. Women, lesbians, and people of color are often tokenized on committees, so that while we are excluded by the sexism, heterosexism, and/or racism of our institutions, we're also curiously centered by institutional needs for diversity in governance, which also increases our labor load. We get trapped into working as a "labor of love"—our political commitments persuade us to work harder, better, and more, but we wind up burnt out and even embittered by making personal sacrifices in the face of increasingly conservative, rather than progressive, institutional change.

Given a climate of budgetary reduction, identity studies programs are too often forced to compete for courses, for faculty lines, for adjunct teachers, and for other institutional resources that allow them to do their best work. The challenge at the end of the millennium is to find ways to rebuild identity studies programs as coalitional sites. We need to consider how team-teaching, properly credited, across for example gay and lesbian studies and women's studies, or women's studies and Asian American studies, might increase available courses, reframe how we deliver knowledge about race, gender, and sexuality, and alleviate high teaching and advising loads for faculty with these areas of expertise; how regular extracurricular colloquia series, lectures, roundtables, and panel discussions, with local faculty and students as participants, might cross-pollinate knowledges in ways that offer greater visibility across fields; and how activist claims against institutional conservatism can only be strengthened by faculty, student, and staff committees that join ideas, commitments, and resources to clamor for employment rights such as pay equity, domestic partnership benefits, living wages for maintenance and service workers, graduate student unions, and antidiscrimination policies. Coalition building could be a progressive institutional value that will help protect marginalized areas of study from the sharp knife of budget cuts, and alleviate the burden of overworked faculty. In addition, true coalitions might reshape the curriculum and research in women's studies and other disciplines. As

Biddy Martin helpfully suggests, in her description of the ways in which our interpretive strategies have become too rigidly organized and isolating, "[I]n order to reorganize education and scholarly exchange around problems so that we bring our different areas of expertise to bear on one another's assumptions, we have to become curious again, curious about what different disciplinary formations and knowledge can contribute to problems or questions that we share."[17]

Feminism and Women's Studies in the Trenches

The classroom provides the micro level at which many of the issues I've addressed here play out. Our classrooms are where we feel—in the dailiness of our academic lives—our affiliations, our labor, our history, our disappointments and hopes influence our choices. Blurred borders characterize my teaching experience. I teach the academic areas of theater studies from a feminist perspective; I teach women's studies from a poststructuralist perspective, often with an emphasis on performance; I teach gay and lesbian theater with an emphasis on social history. Many colleagues whose work overlaps a variety of disciplines share such unstable pedagogical boundaries. While we tend to teach with course numbers resolutely called by discrete departments, the truth of our syllabi belie any neat disciplinary categorizations. My courses are interdisciplinary by nature, and always attract a mixed clientele of students across majors, interests, skill levels, and motivations. These courses become, in effect, models for coalition building in the institution.

I've never taught a large lecture course, but usually medium-sized courses of twenty to fifty on the undergraduate level. I always use a discussion format, however large the class. I give no multiple-choice exams, and I assign quite a lot of writing, from short responses to longer essays or research papers. Whatever the content of any given course, I insist that students be able to think through their ideas on paper with clearly articulated, well-illustrated, well-argued prose. Writing, it seems to me (and sometimes even reading), is too often undervalued in theater studies and women's studies curricula; we need to take responsibility for helping to shape critical thinking through careful articulation and expanded vocabularies. Communicating these values is important for progressive educators mounting a counterdiscourse to the Right's inflated claims that all we teach is politics and advocacy. Many of us teach with fairly conservative forms and expectations to deliver more radical contents.

I firmly believe that knowledge is power, and that the content and methods of academic teaching provide a vital site in which to launch a long-term strategy for social change. My commitment to social activism has influenced my syllabi, but I also communicate certain bodies of knowledge and skills to my students. The notion that advocacy and knowledge are incompatible is a favorite charge from the conservative Right who attack higher education. I believe, on the contrary, that all teaching is advocacy, whether avowedly or not, and that students learn most profoundly from teachers who are clear about their own investments in the material and its relationship to a larger social project.[18]

My aims are socially progressive, but my demeanor in the classroom is fairly traditional. I remain the central authority in the classroom; I stress good writing and reading skills; I set very high standards for students' oral and written assignments; and I require respect for the forms and contents of the knowledge we're addressing. My classrooms are formal, carefully facilitated, and in the best instances, full of vocal, engaged students.[19]

If I were to sum up my feminist teaching strategies, I would say this: I don't see myself as a repository of a great mass of knowledge. I know some things. I read well and can teach people my skills. I can make connections between ideas and help students make their own. I'm very curious about what other people think, and want very much to learn from my students as they're learning from me. There are never right answers in my classroom; in fact, there are rarely answers at all. I think good questions are much more important.

I see myself as a deeply invested, biased facilitator who has some history to share, some contextualizing remarks to offer, some pulling together and traveling forward to try out. I bring a certain expertise to the classroom, but I see my main goal as teaching students how to develop their own expertise. I respect students' potential, although I've learned that some students have more potential than others, and I now understand not to misplace my energies with students who will never care enough to try. I deeply respect effort, which I consistently reward.

I always prepare elaborate handouts to tell students what I expect of their writing and their course projects. I detail my expectations; I give clear examples, often using students' work from earlier semesters of the course; I explain from the first day how and why I grade the way I do; I always give credit for attendance and grade students down when they miss more than three classes. I recommend that students go to one another and to writing labs and other university services for additional help and input.

I keep adequate office hours, but I am not eternally accessible. I keep my office appointments to fifteen minutes, so that my interactions with students are succinct and useful. I don't let students call me at home, as I think it's important for women teachers, especially, and feminist teachers, particularly, to establish and maintain clear boundaries from the outset. Often working in departments in which they're the only woman or the only feminist or the only lesbian faculty person or the only woman of color (or all four), women teachers are susceptible to a host of unmet student needs, which can be overwhelming and impossible to fulfill. I also don't accept late papers, mostly because it's not fair to me or to other students who get their work in on time. I don't give incompletes. I set firm and clear standards and expect students to respect them. I rarely make exceptions, but when I do, I control my own choices. Setting rules frees me to be more giving and open in the classroom because I've already established the sense of order under which I feel comfortable proceeding.

My teaching in Women's Studies at UW–Madison in the late eighties and early nineties was marked by certain intellectual struggles that reflected the political and institutional context of both activism and accommodation. Despite my commitments to feminism, I had never really considered what it might mean to either teach women's studies or to be a feminist pedagogue. I learned on the job, picking up strategies and methods as I went along. I often made my choices in reaction against the tired, tradition-bound teaching I'd typically experienced as a student. Women's Studies faculty at UW–Madison were helpful, to a certain extent, although there seemed a general unwillingness to confront some of the more challenging aspects of teaching in the program. I found it surprising that we didn't talk more, as a faculty, about what exactly we did in class and what we expected of students. Of course, I didn't expect such discussions from the Theatre Department; perhaps my own idealized expectations of women's studies lead me to think that the program would want to carefully hone its faculty's and instructors' teaching skills. My expectations about the Women's Studies Program's institutional self-reflexivity were higher, perhaps unfairly. I expected our faculty to think more analytically about the project of delivering the knowledge we produced.

I taught two courses for Women's Studies during my tenure at Madison. "Feminism and Social Theory" was one of the few required courses in the program. Although other instructors taught it from a historical perspective, starting with Mary Wollstonecraft and working up to the edges of current theorizing, I centered my syllabus on contemporary poststructuralist theory, with a heavy dose of recent feminist thinking on sexuality, as well as gender and race. The first iteration of the class in spring 1990, as I find frequently happens, was most invigorating, as I learned much of the material we studied along with the students. We read Chris Weedon's useful *Feminist Practice and Post-Structuralist Theory*, Foucault's *The History of Sexuality*, selections from Joan Nestle's *A Restricted Country*, Audre Lorde's *Zami*, selections from *This Bridge Called My Back*, and Gloria Anzaldúa's *Making Face, Making Soul*, in addition to many articles in feminist poststructuralist theory.[20] The course argued that theory is a practice of feminism; that experience is a form of theory and can be analyzed accordingly; and that contemporary theory offers useful ways of reenvisioning political practice. We took apart identity, trying to destabilize easy assignments of gender and sexuality; we unsettled notions of eternal, universal truth; and we pushed through the recovery projects of feminist history into an inquiry into the future of feminist activism and communities.

Emotions were often high in the feminist theory class. The project of theory had always been deeply personal for me, as my encounters with continental thinkers had given me a new language and a vital explanatory system at a time when feminist theater criticism was more conventional and (I thought) less effective. I also found continental theory creative and erotic rather than tedious and appreciated its insistence that criticism, too, is a kind of creativity. I read Kristeva and Cixous, Derrida and Barthes, reveling in their language play and the generative force of their thinking, whether or not I understood every word they wrote. Learning poststructuralist thinking on gender and sexuality completely changed my work in feminist performance theory, not to mention significantly shaking my own consciousness. As a result, modeling my belief in the necessity of mixing theory and practice, in both feminism and theater, made me vulnerable to the students in ways that were sometimes productive and sometimes left me too open to their challenges to my authority. I probably revealed more of myself in "Feminism and Social Theory" than I did in other classes, partly because the material was rigorous and partly because it cut closer to my bones.

Since this was the first course I'd taught in Women's Studies, I was excited by the material and enthusiastic in my approach. I talked a lot in class, working hard to make connections between experience and theory, sharing my passion for the ways in which theory had helped me articulate my own feminist commitments. We discussed the material in the large forty-five-student group, and the students worked in small groups, conversing in ways that were both personal and political, both practical and theoretical. Students were moved by the autobiographies and memoirs we read, captivated by Nestle's recitations of butch/femme experience in the fifties, and by Lorde's description of racial divisions in lesbian culture at a similar historical moment. They worked hard on the theory, determined to become adept at what I insisted was a new skill, rather than a foreign language. I explained that reading theory was like hearing new music; at first, it sounds unintelligible, but with repeated listening, the melody starts to separate from the harmony and the lyrics suddenly make sense.

Many of them put a great deal of work into mastering what was an admittedly rigorous and difficult syllabus. One student cried in frustration during class; extending the music analogy, she said she thought theory is just like the Roches' song "Big Nothing," and proceeded to sing some of the lyrics for us. But generally, a productive tension held in the class, an intellectual charge that lead us to investigate this new territory together and see the ways in which it connected to our lives, the possibilities for subjectivity it opened up.

Other iterations of the course were less pleasurable. Because the theory course was required, it gave women's studies students a focus for a certain measure of anti-intellectualism. And because my expectations for writing and thinking and participating stayed very high, women's studies students looking for a "safe" environment in which to learn and share their experiences, unmediated, were resistant. I often had to confront the students' presumption that women's studies courses should somehow be easy, and their animosity because they knew that theory would be difficult. Just as I had looked for a home in women's studies, with all the presumptions of warmth and support that conventionally presumes and rarely delivers, my students, too, wanted to make their home in women's studies a safe harbor in the institutional seas they crossed. And just as I was disappointed by the program's impersonal institutionalization, my students were often disappointed in my conventional, high expectations of them. Teachers are as vulnerable and needy as our students when we teach in women's studies.

But I persevered. I stressed that difficult thinking could also be the basis of feminist activism and that demanding academic and intellectual work might well bear fruit in the social movement. These young women came to feminism through deep and often newly found understandings of injustice and organized their work around activist projects that compelled them outside of class. Feminism was profoundly changing their worldviews, and the new ways in which they understood social arrangements and cultural meanings were still intensely personal. No wonder they couldn't cotton on to a course that appeared to make feminism abstract, elitist, and obtuse. My own goal was to translate for them and to persuade them that feminist theory was in fact an enabling device that would expand the possibilities of their activist work as well as their personal transformations.

It wasn't easy. Many students came in daunted by the prospect of understanding what they perceived as long poststructuralist words with opaque meanings. Because they knew that some of the thinking we read was developed by French men, their newly found gender commitments lead some of them to reject the work out of hand. We also read Barbara Christian's "A Race for Theory," which, through its eloquent and persuasive argument against what she perceives as the hegemony of white European theory, provided grist for some of their antitheory mills.[21] For others, the vocabulary was just too dense and uncomfortable. Part of the resistance, I found, was that students had never been asked to "theorize" and had little practical understanding of what this might mean. One of the course's challenges was to demystify "theory." I tried to persuade them that theory is a common practice, that theories are hypotheses, ways of thinking about social relations that can't be proved empirically, but that can be carefully and ethically argued. Once they understood that theory, too, is various, and that we were learning a certain strain of poststructuralist thought, they began to shift their understanding of their own skills and abilities.

I tried continually to mark how much they were learning. At the end of the course, I passed out a vocabulary sheet with an elaborate list of words they'd come to understand and use. In one version of this class, I asked the students to write questions for the take-home exam. Every student in the class was represented on the test; they could choose to write on the question they submitted, or on one of the other forty or so options. Another of their assignments was to hand in what I called a "theorized question," written on a three-by-five index card, for twelve of our sixteen weeks together. This brief question was meant to be one without a "yes" or "no" answer, one that would provoke discussion or deeper thinking. This challenged their desire to ask questions that could be easily, concretely resolved, or to learn the right answers. I often printed their questions on the board, to share them with the rest of the class, so that people could see how other students were theorizing as we went along. We compiled these theorized questions, and referred to them as a record of the class's thinking.

I used a fair amount of small-group work in this class, a strategy often employed in feminist pedagogy, which assumes that students feel freer to talk when they aren't speaking in a large group. I found that sometimes small groups worked well, that students really did open up and engage with one another on an intellectual and analytical level. Sometimes, the small groups were gossip sessions. One semester, they fostered mutiny, and a group of students went to the chair of Women's Studies to complain about the low grades that I gave them on their papers.

The group that rebelled was furious with me for making what they considered unreasonable demands on their time and abilities. I didn't think the fault was in my teaching methods, as the semester before had gone very well with virtually the same strategies in place. The dynamics of this class were very different, tense and ambivalent and diffident from the outset. The students weren't a particularly strong bunch of thinkers or writers, but I never graded on a curve and always insisted that students strive for the highest level of quality and achievement. Their ringleader was a troubled student who had come to my office to cry on my shoulder about personal matters early in the semester. When I rebuffed her, because I don't feel I'm trained to serve as my students' therapist, she became hurt and angry, and punished me by fomenting revolution in my class.

The mutiny was difficult for me. I knew nothing of their plans until I got a call at home from the chair of Women's Studies, who kindly said that if there were eleven students in her office complaining, then the teacher must not be too happy, either. We talked over some strategies, but essentially, I was left to deal with the students' animosity on my own. I confronted the class about their complaint and reaffirmed my commitment to high standards, telling them I hoped they'd come to me with their issues about the course. Some of them grudgingly came around; others remained hostile until the end. My version of feminist activism contradicted the students' expectations. Their self-righteous presumptions cast me as the villain, a role I couldn't shake until the next semester.

The experience hurt me, and I was surprised at how few outlets there were for talking about these recalcitrant students. When I tried to explain to other faculty what had happened, I sensed an unwillingness to hear, a brushing off of the severity of what I'd felt through the tensest moments. I also sensed my own vulnerability as a junior faculty person, talking publicly about a poor teaching experience. Teaching once again was privatized. Left to my own devices, I decided that some classes go well and others go badly, for a host of unpredictable and often surprising reasons.

The "Lesbian Culture" course I taught (only once) in a four-week summer session was even more overheated. The course had traditionally been offered by a cultural feminist faculty member, who taught the canon of lesbian separatist literature. My course, once again poststructuralist in its orientation, tried to unsettle lesbian identity as an "authentic" subjectivity, while it traced the historical and theoretical underpinnings of current interdisciplinary work in the field. We read performance texts by the internationally known lesbian artist Holly Hughes and by the feminist trio, Split Britches; theoretical and historical work by John D'Emilio and Estelle Freedman, Sue-Ellen Case, Teresa de Lauretis, and Esther Newton; some of Lillian Faderman's history of lesbians in the United States in the twentieth century, *Odd Girls and Twilight Lovers*; along with Judith Butler's influential theory volume, *Gender*

Trouble, and selections from Diana Fuss's early collection of lesbian/gay theoretical writing, *Inside/Out.*[22]

These students were primed for the theoretical investigation; many of them had taken the theory class and chose "Lesbian Culture" as an elective. My challenges in this class were more political and historical. Coalition building around identity studies means that you can't always presume that students who want to take, say, a class in lesbian culture, will all be lesbians. Anyone with an interest in progressive ways of thinking about sexuality should or might be interested in this knowledge. But my poststructuralist approach to identity created an environment in which these young students seemed almost too willing to throw over the trappings of identity, even parodying lesbian feminist presumptions about sexuality and gender. Although the word wasn't used then, in the very early nineties, these women were acting "queer," and I found myself unsettled by this new style.

When we read *Beebo Brinker,* Ann Bannon's classic lesbian pulp novel, for example, my students scoffed at Beebo's experiences, her inability to connect with a self-defined and self-approving lesbian community.[23] Where I read the novel as a chestnut, but one that revealed something of what it meant to be a lesbian in the fifties (if in lurid, melodramatic detail), my students found it tacky and ridiculous. They refused to make the historical connections and couldn't find themselves in Beebo's angst. This was the first time I noticed my age, as a teacher. Immediately after that class, I began to embrace more fervently a historical and historicizing approach to lesbian studies. I realized that while I understood the importance of institutional history in fields like women's studies or gay/lesbian/queer studies, it's also important continually to ground new ideas in their genesis out of intellectual history. Teaching Mary Wollstonecraft or Sojourner Truth alongside Foucault, or Sappho beside Judith Butler, suddenly seemed like a very sound idea.

Theater Studies and Writing across the Curriculum

Teaching in a theater department presents its own challenges. Students who decide to major in theater are often iconoclasts, willing to buck their parents' inevitable concerns about the lack of marketability in an arts degree. Many of them are would-be actors, who see themselves becoming not thinking artists, but stars, celebrities-in-the-making who have no need for a liberal arts education. Many departments, with their heavy emphasis on production and on grooming students for careers in the theater, film, or television industry, foster an environment in which getting cast in mainstage shows determines a student's rate of success, regardless of his or her grades or how well the student does in their academic studies. The history of ideas, as a result, tends to be low on the priority list of many theater majors.

In addition, because of heavy production schedules, their location in performing arts centers set off from the rest of the campus, and their tendency to overwork faculty and students, theater departments are often isolated from campus life, as well as from national discussions about the arts and their survival. With such isolation comes a perception of theater majors as different from other students, as more creative, perhaps more romantic, but also as less intellectually inclined. When I taught "Writing about Performance" at UW–Madison, a course mandated to fill the English competency requirement for theater majors, I encouraged a simple sense of pride in the students' intellectual work while I taught them critical thinking and clear writing skills. I wanted these students to learn that it's okay to be smart and creative at once. I wanted them to believe, as I do, that writing and rigorous thinking is important to their work as actors or designers or directors. So few people in universities or in American culture have deep respect for people who dedicate their lives to theater; I wanted them to take pleasure and pride in a community that shared common goals.

We focused on various kinds of critical analysis and their articulation, from historical and biographical to feminist and psychoanalytical. The students wrote a series of papers applying critical methods to various plays or performances. They wrote and rewrote a number of drafts that they shared with me and with one another. We read Strunk and White; we used William Zinsser's *On Writing Well*; we read theater criticism from the *New York Times* and the local newspapers.[24] I used quite a lot of peer review in this course; students worked in groups or pairs, circulating their drafts. This helped to demystify the process of writing by allowing students to look at one another's work for clarity, interest, construction, grammar, syntax, and style. Because students tend not to see one another's written work, they have no idea how their peers write, or how to judge their own work in relation to their cohort (learning, like teaching, is too frequently privatized).

The course also encouraged them to see writing as a process, work as meticulous as building a character, or blocking a scene, or designing a set. Students read work aloud in class; we worked on constructive criticism; we learned to isolate problems and tried to solve them. I gave them sheets that asked them to rate themselves on structure, on style, on clarity and persuasiveness, so that they could learn to think critically about their own work. I asked them to be self-critical, to give themselves grades on papers as a practice exercise. (They hated grading themselves.) I asked them to read writing about theater, or critical writing in general, since they have very few models and didn't understand that they could emulate authors they like. We read Anna Quindlen's collection of essays, *Living Out Loud*, as a model of invested, clear, persuasive style.[25]

Required courses like "Writing about Performance" have their own challenges, especially for feminist teachers who want everyone to be enthralled and moved by what we're doing. But meeting with theater majors to encourage their critical thinking skills was invariably rewarding. The course was inspired by UW's mandate for writing across the curriculum, which insists on writing as a disciplinary skill intimately connected to the acquisition and distribution of knowledge. And the course did, in many cases, instill pride in both intellectual and artistic work in our department.

Another course I developed for the Theatre Department at UW–Madison and cross-listed with Women's Studies was called "Introduction to Contemporary Feminist Theatre and Criticism." This course was designed as an overview of the field. We read plays with forms and contents students had never encountered before (Joan Schenkar's deconstructionist literary and cultural history, *Signs of Life*; Susan Yankowitz's 1960s expressionistic tract about racism, *The Slaughterhouse Play*; and Cherríe Moraga's early, evocative Chicana lesbian text, *Giving Up the Ghost*), and theory by Sue-Ellen Case, Lynda Hart, Peggy Phelan and others that sometimes frustrated but always intrigued them.[26] In this course, the women's studies students were much less resistant to theory, perhaps because the course wasn't required, or because its disciplinary base in theater created different expectations.

I set two goals for the course: First, I intended the students to acquire analytical skills that would let them do original close readings of plays and performances, paying particular attention to form, structure, content, and the workings of ideology in the text. I wanted them to be able to use these skills to write critically. Second, I wanted students to understand the social and political bias of all theater, whether feminist or overtly political or not. I wanted them to see our complicity in representation and to learn to take a stand about the meanings of theater and performance. Since the course was about the politics of performance, my own political readings were very much in evidence. I tend to be very open about my ideological foundation, my beliefs, and my opinions as a teacher. Students are then free to develop their own political analyses and recognize them as such. I tell them they don't have to agree with me (and many students vocally express their differences), but I won't hide my politics or pretend that the representations we study are objective or unaligned.

The clientele for the feminist theater class was always mixed. Theater students enrolled who had some expertise in reading plays and performance; women's studies majors enrolled who knew something about feminist critical strategies or American women's history. These two camps tended to regard each other suspiciously over what was often a physical divide in the class-room. The women's studies students came to class gripping coffee mugs with political bumper stickers pasted over them, while the theater students came groggy from late-night rehearsals, resolved not to be politicized, but to talk about universality and art. My mission was to bridge these practical and ideo-logical gaps and get everyone to share knowledge, questions, ideas, and pleasures.

One strategy that worked well, which tends to be used frequently in fem-inist pedagogy, was asking them to keep a critical journal. The productive as-pect of a journal is that it's not as closely structured as a formal paper and asks students to imbue their thoughts with a sense of their own relationship to a text or a performance. The journals let me have a dialogue with students in writing, one that felt less rigid than assessing their organizational skills and argumentation. I explained that I expected close textual analysis of the plays and theory we read and the performances we saw. But journal writing also let students approach their critical work from a more invested position. They struggled to put themselves in their writing, since so many are still taught that they can't use "I" in their academic work. But while the journals invited a kind of personal reflection, I wanted them to use the exercise to un-derstand the importance of who they are in more than a personal sense, to understand that what they think means something to a larger cultural and social space. I reminded them, often, that I could grade their analysis but not their lives. Sometimes, still, people used the occasion of journalizing to re-veal personal things I would rather not have known or to critique the pro-gress of the class, a venting I encouraged them to bring to office hours, in-stead. I gave them very specific feedback on their journals and firmly corrected their tendencies to misuse the occasion of this writing.

Theater and Social Change: Institution as Microcosm

Another course I developed at UW–Madison was "Theater and Society," a course that met the university-wide ethnic studies requirement for the mostly white student population. As a result, students signed up from across the campus; this course, more than any other I taught at UW, enrolled a diversity of majors and status levels, although the racial composition of the course re-mained at least 95 percent white. The upper-level literature and theory course focused on identity politics around race, through a framework that asked students to consider what it means to be inside or outside racial or ethnic or sexual categories. The course started with identity politics and ended with much more fluid, unstable understandings of race and ethnicity, as well as gender and sexuality, in some ways anticipating the current work in queer theory. The course argued for performance as a profitable site at which to think about the construction of identities, whether as performers or spectators, in communities or universities.

We began with eight weeks of interdisciplinary theory and criticism that addressed spectatorship in theater and performance, race theory, questions of "authenticity" and ownership in representation, stereotyping, and various strategies for reading representation and "community." We read Susan Bennett's book *Theatre Audiences* and Skip Gates's *New York Times* piece on the authorship of *The Education of Little Tree* and its racial implications, and other articles that broached a suspicion of firmly held, stably conceived identity positions.[27] We then spent four two-week units in distinctly marked race or ethnic or sexual communities (African American, Asian American, Latino, gay/lesbian). We questioned how the plays and theory we read drew their boundaries, asked how race and ethnicity and sexuality are constructed and by whom, and allowed students to place their bodies in relation to the communities presented by the plays. We asked how these plays constructed the identities of their characters and which audiences they seemed to address. We looked at how "inside" and "outside" worked as locations around the texts and asked where each student and we as a class seemed to be positioned. We asked how reading these plays in an academic context changed them. And we asked ourselves what we don't know in relation to these texts or communities, how we might know more, and why we should try to teach ourselves. What would a "fuller" understanding offer, and how might it be useful in trying to change social relations between races, genders, sexualities, through performance? How might we even approach Phelan and Young's notion of productive misunderstanding by engaging at these sites?

For the first four weeks of class, I required weekly response papers that commented critically on our reading. These entailed a one-page close analysis of a line, a paragraph, or a piece of a play, and were not graded. They let me interact with students' writing early and frequently, so that I could predict problems and begin to address them. The second four-week segment required a five-page essay, in which I expected a clearly structured argument, solid critical evidence, and smooth presentation.

For the last eight weeks of the class, student groups facilitated the presentation of scene projects on which each student wrote a three-page paper analyzing the play and their group's performance process. The students' assignment was to read and analyze the play; to choose a short scene to perform in class, making bold choices about performance style and audience constitution; and to facilitate a discussion after the scene. Each group produced a program that situated the performance within a speculative (but specific) audience community, that iconographically illustrated their interpretation of the scene, and that posed questions for group discussion after the performance. The programs often raised discussion questions around the legibility and consequences of the students' choices, which typically were brave and unusual. The students didn't take the texts at face value, but freely reinterpreted them, changed their location, moved around the chairs and tables in the classroom or moved us elsewhere all together, and brought in costumes and props that illustrated the new values through which they were reading the play.

Many of the scenes were deconstructive, and helped students give up tenacious attachments to author's intent. That is, rather than doing the play as written, they would make radical choices about where the play should be set, its location, characters, and meanings, sometimes abstracting the texts, sometimes metaphorizing them, sometimes making them allegories. We respected the plays we read, but explored them as living, writable documents. The performances also tended to be funny and poignant, but all of them met the challenge of the class to address what racial, gender, sexual, and ethnic embodiments mean in performance, as well as in daily life. Cross-gender and cross-racial casting happened of necessity in these scenes, but the crosscasting also prompted some investigation into what it might mean both to act and to be a person of a different race or gender. The scenes accomplished some new understandings about identity politics, freeing students from rigid presumptions about the origin of race and ethnicity, sexuality and gender.

Because students worked closely together, they taught one another in their scene-work groups and then went on to teach their colleagues in class. This kind of mutual support, often around discussions of racial or sexual communities for which few people in the class had firsthand knowledge, let people cross that threshold of polite hesitation that tends to dampen discussions of gender, race, and sexuality. Students generally agreed that gender and sexuality are performances, in Butler's definition, early in the class. But later, race, too, lost its status as a metaphysics of substance and became a productively fluid performance without the requirement of authenticity. The scene work helped students discover the differences between theatrical performance and performativity, as the frame of theater, even in a shabby, windowless classroom, provided an aura of expectation (and spectating) that they saw was missing from performativity's more social excursions. That is, while it's helpful to think of gender, race, and sexuality as social perform-ances, staging them as theatrical performance allowed a more focused critical study in the laboratory of the classroom.

The characters in most of the plays we read were markedly different racially or ethnically from the students performing them, so everyone had to think about what it meant to embody these differences and perform them for an audience. In Alexis DeVeaux's *Tapestry*, a poetic drama about an African American woman trying to sort out her life, a group of white women felt ut-terly inadequate to perform the African American dialect in which most of the poetic, imagistic play is written.[28] They transposed the language and the ref-erences to a kind of redneck whiteness, to try to point out how race is marked in the text. I think the choice erased blackness more than it foregrounded race as a construct, but it prompted a discussion about fear and why these women didn't feel it appropriate to adopt a dialect that they couldn't "authenticate." The choice was bold, even if I disagreed with it; the students and I critiqued all the scene-work choices for their efficacy and persuasiveness, for what they opened up about the play and the issues it addressed.

Students also learned to poke fun at their own outsiderness, in ways that brought inside and outside closer together. Humor was invaluable in these moves. The several students of color in the class offered useful information when they thought it necessary and also performed against their own so-called communities of origin. Cross-gender casting became quickly natural-ized. By the end of the semester, two heterosexual white men played the white lesbians Deeluxe and Michigan, originally played by Lois Weaver and Peggy Shaw, in Holly Hughes's *Dress Suits to Hire* and somehow, remarkably, captured the text's eroticism and its evocative language play.[29]

The scenes also interrogated production context, commenting wryly on the spectacle and commodification of *Angels in America* on Broadway, for ex-ample. But students also appreciated the two-part text's productively contra-dictory characters, its linking of the erotic with the spiritual, and its desire to infuse people with belief and agency.[30] Broadway didn't become villainous just because of its mainstream values; students recognized that even in main-stream contexts, productions might be used differently by different specta-tors. They understood that not all readings are politically progressive, and that readings and uses, no matter how various, have different effects in differ-ent contexts, on different spectators. We came to agree that identity cate-gories in this play and in many productions are merely functional, and that their functions and affiliations and meanings change across context. These ideas were usefully extrapolated to other plays and other contexts.

The scenes required students to put their bodies on the line, and I appreciated their willingness to ask, through embodiment, various questions prompted by the plays we read. For example, per *Angels in America*: What does faith mean? In what do we believe? Who do we love? Why do we care? These, I believe, are questions that have to be asked, to prompt students to think about their investments in knowledge and its social effects. Using strategies from drag, to cross-gender, to cross-racial, to "method," to parodic, to deconstructive, the class let bodies signify wildly. Desire circulated freely, as we took pleasure in one another's interpretations, presences, and performances, which were rarely virtuosic, but always dangerous and always committed. It turned out to be really good theater.

The course also turned out to be an example of local social change. One student in the class—a physics major who took it to meet the ethnic studies requirement—wrote to me at the end that he'd had no idea about what it meant to be of a different race or gender, never really thought it mattered. Now, he said, he sees it, and wants to work at understanding it and his relationship as a heterosexual white man to everything that means. At the beginning of the semester, we used "social change" as a term so often it became a kind of mantra, emptied of all but the best intentions because of our inability to make the leap from here to there. We finally realized that we can't assume that the social is out there, but in fact was in here, in class, all along.[31]

My "Ten Commandments" for Teaching

Finally, my ten personal commandments for teaching. I have to stress that these are my own; they've worked for me and they might work for others.

1. Teach to the highest common denominator. Students will rise to the occasion. Learning should be hard.

2. Teach for questions, not for answers. Focus on the gaps, the omissions, the whys, the maybes, but always take a stand around the knowledge you share or discover.

3. Teach to unsettle, not to create a safe space. Learning should be dangerous, because ideas and what they can do have real meanings and real effects.

4. Teach to learn something. Never teach the exact same syllabus twice, but always look for different readings, new input. Learn in front of your students, as you teach.

5. Believe that good writing is fundamental to learning anything and insist that students do it well.

6. Believe that students have a lot to teach one another. The teacher isn't the only one in the classroom with something important to say.

7. Believe that humanities/arts classrooms should be about learning the skills of analysis, about how to ask questions more than about transmitting correct readings of canonical texts.

8. Believe in embodied learning and teaching. Everyone's body should be on the line in the classroom, even if no one leaves their chair.

9. Be responsible to your own authority and power as a teacher. I give the grades, so I have to be as organized, committed, and well prepared as I expect the students to be.

10. Believe in a classroom in which pleasure circulates freely: as desire, as humor, as intellectual inquiry, as the passionate commitment to ideas, theories, and practices.

epilogue
On Pleasure

*By political struggle . . . I am referring to a social movement
with a radical democratic vision, a way of imagining and re-
making the world in a manner we have never seen.*
—Robin Kelley

Geographies of Learning has, I hope, addressed the myriad
ways in which progressive academics, activists, and artists negotiate the vicis-
situdes of often conservative institutional environments, trying to translate
their theory into various practices and vice versa across constituencies, from
students to community activists to audiences. In addition to charting the
challenges, I've attempted to describe the pleasures of being a progressive
academic—teaching, lecturing, and writing with a number of different audiences and communities in mind. I've insisted that part of our project can be
to assert a different cosmology of values and that one of those values is the
pleasure derived from politically inflected intellectual work.

The classroom is an intimate place. Any place where people meet, where
live bodies and minds come into contact to think, to read, to analyze together, to perform for each other, whether a classroom or a theater, will be
charged with the mysteries of presence and charisma, with curiosity and
longing, with private passions that illuminate public debate. When a course
meeting "clicks," students and teachers are linked together in a moment as
profound and fleeting as performance. Teaching is like performance, and
classrooms are like theatre; our encounters there are ephemeral, unrepro-
ducible. Teaching the same text never feels the same way twice, and each audience of students responds differently. Students are transitory; their goal is
to leave. Professors stay on, influencing and being shaped by new generations of desiring subjects. Professors are role models; students desire to be
like us. Students remind us of ourselves; we desire to replicate ourselves
through them.[1] Classrooms are places of longing and loss, in which embodied emotions roil to prompt the pursuit of intellectual fulfillment, a state that
can only be attained for a moment. This is the stuff of desire.

Just as we need to reclaim theatre and performance as honorable sites of
pleasure, progressive academics might begin to publicly value the pleasure of
their teaching and their research. Michael Bronski argues that pleasure scares

conservatives because it's nonreproductive. Indeed, conservatives devalue lesbian/gay/queer and feminist studies because they fail to reproduce the canon or traditional value systems. They disparage theater and performance scholarship because it's seen as mere entertainment, the study of pleasures that usually offend family values, as the NEA debacle proves. But exactly these "nonreproductive" pleasures afford hope to progressive scholars, activists, and artists. What's productive here is the pleasure of imagining different futures in which social justice might prevail. In classrooms coursing with the desire for knowledge, for clarity, for new social relations, we might be able to practice, try on, and perform such utopian visions.

I love teaching for precisely these reasons. By thinking with a group of people, I move closer to my own beliefs and values. I clarify my commitments and learn how to better articulate them. Because I'm passionate about my ideas, teaching engages me ethically. Teaching uses all of me and taps into sources that are deeply personal. Sharing these emotions and this intellectual momentum with a group of students that forms its own community over the course of a semester leaves me vulnerable to them as well as to myself.

Relationships of respect and caring and even love are a very good thing for students and teachers, critics and artists, academics and activists. Teaching in intense classrooms of politically and intellectually and artistically committed students provides me with community that I sometimes don't have time to form elsewhere. I know that my university-based relationships are scored with power differences; after all, I give grades and often make decisions that affect my students' lives. I try to stay aware of my power and responsible to its effects. But my students and my colleagues provide an extended kinship structure that feeds me, and to which I often turn for personal as well as professional support. My students—not my children, since I've chosen not to bear or adopt any—are my progeny, my inheritors, my tiny glimpse of immortality.

Likewise, the community I form with friends and colleagues who are artists and activists and academics elsewhere sustains me and feeds me, challenging me to justify my choices of where to work, what to teach, where to live, what to write, what to create, who to love. I treasure the camaraderie of going to conferences and attending performances, of roundtable discussions where we share our thinking and frustrations. I even enjoy committee meetings, because I believe they're the micro level of academic, activist, and artistic engagement. I've tried to think through the process of building coalitions, alliances, and affiliations, a process that happens daily, on the local levels where we teach, meet in committees, and attend rallies, demonstrations, lectures, discussions, conferences, and performances. No wonder I feel shattered when I'm implicitly called a "dirty academic," someone whose language is ugly and indulgent. No wonder I despair at coalition when walls seem erected so thoughtlessly between people with mutual goals.

I'm bemused, for a moment, that I'm ending a book about theory and practice, academics and activism, artists and critics, with a discourse on kinship, on utopia, on love. But on reflection, it strikes me that this is what *Geographies of Learning* has been at least tacitly about. Don't we work—at theater and art, scholarship and teaching, at activism and social justice—because we have a vision for how they can make the world different? Here, too, I try to stay aware of power differentials. I'm a professor in a major research university, which provides me a steady salary, benefits, perks, and security that aren't available to many of my artist and activist friends. I'm empowered and enabled by my position. But I use that power and those resources toward activist goals and try to share them with artists as much as possible. My position is not a place to which I retreat; my university is not an ivory tower.

Regardless of our methods and contexts—whether theoretical or practical or both, in the academy, in the street, in the theatre, or all three—aren't those of us committed to progressive change united by a deep desire to see more love determine the course of events in the world, and less oppression, cruelty, and exploitation in the name of profit, religion, colonialism, or imperialism? Don't we all hope that how we move across geographies of learning, of art making, of idea generating, of policy making, of world building, of culture forming will reconfigure them radically, making them more humane, valuing all their subjects, finding in them pleasure, fleetingly fulfilled desire, and even peace?

I hope so. Let's respect one another, admire one another, and even love one another, while our mutually great work continues.[2]

notes

Chapter 1

1. I'm not sure, frankly, what constitutes "grass roots" in the twenty-first century. But the term is still used, in political circles, to refer to those who work "on the ground" in political organizing, rather than in larger organizations or institutions perceived to be more removed from people's lives. In another project, it might be worth researching the use and abuse of this term.

2. See bell hooks, *Ain't I a Woman? Black Women and Feminism* (Boston: South End, 1981), and her *Feminist Theory: From Margin to Center* (Boston: South End, 1984).

3. White made these remarks on the morning plenary session at the Barnard College "The Feminist and the Scholar" conference, 28 March 1998, in New York City.

4. The conference, "Women in Theatre: Mapping the Sources of Power," was organized by the Women's Project and Productions and funded by the Ford Foundation. It was held 7 and 8 November 1997, at the New School for Social Research in New York City.

5. I disagree, for example, with Richard Rorty, who, in "The Inspirational Value of Great Works," in *Achieving Our Country: Leftist Thought in Twentieth-Century America* (Cambridge: Harvard UP, 1998), suggests, "You cannot, for example, find inspirational value in a text at the same time that you are viewing it as the product of a mechanism of cultural production. To view a work in this way gives understanding but not hope, knowledge but not self-transformation" (133). On the contrary, I believe that understanding the mechanisms of culture, and how it produces its meanings, provides hope for a transfigured future.

6. Many of these attacks are published in *Lingua Franca*, which delights in academics trashing one another, and the more sober but often prurient *Chronicle of Higher Education*. See also Martha Nussbaum's critique of Judith Butler, "The Professor of Parody: The Hip Defeatism of Judith Butler," *New Republic* 23 February 1999, 37+, and see Butler's self-defense of theoretical language in her op-ed, "A 'Bad Writer' Bites Back," *New York Times* 20 March 1999, A15.

7. I'd like to thank Juanita Rockwell, of Towson University, for this catchy and descriptive phraseology.

8. See, for only a few examples, Roger Kimball, *Tenured Radicals: How Politics Has Corrupted Our Higher Education* (New York: Harper and Row, 1990); William J. Bennett, *The Death of Outrage: Bill Clinton and the Assault on American Ideals* (New York: Free, 1998); Lynne V. Cheney, *Telling the Truth: Why Our Culture and*

Our Country Have Stopped Making Sense (New York: Simon and Schuster, 1995); and Lynne V. Cheney, *Fifty Hours: A Core Curriculum for College Students* (Washington, D.C.: US GPO, 1989).

9. See *Chronicle of Higher Education* 12 January 1998, A33–35.

10. See Cary Nelson, *Manifesto of a Tenured Radical* (New York: New York UP, 1997), for a discussion of the MLA and graduate student employment, as well as other labor issues vital to the contemporary academy. See also his edited volume, *Will Teach for Food: Academic Labor in Crisis* (Minneapolis: U of Minnesota P, 1997).

11. See, for example, Todd Gitlin, *Twilight of Common Dreams: Why American Is Wracked by the Culture Wars* (New York: Metropolitan Books, 1995), and John Wilson, *The Myth of Political Correctness: The Conservative Attack on Higher Education* (Durham: Duke UP, 1995), for a conservative and a liberal, respectively, reading of these debates; Katie Roiphe, *The Morning After: Sex, Fear, and Feminism on Campus* (Boston: Little, Brown, 1993), Susan Faludi, *Backlash: The Undeclared War against American Women* (New York: Crown, 1991), and Camille Paglia, *Sexual Personae* (New Haven: Yale UP, 1990), for various readings of contemporary feminism that have added to or commented on the hostile climate on campus for feminism, in particular.

12. Rorty, for instance, says, "If the intellectuals and the unions could ever get back together again, and could reconstitute the kind of Left which existed in the Forties and Fifties, the first decade of the twenty-first century might conceivably be a Second Progressive Era" (56). Robin D. G. Kelley, in *Yo' Mama's Disfunktional!* (Boston: Beacon, 1997), responds to Rorty's and Gitlin's privileging of class: "The implications are frightening: the only people who can speak the language of universalism are white men (since they have no investment in identity politics beyond certain white working-class ethnic movements) and women and colored people who have *transcended or rejected* the politics of identity" (108–109), italics in original.

13. See, for example, James Clifford, *Routes: Travel and Translation in the Late Twentieth Century* (Cambridge: Harvard UP, 1997); Paul Gilroy, *The Black Atlantic: Modernity and Double Consciousness* (Cambridge: Harvard UP, 1993); and Arjun Appadurai, *Modernity at Large: Cultural Dimensions of Globalization* (Minneapolis: U of Minnesota P, 1997), for useful investigations of postcolonial theory.

14. Kelley, 139.

15. Bonnie Marranca, "Theatre and the University at the End of the Twentieth Century," *Performing Arts Journal* 50/51.2/3 (May/September 1995): 57.

16. Anna Deavere Smith, "Not So Special Vehicles," *Performing Arts Journal* 50/51.2/3 (May/September 1995): 80. She says, "We have spent too much time training our students to mirror ourselves, to show the world what's *inside* of the artist rather than the world *around* the artist" (81). Smith suggests that "we have to find new collaborators within the university that will allow us to look at acting as a study of human behavior and as a tool for researching communication skills, and for expanding our knowledge of what expression is" (84). In conjunction with Robert Brustein, artistic director of the ART Repertory Theatre at Harvard University, Smith has established a summer institute on theater and social change that brings together artists and academics to investigate social issues through performance.

17. Smith, 84.

18. Smith, 84.

19. Dwight Conquergood, "Rethinking Ethnography: Towards a Critical Cultural Politics," *Communication Monographs* 58 (1991): 187.

20. See Peggy Phelan, *Unmarked* (New York: Routledge, 1993), especially the final chapter, for a persuasive argument about generative misunderstandings. On the specific misunderstandings that occur around sexual harassment, desire, and knowledge in educational institutional settings, see thoughtful work by Jane Gallop, *Feminist Accused of Sexual Harassment* (Durham: Duke UP, 1998), and her "Resisting Reasonableness," *Critical Inquiry* 25.3 (spring 1999): 599–609. See also Ann Pellegrini, "Critical Response (to Jane Gallop) II: Pedagogy's Turn: Observations on Students, Teachers, and Transference-Love," *Critical Inquiry* 25.3 (spring 1999): 617–625.

21. Attempts to unmask the academy's political irrelevance have been regular in the past several years. For instance, on the Q-Studies listserver a couple of years ago, Daniel Harris staged a cheap hoax. He posed a theoretical question drawing on the work of a fictitious scholar, simply to provoke the list to examine what he considers its jargon-heavy self-satisfaction.

22. See Judith Butler, *Gender Trouble* (New York: Routledge, 1990), and *Bodies That Matter: On the Discursive Limits of "Sex"* (New York: Routledge, 1993); and Eve Kosofsky Sedgwick, *Epistemology of the Closet* (Berkeley: U of California P, 1990), and also her *Tendencies* (Durham: Duke UP, 1993) for an elaboration of these ideas.

23. Some theater and performance studies scholars read my argument as conservative, although I don't intend it that way. See for example, Joseph Roach, "Economies of Abundance," *TDR (The Drama Review)* 39.4 (fall 1995): 164, in which he suggests I "attack" performance studies.

24. See Gitlin and Rorty.

25. Kelley, 111.

26. See Nancy K. Miller, *Getting Personal: Feminist Occasions and Other Autobiographical Acts* (New York: Routledge, 1991), for a justification of situated, personally inflected writing. See also her *Bequest and Betrayal: Memoirs of a Parent's Death* (New York: Oxford UP, 1996), for a lovely example of personal yet critical writing. See, too, Susan David Bernstein, *Confessional Subjects: Revelations of Gender and Power in Victorian Literature and Culture* (Chapel Hill: U of North Carolina P, 1997), in which she critiques the "confessional" subject in feminism.

Chapter 2

1. Edward Said, "Opponents, Audiences, Constituencies, and Community," *Critical Inquiry* 9.1 (September 1982): 2.

2. Lisa Duggan, "Introduction," in Lisa Duggan and Nan Hunter, *Sex Wars: Sexual Dissent and Political Culture* (New York: Routledge, 1995) 2.

3. The "Queer Theater" conference was presented by the Center for Lesbian and Gay Studies in April 1995. See chapter 3 for an analysis of this event.

4. Escoffier made these remarks on a plenary panel at the "Forms of Desire"

conference, sponsored by CLAGS, at the CUNY Graduate Center, 3–5 April 1997. It's also worth noting that at the "Creating Change 2000" conference, Dr. Manning Marable presented one of the keynotes. Marable is a the founding director of the Institute for Research in African American Studies at Columbia University, and also one of the founders of the Black Radical Congress, a "center without walls" for transformative politics that focuses on the conditions of black working and poor people, which includes a specific platform plank supporting bisexual and transgender people, gay men, and lesbians (see NGLTF's promotional materials for "Creating Change 2000"). Since his work so importantly crosses the academy and activism, Marable is a model speaker for addressing the kinds of issues that concern me here in a wide, activist context.

5. Quoted in Steven Drukman, "Writers and Their Work: Holly Hughes Interviewed by Steven Drukman," *Dramatists' Guild Quarterly* (summer 1996): 40.

6. See, for example, Urvashi Vaid, *Virtual Equality: The Mainstreaming of Gay and Lesbian Liberation* (New York: Anchor Books, 1995); Andrew Sullivan, *Virtually Normal: An Argument about Homosexuality* (New York: Random House, 1995); Gabriel Rotello, *Sexual Ecology: AIDS and the Destiny of Gay Men* (New York: Dutton, 1997); Michelangelo Signorile, *Life Outside: The Signorile Report on Gay Men: Sex, Drugs, Muscles, and the Passages of Life* (New York: HarperCollins, 1997); Sarah Schulman, *Stagestruck: Theater, AIDS, and the Marketing of Gay America* (Durham: Duke UP, 1998); and some of the contentious arguments about these books.

7. Duggan and Hunter, 177.

8. Holly Hughes, e-mail correspondence, July 1996.

9. See my article on the status of gay and lesbian faculty and an overview of institutional issues in the field of lesbian/gay/queer studies, in *Academe* 84.5 (September/October 1998): 40–45. See also George Chauncey, "The Ridicule of Gay and Lesbian Studies Threatens All Academic Inquiry," *Chronicle of Higher Education* 3 July 1993, A40.

10. We need to take care, however, that we build new programs with an awareness of interlocking issues. For instance, at a conference on lesbian/gay/queer studies organized by Miranda Joseph and Janet Jakobsen at the University of Arizona on 25 April 2000, David Eng commented that we're attempting to build new programs in queer studies in the context of a backlash against affirmative action. He suggested we not sacrifice racial issues on campus to those of sexuality.

11. Michael Warner, "No Special Rights," in *Higher Education under Fire: Politics, Economics, and the Crisis of the Humanities*, ed. Michael Bérubé and Cary Nelson (New York: Routledge, 1995) 285.

12. Of the many series now collecting work in lgbtq studies, one is my own series with David Román at the University of Michigan Press, Triangulations: Lesbian/Gay/Queer Drama/Theatre/Performance, and a second is CLAGS' series at New York University Press, Sexual Cultures: New Directions from the Center for Lesbian and Gay Studies, edited by Ann Pellegrini and José Muñoz, for which I serve on the editorial board. I don't mean to imply, therefore, that I'm outside the forces of the market or publishing trends.

13. Gayle Rubin with Judith Butler, "Interview: Sexual Traffic," *differences: A Journal of Feminist Cultural Studies* 6.2/3 (1994): 89.

14. Biddy Martin, "Sexualities without Genders and Other Queer Utopias," *Femininity Played Straight: The Significance of Being Lesbian* (New York: Routledge, 1996) 73.

15. The conference was called "Identity/Space/Power: Lesbian, Gay, Bisexual, and Transgender Politics" and was hosted by the Center for Lesbian and Gay Studies at the Graduate Center of the City University of New York, 8 February 1996.

16. News blurb, *Advocate* 2 April 1996.

17. Pat Califia, column, *Girlfriends* March/April 1996, 38.

18. Suzanna Walters, "From Here to Queer: Radical Feminism, Post-Modernism, and the Lesbian Menace (Or, Why Can't a Woman Be More Like a Fag?)," *SIGNS* (summer 1996): 855.

19. Sue-Ellen Case, "Toward a Butch-Feminist Retro Future," in *Cross Purposes: Lesbians, Feminists and the Limits of Alliance*, ed. Dana Heller (Bloomington: Indiana UP, 1997) 210.

20. Case, 215.

21. Walters, 843.

22. Walters, 865.

23. See Martha C. Nussbaum, "The Professor of Parody: The Hip Defeatism of Judith Butler," *New Republic* 23 February 1999, 37+.

24. In the outcry against racial profiling by New Jersey state troopers on the New Jersey Turnpike in spring and summer 1999, spokespeople for the troopers explained that they weren't being personally racist, but they were influenced by unfortunate stereotypes of people of color as criminals. This is certainly an example of the ways in which critical intervention in cultural representation might shift public attitudes.

25. Cohen made these remarks at the "Identity/Space/Power" conference. They were subsequently published in Cathy J. Cohen, "Punks, Bulldaggers, and Welfare Queens: The Radical Potential of Queer Politics?" *GLQ* 3.4: 437–466.

26. Or, as Lynda Hart argues in *Fatal Women*, the white lesbian and the single woman of color are linked "in the white masculine imaginary as figures who constitute serious threats to the reproduction of white men—both fail to reproduce *him*, even when they do reproduce." *Fatal Women: Lesbian Sexuality and the Mark of Aggression* (Princeton: Princeton UP, 1994) 117, quoted in Kate Davy, "Outing Whiteness: A Feminist/Lesbian Project," *Theatre Journal* 47:2 (May 1995): 191.

27. Urvashi Vaid, remarks on "Constituencies, Organizing, Political Formations" panel at the "Identity/Space/Power" conference.

28. Rubin, 93.

29. See Esther Newton, "Dickless Tracy and the Homecoming Queen: Lesbian Power and Representation in Gay Male Cherry Grove," in *Inventing Lesbian Cultures in America*, ed. Ellen Lewin (Boston: Beacon, 1997) 162–230.

30. Said, 19.

31. See, for example, my chapter, "'Lesbian' Subjectivity in Realism," in my

book, *Presence and Desire: Essays on Gender, Sexuality, Performance* (Ann Arbor: U of Michigan P, 1993), for a discussion of how particular forms and their contents teach spectators ideological meanings regarding especially lesbians and other marginalized subjects.

32. Said, 25.

33. I have to say, too, that the Women and Theatre Program of the Association for Theatre in Higher Education worked for years to successfully, finally create a forum in which feminist and lesbian performers and critics could speak with one another openly about theory and practice. We need to work harder to create more such critical spaces and borrow feminist strategies to enhance gay and lesbian and queer work.

34. Babs Davy, e-mail correspondence, July 1996.

35. Peggy Phelan, "Serrano, Mapplethorpe, the NEA and You: 'Money Talks,'" *TDR* 34.1 (spring 1990): 4–15.

36. Urvashi Vaid 25. Richard Rorty, on the other hand, argues that "Leftists in the academy have permitted cultural politics to supplant real politics, and have collaborated with the Right in making cultural issues central to public debate," in *Achieving Our Country: Leftist Thought in Twentieth-Century America* (Cambridge: Harvard UP, 1998) 14.

37. See, for example, Duggan and Hunter, 154.

38. Despite these bureaucratic entanglements and paternalisms, the Graduate Center administration, especially President Frances Degan Horowitz, then-Dean Alan Gartner, Vice Provost Stephen Brier, Provost William Kelly, and Assistant to the President Steve Gorelick, have been unimpeachably, actively supportive of CLAGS at CUNY.

39. One of the most successful fund-raising campaigns CLAGS has run in recent years was for fellowships for gay and lesbian students and scholars. Perhaps because of the media around Kramer, and because of gay university student Matthew Shepard's brutal beating death in Wyoming, which called attention to the status of lesbian/gay/queer/transgender students on university campuses, more people understand the need to directly support lesbian/gay/queer scholars and students. These two incidents, the one unfortunate and the other tragic, demonstrated that what looks like security is really a much more tenuous, even threatened, state of affairs for gays and lesbians and queer studies on some college and university campuses.

40. Given the HRC's recent gerrymandering of the 2000 March on Washington, I have to say I don't think the group represents grassroots organizing in the United States. HRC staff decided to force the issue of a national gay and lesbian march, rather than cooperating with grassroots groups. The National Gay and Lesbian Task Force and the statewide federation of gay and lesbian lobbying groups argued for state-based efforts rather than an expensive, draining, ultimately less effective gesture made in Washington. The HRC went forward with plans for the march despite these protests.

Chapter 3

1. See W. B. Worthen, "Drama, Performativity, and Performance," *PMLA* 113.5 (October 1998): 1093–1107; Joseph Roach, "Reconstructing Theatre/History," *Theatre Topics* 9.1 (March 1999): 3–10; and Josephine Lee, "Disciplining Theatre and Drama in the English Department: Reflections on 'Performance' and Institutional History," *Text and Performance Quarterly* 19.2 (April 1999): 145–158, for various readings of this history.

2. In many ways, this is the chasm over which theater studies plays out its own version of the so-called culture wars. See, for example, Jeffrey Williams, ed., *PC Wars: Politics and Theory in the Academy* (New York: Routledge, 1995); John Wilson, *The Myth of Political Correctness: The Conservative Attack on Higher Education* (Durham: Duke UP, 1995); Lawrence W. Levine, *The Opening of the American Mind: Canons, Culture, and History* (Boston: Beacon, 1996); Todd Gitlin, *The Twilight of Common Dreams: Why America Is Wracked by Culture Wars* (New York: Metropolitan Books, 1995), for various readings of the culture war debates.

3. Michael Dyson, "Contesting Racial Amnesia: From Identity Politics toward Post-Multiculturalism," in *Higher Education under Fire: Politics, Economics, and the Crisis of the Humanities,* ed. Michael Bérubé and Cary Nelson (New York: Routledge, 1995) 341.

4. Yet the worst-case uses of identity studies can be as modernist and ahistorical as those conservative reifiers of the past, rigid in their presumptions about how experience becomes knowledge. Gender, sexual, or racial separatists, or any identity group faction that shores up the borders of their own differences through essentialist reasoning, perhaps fit this description. But how identity is produced—and how race and ethnicity, sexuality and gender, and all their intersections are understood—has been profoundly changed by poststructuralist and postcolonial critiques of subject formation and essentialism. More complicated, subtly nuanced work around identity in theater studies proceeds from a materialist understanding of history and socioeconomic systems, and doesn't hide behind purely aesthetic postmodern reasonings.

5. Bérubé and Nelson, "Introduction," 19.

6. See, for example, Michiko Kakutani, "Portrait of the Artist as a Focus Group," *New York Times Sunday Magazine* 1 March 1998, 26.

7. For a very thoughtful, compelling critique of celebrity culture, and of life as a performance, see Neil Gabler, *Life, the Movie: How Entertainment Conquered Reality* (New York: Knopf, 1998).

8. See Pierre Bourdieu, *Distinction: A Social Critique of the Judgement of Taste,* trans. Richard Nice (Cambridge: Harvard UP, 1984).

9. Graham made these remarks at a roundtable discussion among chairs of theater departments in the CUNY system, held at the CUNY Graduate Center on 30 September 1996. A new proposal is now afloat in the system, proposed by Kingsborough Community College, which lost its theater department in 1995. The proposal offers a major in performing arts that's based not on liberal arts educational values, but on a savvy awareness of the growing employment opportunities for

New York City students trained in mostly vocational aspects of the entertainment business (stagehands, grips, managers). The rise in employment in these craft fields, the proposal suggests, is particularly tied to the "Disneyfication" of Times Square. The presumption here, however, is that a community college should train laborers in the theater industry, rather than spectators or art appreciators. The class bias, then, holds.

10. See Stacy Wolf, "Theatre as Social Practice: Local Ethnographies of Audience Reception," dissertation, University of Wisconsin–Madison, 1994, and her "Civilizing and Selling Spectators: Audiences at the Madison Civic Center," *Theatre Survey* 39.2 (November 1998): 7–23, for explications of the "localness" of theater.

11. See Carol Becker, "A New Generation of Artists and Art Schools," *Chronicle of Higher Education* 8 November 1996, B8–9, for a creative, politicized, and pragmatic approach to training artists in a postmodern era. See also her *Zones of Contention: Essays on Art, Institutions, Gender, and Anxiety* (Albany: State U of New York P, 1996), and her edited collection, *The Subversive Imagination: Artists, Society, and Social Responsibility* (New York: Routledge, 1994).

12. For her argument on nonreproductivity, see Phelan's *Unmarked* (New York: Routledge, 1993).

13. Sandra L. Richards, "Writing the Absent Potential: Drama, Performance, and the Canon of African-American Literature," in *Performance and Performativity*, ed. Andrew Parker and Eve Kosofsky Sedgwick (New York: Routledge, 1995) 67.

14. Richards, 69.

15. Richards, 69.

16. Carole A. Stabile, "Another Brick in the Wall: (Re) Contextualizing the Crisis," in Bérubé and Nelson, 108–125.

17. Henry Giroux, "Beyond the Ivory Tower: Public Intellectuals and the Crisis of Higher Education," in Bérubé and Nelson, 249.

18. Gregory Jay and Gerald Graff, "A Critique of Critical Pedagogy," in Bérubé and Nelson, 210, 212.

19. These debates and responses can be found in *American Theatre*'s September–December 1996 issues. Hartigan's response is in *American Theatre* (December 1996): 63.

20. See William Grimes, "Face-to-Face Encounter on Race in the Theatre," *New York Times* 29 January 1997, C9, for an account of the event.

21. Unfortunately, the racial lines drawn among gays and lesbians mean that sexuality alone is not enough to create political unity. Esperanza's case is one in which white gay men supported conservative politicians' efforts against a racially affiliated performance space.

22. When city councilperson Jack Finger attended the plenary session on Esperanza's defunding at the 1998 ATHE conference in San Antonio, he waved a flier for its lesbian and gay film festival as evidence when he spoke about why the group had to be "stopped."

23. For an evocative and brilliant reading of the NEA Four's debacle, and its effects on the four artists, see Holly Hughes's performance piece, *Preaching to the Perverted* (work in progress, Dixon Place, New York City, 10 July 1999, and perform-

ance, Off Center, Austin, Texas, 21 and 23 September 2000). See also Wendy Steiner, *The Scandal of Pleasure* (Chicago: U of Chicago P, 1995) for an early reading of the NEA situation.

24. The roundtable discussion took place at the CUNY Graduate Center on 7 February 1998 and was organized by CLAGS.

25. The "Sensation" exhibit at the Brooklyn Museum in fall 1999 provides another example of such media attention. New York City mayor Rudy Giuliani threatened to cut city funds from the museum because he was offended by a piece created by a British artist with an African background that depicted the Virgin Mary decorated with elephant dung. This exhibit raised a hue and cry from conservatives and an aggressive free speech argument from liberals. The courts prohibited the mayor from cutting the museum's funding. But the Brooklyn Museum is much better established and able to defend itself than individual, struggling gay and lesbian performance artists.

26. See Gerald Graff, *Beyond the Culture Wars: How Teaching the Conflicts Can Revitalize American Education* (New York: Norton, 1992), to which my own adaptation of teaching the conflicts is indebted.

27. At an interview/discussion at the CUNY Graduate Center on 23 February 1997, sponsored by its Ph.D. Program in Theatre, Holly Hughes mourned the demise of a counterculture, without which she feels it's impossible for alternative, politically critical performance work to survive.

28. See Catharine R. Stimpson, "Activist Trustees Wield Power Gone Awry," *Chronicle of Higher Education* 16 January 1998, B4–5.

29. A number of examples illustrate the ways in which freedom of speech is being squelched on campuses, from the surveillance systems installed to watch graduate students in their governance offices at City College in the CUNY system, to the attacks on tenure around the country, most notably at Bennington College and at the University of Minnesota.

30. At the same time, the legislator was told by one of her constituents that the constituent's daughter was being exposed to lesbian material in a course taught by the English Department and cross-listed with Women's Studies at the University of Arizona. The constituent also objected that her daughter had to buy books from a local feminist bookstore in Tucson. As a result, the politician proposed legislation that would ban teachers from requiring students to purchase obscene materials and would force faculty to order course materials only at the university bookstore. A bill was also proposed, and later tabled, that would require faculty to label their syllabi if they included materials with "objectionable content" in their courses. The furor seems to have died down, but it shook women's studies faculty in Tucson deeply. For details, see Jon Bowen's 7 April 1999 report in *Salon*, the Web-based magazine. I'd like to thank Miranda Joseph for providing me with very helpful information about this case.

31. See arguments for and against pedagogical advocacy in Patricia Meyer Spacks, ed., *Advocacy in the Classroom: Problems and Possibilities* (New York: St. Martin's, 1996), which culls papers from a 1995 conference entitled "The Role of Advocacy in the Classroom," which was sponsored by sixteen scholarly organiza-

tions representing diverse academic disciplines. See also the "Activism and the Academy" section of the *Minnesota Review* 50/51 (October 1999): 55–270, for a series of articles, interviews, and discussions of advocacy and activism in colleges and universities.

32. Levine, 43.

Chapter 4

The epigraph is from David Cole, *Acting as Reading* (Ann Arbor: U of Michigan P, 1992) 23.

1. Bonnie Marranca, in "Performance World, Performance Culture," (*Performing Arts Journal* 10 1987): 21, asks, "What will theatre do, now that life itself is experienced more and more according to a theatrical paradigm?" She cites discos, personal ads, custody battles, "nuclear theatre," and Hollywood tours of stars's homes as examples of "performance culture." See also Neil Gabler, *Life, the Movie: How Entertainment Conquered Reality* (New York: Knopf, 1998), who reads through the whole of American culture—from consumer products, to television, to politics, to identity construction—as performance. Operation Rescue, on which Peggy Phelan has written, and ACT-UP, are both examples of political activist organizations whose interventions in the social use street performance to communicate their goals through the media; see her *Unmarked* (New York: Routledge, 1993). See also David Román, "Performing All Our Lives: AIDS, Performance, Community," in *Critical Theory and Performance*, ed. Janelle Reinelt and Joseph Roach (Ann Arbor: U of Michigan P, 1992), especially 214–215, and his book, *Acts of Intervention: Performance, Gay Culture, and AIDS* (Bloomington: Indiana UP, 1998), for discussion of performance as activism in gay politics. Judith Butler writes about similar strategies as "theatricalizing activism": "Both [Queer Nation and ACT-UP] also have engaged theatrical venues for politicization. . . . It's a certain theatricalization, and a certain performative production of identity, that is utterly strategic" (Judith Butler, as quoted in "The Body You Want: Liz Kotz Interviews Judith Butler," *Artforum International* 31 [November 1992]: 83). These quotes indicate the overlapping discourses of performance in "life" and performance as politics.

2. See, for instance, Eve Kosofsky Sedgwick's *Epistemology of the Closet* (Berkeley: U of California P, 1990).

3. Biddy Martin and Chandra Talpade Mohanty, "Feminist Politics: What's Home Got to Do with It?" in *Feminist Studies/Critical Studies*, ed. Teresa de Lauretis (Bloomington: Indiana UP, 1986) 191, 196. Their discussion of home is centered on the politics of difference between white women and women of color, through their explication of Minnie Bruce Pratt's "Identity: Skin Blood Heart," revised version in *Rebellion: Essays, 1980–1991* (Ithaca: Firebrand Books, 1991) 27–81.

4. See Michael Warner, "From Queer to Eternity: An Army of Theorists Cannot Fail," *Voice Literary Supplement* (June 1992): 18–19, for a description of gay and lesbian studies' place in critical theory and the academy. See also Michael Warner, ed., *Fear of a Queer Planet* (Minneapolis: U of Minnesota P, 1993), and Henry Abelove, Michele Aina Barale, and David M. Halperin, eds., *The Lesbian and Gay Studies*

Reader (New York: Routledge, 1993), for foundational texts in queer theory and gay and lesbian studies. See also my article on gay/lesbian/queer studies in *Academe* 84.5 (September/October 1998): 40–45.

5. Lawrence Grossberg, Cary Nelson, and Paula Treichler, eds., *Cultural Studies* (London: Routledge, 1992). The only exception in the book is Peter Stallybrass's article, "Shakespeare, the Individual, and the Text" (593–609), which keeps theater confined to its canonical, high-art status. The book gathers the proceedings of the "Cultural Studies Now and in the Future" conference at the University of Illinois at Champaign-Urbana in April 1990. See also Simon During, ed., *The Cultural Studies Reader* (New York: Routledge, 1993).

6. Cultural studies' orientation toward studying "low art," which is generally considered cultural objects of mass distribution, is partly a result of its origins in media studies. Whether or not theater and performance are "eligible" for "low" status seems part of what's implicitly challenged in these exclusions and absences. See Lawrence Levine, *Highbrow/Lowbrow: The Emergence of Cultural Hierarchy in America* (Cambridge: Harvard UP, 1988). Nonetheless, cultural studies methods, particularly its emphasis on Gramsci's notions of articulation, hegemony, and resistance, can be very useful to theater studies. See, for example, Elin Diamond's important anthology, *Performance and Cultural Politics* (New York: Routledge, 1996).

7. Robert Allen, in *Horrible Prettiness: Burlesque and American Culture* (Chapel Hill: U of North Carolina P, 1991), writes disparagingly, "But obviously, theatre can be and has been 'tamed.' . . . The potentially subversive qualities of the theatre have been obscured in modern times by its full incorporation into mainstream, middle-class culture: theatre is taught in universities and kept alive as a cultural phenomenon by government grants. Moreover, the usurpation of the dramatic theatre as a form of popular entertainment, first by the movies and then by television, has rendered it all but moribund as a social force" (39). I find it troubling that Allen can be so shortsighted and dismissive about contemporary theater's potential to engage with social transformations, but his tone seems indicative of how our discipline is viewed from elsewhere.

8. See for example, Joseph Roach, *Cities of the Dead* (New York: Columbia UP, 1996); Bruce McConachie, *Melodramatic Formations: American Theatre and Society, 1820–1870* (Iowa City: Iowa UP, 1992); Diamond; and Sue-Ellen Case, *The Domain-Matrix: Performing Lesbian at the End of Print Culture* (Bloomington: Indiana UP, 1996). Many performance scholars of an institutionally younger generation are also applying cultural studies and performance studies models to performance. See Ann Pellegrini, *Performance Anxiety: Staging Psychoanalysis, Staging Race* (New York: Routledge, 1997); José Estaban Muñoz, *Disidentifications* (Minneapolis: U of Minnesota P, 1999); and David Román, *Acts of Intervention: Performance, Gay Culture, and AIDS* (Bloomington: Indiana UP, 1998).

9. Diana Fuss, *Inside/Out: Lesbian Theories, Gay Theories* (New York: Routledge, 1991).

10. Abelove, Barale, and Halperin; Corey K. Creekmur and Alexander Doty, eds., *Out in Culture: Gay, Lesbian, and Queer Essays on Popular Culture* (Durham: Duke UP, 1995).

11. See some of the essays in Thomas Postlewait and Bruce A. McConachie, eds., *Interpreting the Theatrical Past* (Iowa City: U of Iowa P, 1989), particularly R.W. Vince, "Theatre History as an Academic Discipline," 1–18, for narratives of theater scholarship's "tradition."

12. Reinelt and Roach, "General Introduction," *Critical Theory and Performance*, 5, cf. 3–4. See also Joseph Roach, "Reconstructing Theatre/History," *Theatre Topics* 9:1 (March 1999): 3–10.

13. Roach made these remarks on a panel at the "Reconstructing Theatre/History" symposium, hosted by the Department of Theatre and Dance, University of Texas at Austin April 1998.

14. See Gabler.

15. See the anthologies in theater studies that illustrate such interdisciplinary critical/theoretical influences: Sue-Ellen Case and Janelle Reinelt, eds., *The Performance of Power: Theatrical Discourse and Politics* (Iowa City: U of Iowa P, 1991); *Interpreting the Theatrical Past*; *Critical Theory and Performance*; and Sue-Ellen Case, ed., *Performing Feminisms: Feminist Critical Theory and Theatre* (Baltimore: Johns Hopkins UP, 1990). Ellen Donkin and Sue Clement, eds., *Upstaging Big Daddy* (Ann Arbor: U of Michigan P, 1993), is another volume that uses interdisciplinary critical theory to study work by feminist directors, explicitly challenging many of theater's old-fashioned ideologies about "high art." See also Lynda Hart and Peggy Phelan, eds., *Acting Out: Feminist Performances* (Ann Arbor: U of Michigan P, 1993).

16. Reinelt and Roach, 5.

17. For excellent examples of work in critical race studies in theater studies and performance studies, see José Estaban Muñoz, *Disidentifications*; Alberto Sandoval, *José, Can You See? Latinos On and Off Broadway* (Madison: U of Wisconsin P, 1999); Román; Harry Elam, *Taking It to the Streets: The Social Protest Theatre of Luis Valdez and Amiri Baraka* (Ann Arbor: U of Michigan P, 1997); and Alicia Arrizón, *Latinas and Performance: Traversing the Stage* (Bloomington: Indiana UP, 1999).

18. Margaret Wilkerson, "Demographics and the Academy," in Case and Reinelt, 239.

19. James V. Hatch, "Here Comes Everybody: Scholarship and Black Theatre History," in Postlewait and McConachie, 149.

20. Wilkerson, 240.

21. The panel took place on 13 August 1998, in the San Antonio RiverCenter Hotel, and was organized by Elizabeth Ramirez and Kathy Perkins. Considering the large audience for the discussion, these issues are clearly still felt and worried in numerous institutional settings, and ATHE, as a professional organization, still hasn't done enough to focus the field's energy to think creatively about new production and curricular possibilities.

22. Roach, "Introduction" [to "Cultural Studies" section], in Reinelt and Roach, 11.

23. She made these remarks as an audience member at an ATHE conference panel in 1998 on emerging scholarship and institutional issues in the field. This panel took place on 14 August 1998. Panelists included Shannon Jackson, Jay Plum, and Stacy Wolf, and I moderated.

24. The epigraph to this section is from George Marcus, ed., *Rereading Cultural Anthropology* (Durham: Duke UP, 1992) ix.

25. See "Schechner Advocates Radical Rethinking," an unsigned article in the *ATHENEWS* 6.4 (September 1992): 1, for a report on the speech and the panel, in which Schechner is quoted as saying, "Get out of the phony training business and into the culture business." See also his *TDR* "Comment," "Transforming Theatre Departments," *TDR* 39.2 (summer 1995): 8. A performance studies focus group for ATHE formed, thanks to the motivating energy at the 1992 conference, portraying itself in its invitational literature as an underdog who must win a place as a family member in the parent organization. Eight years later, it has become an established ATHE focus group, and has been instrumental in the formation of a new association called Performance Studies International. PSI intends to remake the practices of professional associations, attempting to resist the typically conservative impulses of institutionalization while it charts new territory in this still growing field.

26. Dwight Conquergood, "Rethinking Ethnography: Towards a Critical Cultural Politics," *Communication Monographs* 58 (1991): 187.

27. Dick Hebdige, *Subculture: The Meaning of Style* (London: Methuen, 1979).

28. James Clifford, "On Collecting Art and Culture," in During, 68.

29. Richard Schechner, "Restoration of Behavior," *Between Theatre and Anthropology* (Philadelphia: U of Pennsylvania P, 1985).

30. Lawrence W. Levine, *Highbrow/Lowbrow: The Emergence of Cultural Hierarchy in America* (Cambridge: Harvard UP, 1988).

31. For further explication of the centrality of New York as the scale by which all theater is measured, university and otherwise, see Stacy Wolf, "Theatre as Social Practice: Local Ethnographies of Audience Reception," dissertation, University of Wisconsin–Madison, 1994. See also her "Civilizing and Selling Spectators: Audiences at the Madison Civic Center," *Theatre Survey* 39:2 (November 1998): 7–23.

32. Marvin Carlson, "Theatre History, Methodology, and Distinctive Features," *Theatre Research International* 20.2 (summer 1995): 92.

33. These misreadings of our program as only about entertainment or theater practice persisted. In preparation for the opening of the Graduate Center's new building at thirty-fourth Street and Fifth Avenue in fall 2000, I was asked to serve on the "Arc of Celebration" committee. People couldn't fathom why I wasn't interested in encouraging students to do some performances to honor this event. My explanation that our program is strictly academic, rather than one in which students act and direct, was completely opaque to my colleagues on the committee. This still seems to me a misunderstanding of the intellectual, as well as the practical, value of theater studies.

34. Phil Auslander, "Evangelical Furor," *TDR* 39.4 (fall 1995): 178–183.

35. Phillip Zarrilli, "Toward a Definition of Performance Studies, Part I," *Theatre Journal* 38.3 (October 1986): 374.

36. Bruce A. McConachie, "New Historicism and American Theatre History: Toward an Interdisciplinary Paradigm for Scholarship," in Case and Reinelt, 267.

37. As Michele Aina Barale cautions in another context, "This notion of progress assumes that the existing ideology has permitted entrance of the previously un-

speakable because a new and uncensored discourse has begun. Such cultural self-visioning proceeds from a larger and more encompassing vision of history itself as a process of ideological liberation, and provides a means of appropriating the subcultural text so as to enable it to seem consonant with existing ideology." Michele Aina Barale, "Below the Belt: (Un)Covering *The Well of Loneliness*," in Fuss, 235.

38. Vicki Patraka pointed out to me that this "promiscuous citation" also threatens to subsume the founding discourses about performativity in gay and lesbian theory. There is a clear and present danger of appropriating language without the identity referents that secure its politics.

39. John Fiske, "British Cultural Studies and Television," in *Channels of Discourse: Television and Contemporary Criticism*, ed. Robert Allen (Chapel Hill: U of North Carolina P, 1987) 260.

40. Ellen Rooney, "Discipline and Vanish: Feminism, the Resistance to Theory, and the Politics of Cultural Studies," *differences: A Journal of Feminist Cultural Studies* 2.3 (1990): 16.

41. Rooney, 22, 23.

42. Terry Eagleton once warned the same thing about Marxist criticism, hoping that it wouldn't simply become another in a long line of methodologies useful to reading a text, detached from the political motivation in which it's founded. See his *Marxism and Literary Criticism* (Berkeley: U of California P, 1976), cf. vii.

43. See, for example, John J. MacAloon, ed., *Rite, Drama, Festival, Spectacle: Rehearsals toward a Theory of Cultural Performance* (Philadelphia: Institute for the Study of Human Issues, 1984); Richard Schechner, *Performance Theory*, rev. ed. (New York: Routledge, 1988); Schechner, *Between Theatre and Anthropology*; Schechner and Willa Appel, eds., *By Means of Performance: Intercultural Studies of Theatre and Ritual* (New York: Cambridge UP, 1990); Dwight Conquergood, "Poetics, Play, Process, and Power: The Performative Turn in Anthropology," *Text and Performance Quarterly* 91.1 (1989): 82–88; and Margaret Thompson Drewal, "The State of Research on Performance in Africa," *African Studies Review* 34.3 (December 1991): 1–64.

44. For an elegant analysis of the ways in which performance studies remains textually indebted, even as it tries to dislodge conventional ways of thinking about performance objects, see W. B. Worthen, "Drama, Performativity, and Performance," *PMLA* 113.5 (October 1998): 1093–1107.

45. See in particular Susan Bennett, *Theatre Audiences*, 2nd ed. (1990; New York: Routledge, 1996), for discussion of the impact of location on reception and production. See also Marvin Carlson, *Places of Performance: The Semiotics of Theatre Architecture* (Ithaca: Cornell UP, 1989), and his *Theatre Semiotics: Signs of Life* (Bloomington: Indiana UP, 1990).

46. I don't mean to idealize the "real," but to suggest that "liveness," while obviously more and more technologically mediated, still offers something unique and useful to a community. For an argument against this position, see Philip Auslander, *Liveness: Performance in a Mediatized Culture* (New York: Routledge, 1999), and his *From Acting to Performance: Essays in Modernism and Post-modernism* (New York: Routledge, 1997). See also Marvin Carlson's useful book, *Performance: A Critical Introduction* (New York: Routledge, 1996).

47. Quoted in Zarrilli, 372. See also Erving Goffman, *The Presentation of Self in Everyday Life* (New York: Doubleday, 1959).

48. Fiske, 285.

49. Zarrilli, 372.

50. Turner, quoted in Zarrilli, 373.

51. Performance studies, because it has rejected the limiting convention of the dramatic text, is free to look elsewhere for contextualizing narratives. In its oral interpretation variety, performance studies might borrow literary texts from other contexts and write them across the body of the performer, or provide texts crafted of other social experiences. As Beverly Long, the first editor of *Literature in Performance*, wrote in 1980, "Literature is viewed as a verbal art, completed or fulfilled by performers, a provisional completion that may be public or private, individual or ensemble." She set out the field's intent to "explore interactions between composition, performance, and context," in ways that are already interdisciplinary and process oriented (editor's comment, *Literature in Performance* 1.1 [November 1980]: v). When *Literature in Performance* changed its title and its focus in 1989, Wallace A. Bacon, the editor of the newly named *Text and Performance Quarterly*, wrote of the "expansion of text and performance interests in recent years in areas beyond the traditional limits of interpretation. The term 'performance studies' embraces much current research in anthropology and ethnography . . . as well as the usual fields of interpretation and theatre." He wrote that *TPQ* would be interested in "the whole process from the creation and criticism of text through the creation and criticism of performance, together with the history and theory of both ends of the spectrum" (Wallace A. Brown, editor's comment, *Text and Performance Quarterly* 9.2 [April 1989]: n.p.). While Schechner's variety of performance studies has perhaps dominated some aspects of the field, especially as it relates to theater studies, the shared concerns of theater studies and performance of the once oral interpretation variety perhaps need to be revisited and revised. Darlene Hantzis, of Indiana State University, has been persuasive for me in thinking about the potential of these intersections.

52. Ed Cohen's "Who Are 'We'? Gay 'Identity' as Political (E)motion (A Theoretical Rumination)," in Fuss, *Inside/Out*, was especially instrumental to our thinking about moving spectators emotionally and therefore politically. I'd like to thank Krista Bourquein, who played the Young Woman in *Machinal*, for her commitment to exploring these issues with me in our production.

53. See Josephine Lee, "Disciplining Theatre and Drama in the English Department: Reflections on 'Performance' and Institutional History," *Text and Performance Quarterly* 19.2 (April 1999): 145–158.

54. See, for example, Judith Butler, *Gender Trouble: Feminism and the Subversion of Identity* (New York: Routledge, 1990), and her earlier *Theatre Journal* article, "Performative Acts and Gender Constitution: An Essay in Phenomenology and Feminist Theory," anthologized in Case, *Performing Feminisms*, 270–282. See also her *Bodies That Matter: On the Discursive Limits of "Sex"* (New York: Routledge, 1993).

55. See also Laurence Senelick, ed., *Gender in Performance: The Presentation of*

Difference in the Performing Arts (Hanover, N.H.: U Presses of New England, 1992); Lesley Ferris, ed., *Crossing the Stage: Controversies on Cross-Dressing* (New York: Routledge, 1993); and Moe Meyers, ed., *The Politics and Poetics of Camp* (New York: Routledge, 1994) for collections of articles on gender performances located specifically in theater.

56. Teresa de Lauretis, "The Technology of Gender," *Technologies of Gender: Essays on Theory, Film and Fiction* (Bloomington: Indiana UP, 1987) 3. See also Kate Davy, "Fe/male Impersonation: The Discourse of Camp," in *Critical Theory and Performance*, 242, for a reading of this article through critical strategies in theater; and Janelle Reinelt, "Staging the Invisible: The Crisis of Visibility in Theatrical Representation," *Text and Performance Quarterly* 14.2 (April 1994): 97–107, in which she charts a similar critical move from de Lauretis to Butler.

57. Butler, "Performative Acts," 277.

58. Butler, "Performative Acts," 277.

59. See, for example, Rhonda Blair, "'Not . . . But'/'Not-Not-Me': Musings on Cross-Gender Performance," in *Upstaging Big Daddy: Directing Theatre as if Gender and Race Matter*, ed. Ellen Donkin and Susan Clement (Ann Arbor: U of Michigan P, 1993) 291–307.

60. Butler, "Performative Acts," 273.

61. See Marjorie Garber's extensive study, *Vested Interests: Cross-Dressing and Cultural Anxiety* (New York: Routledge, 1992), in which she takes up many of these issues. Garber's book, however, participates in the same shortsightness about theatrical performance I've been outlining here. She engages with very few, and mostly mainstream, examples of performance to make her point about the transvestite as the "third term" in binaries of gender (and sometimes race). See also Alisa Solomon's insightful review of Garber's book, "Queen for a Day: Marjorie Garber's Drag Race," *Voice Literary Supplement* (June 1992): 23, in which she chastises Garber for ignoring "any of a number of . . . sophisticated gender-bending performances" that were playing in downtown venues during the period of Garber's research.

62. Butler says, "[T]hat culture so readily punishes or marginalizes those who fail to perform the illusion of gender essentialism should be sign enough that on some level there is social knowledge that the truth or falsity of gender is only socially compelled and in no sense ontologically necessitated" ("Performative Acts"): 279.

63. Reinelt's "Staging the Invisible," for example, uses evocative metaphors to refer to the "sweat" of the body, as it labors to signify on stage.

64. Fornes made these remarks in her eloquent speech at the 1992 ATHE conference, when she won the organization's Career Achievement Award for professional theater.

65. Fuss, "Inside/Out," in Fuss, *Inside/Out*, 6–7.

66. Cohen, in Fuss, *Inside/Out*, 87, 86. Like Martin and Mohanty, Cohen, too, is explicating Minnie Bruce Pratt's essay, "Identity: Skin Blood Heart," to make this part of his argument. Cohen persistently spells emotion "(e)motion"—I don't mean to neutralize his argument by my more traditional spelling here.

67. The epigraph for this section is from Peggy Phelan, *Unmarked* (London: Routledge, 1993) 174.

68. Susan Bennett, on a panel at the 1992 Women and Theatre Program Conference in Atlanta, cautioned participants about how easily the visible can be aligned with a kind of tourist gaze, especially when looking at productions by subjects marginalized from dominant discourse. See also her letter to *TDR*, "Subject to the Tourist Gaze," in which Bennett argues eloquently about the necessity to consider the "privilege of articulation" in discussions of multicultural work (37.1 [spring 1993]: 9–13). See also James Moy, "The Anthropological Gaze and the Touristic Siting of Chinese America," *Modern Drama* 35.1 (1992): 82–89, and his book, *Marginal Sights: Staging the Chinese in America* (Iowa City: U of Iowa P, 1993). The now burgeoning literature on tourism and performance is useful in parsing out these ideas. See, for just two brief examples, Jane Desmond, "Invoking 'the Native': Body Politics in Contemporary Hawaiian Tourist Shows," *TDR* 41.4 (winter 1997): 83–109, and Christopher B. Balme, "Staging the Pacific: Framing Authenticity in Performances for Tourists at the Polynesian Cultural Center," *Theatre Journal* 50.1 (March 1998): 53–70.

69. Gloria Anzaldúa, "Introduction," in *Making Face, Making Soul: Creative and Critical Perspectives by Women of Color*, ed. Gloria Anzaldúa (San Francisco: Aunt Lute Foundation Books, 1990) xv. Parts of the following portion of this argument are revised from my "Rethinking the Radical: Strategies of Engagement for Feminist Theatre," a paper I delivered at the 1992 ATHE conference. I'd like to thank Sandra Richards and Susan Bennett for their provoking criticisms of the earlier version, which has been significantly adapted here.

70. Anzaldúa, xvi.

71. Anzaldúa, xviii.

72. For a useful analysis of identification as appropriation, see Rebecca Schneider's discussion of Spiderwoman Theatre in her book *The Explicit Body in Performance* (New York: Routledge, 1997).

73. Iris Marion Young, "The Ideal of Community and the Politics of Difference," in *Feminism/Postmodernism*, ed. Linda Nicholson (New York: Routledge, 1990) 317.

74. Young, 318.

75. Young, 319.

76. Phelan, 174. The metaphors of location I'm employing here refer to a number of play anthologies published in the late eighties and early nineties, which described the work they collected as moving from the margins to the center of American theater discourse through some sort of spatial reference. See, for example, Misha Berson, ed., *Between Worlds: Contemporary Asian-American Plays* (New York: Theatre Communications Group, 1990); Lenora Champagne, ed., *Out from Under: Texts by Women Performance Artists* (New York: Theatre Communications Group, 1990); M. Elizabeth Osborn, ed., *On New Ground: Contemporary Hispanic-American Plays* (New York: Theatre Communications Group, 1987); and Don Shewey, ed., *Out Front: Contemporary Gay and Lesbian Plays* (New York: Grove, 1988).

77. Maria Lugones, "Playfulness, 'World'-Travelling, and Loving Perception," in Anzaldúa, *Making Face, Making Soul*, 393.

78. Lugones, 394, italics in original.

79. Lugones, 395.

80. Lugones, 396.

81. Lugones, 400.

82. Young, 311.

83. Elin Diamond, "The Violence of 'We': Politicizing Identification," in Reinelt and Roach, 396.

84. Diamond, 396, italics in original.

85. Diamond, 396.

86. Thulani Davis, *All Things Considered*, National Public Radio, WNYC, New York, June 1992.

87. Anna Deavere Smith, *All Things Considered*, National Pubic Radio, WNYC, New York, June 1992.

88. Phelan, 174, italics in original.

89. Sandra Richards, in "Caught in the Act of Social Definition: *On the Road with Anna Deavere Smith*," in Hart and Phelan, *Acting Out*, argues that "theatre, because it deploys multiple sign systems within a public arena, can serve as a particularly powerful realm for the renegotiation of identity(ies)" (50). She suggests that rejecting a metaphysics of substance about race might allow spectators, performers, and critics to look at the material effects of racial discourse, "particularly on . . . those who are identified as being other than the (white) norm" (44). Along with Smith's insistence on the inadequacies of humanistic understanding comes a critique of racial essentialisms that increases possibilities for different identifications.

90. I don't necessarily mean to lionize Smith's performances over other performers who attempt similar strategies. Smith's second popular performance piece, *Twilight, Los Angeles*, was constructed in much the same way, but apparently, Smith's engagements with the South Central community were perceived as a bit more imperialist. Danny Hoch, who doesn't perform other people's words verbatim, but who does impersonate cross-cultural accents and gestural styles with remarkable fluency, as I suggest here, is another useful example of a performer whose intent is to directly engage and to embody marginalized subjects in communities not regularly represented in performance. For biographical information and excerpts from Smith's and Hoch's work, see *Extreme Exposure: An Anthology of Solo Performance Texts from the Twentieth Century*, ed. Jo Bonney (New York: Theatre Communications Group, 2000).

91. I would like to thank Bill Worthen, Vicki Patraka, and Stacy Wolf for their comments on various drafts of this chapter.

Chapter 5

1. Edward Said, "Opponents, Audiences, Constituencies, and Community, *Critical Inquiry* 9.1 (September 1982): 9.

2. The conference took place in New York City 27–29 April 1995. It was presented by the Center for Lesbian and Gay Studies at the Graduate Center of the City University of New York and cosponsored by the CUNY Graduate Center's Theatre Program; it was cohosted by the Arts Program at the Judson Memorial

Church, New York Theatre Workshop, La Mama E.T.C., and the Joseph Papp Public Theatre. Alisa Solomon and Framji Minwalla coordinated the conference, working with a thirteen-person planning committee comprised of academics, artists, producers, and administrators. In addition to delivering the keynote on 27 April, at the Judson Memorial Church, I was also a member of the planning committee.

3. See Alan Sinfield, *Out on Stage: Lesbian and Gay Theatre in the Twentieth Century* (New Haven: Yale UP, 1999).

4. See Nancy K. Miller, *Getting Personal: Feminist Occasions and Other Autobiographical Acts* (New York: Routledge, 1991), for a persuasive argument about the importance of what she calls "occasional" writing.

5. A special issue of *Modern Drama* devoted to gay and lesbian theater in which a version of this chapter was previously published (32.1 [spring 1996]) followed on the heels of *Theatre Journal*'s special issue, "Gay and Lesbian Queeries," 47.2 (May 1995). It probably wouldn't be excessive to say that most professional journals in most fields have devoted an issue or two to gay and lesbian and/or queer studies over the last several years. Whether this spurt of attention signals the arrival of gay and lesbian and/or queer studies as a fixture on the academic scene is another question.

6. Because of its more intellectual, historical, and political sweep, Tony Kushner's *Angels in America* might not be taken as such an index to white gay male lifestyles. But David Savran, in "Ambivalence, Utopia, and a Queer Sort of Materialism: How *Angels in America* Reconstructs the Nation," *Theatre Journal* 47.2 (May 1995): 207–227, argues persuasively that if "queer drama [has] become *the* theatrical sensation of the 1990s" (208), it may be because so much of it is squarely liberal pluralist in its political orientation. Using Kushner's *Angels in America* (parts 1 and 2) as axiomatic, Savran argues that such liberalism also retains a masculinist underpinning that belies the utopian promise of Queer Nation. He writes, "I wonder finally how subversive this queering of Broadway is when women, in this play at least, remain firmly in the background. What is one to make of the remarkable ease with which *Angels in America* has been accommodated to that lineage of American drama (and literature) that focuses on masculine experience and agency and produces women as the premise for history, as the ground on which it is constructed? Are not women sacrificed—yet again—to the male citizenry of a (queer) nation?" (226).

7. See Tim Miller and David Román, "Preaching to the Converted," *Theatre Journal* 47.2 (May 1995): 169–188, for a personal description of the creation and reception of Miller's work and an important argument about reinvigorating the notion of "preaching to the converted" for community-based theater. See also Miller's book *Shirts and Skins* (Boston: Alyson P, 1997), which transcribes several of his solo performances. See also Peggy Phelan, "Tim Miller's *My Queer Body*: An Anatomy in Six Sections," *Theater* 24.2 (1993): 30–34, for an argument with the ways in which Miller figures his own "young gay white male" body as the ontological center of "queer."

8. Especially not since Miller's performances and McNally's play both rely on revealing and recognizing the naked white gay male body as a supreme and formative

ontological moment. Many of the gay male plays that have arrived at the center of critical attention in the theater trade in the naked white gay male body to secure their aesthetics. Miller's *My Queer Body* and his *Naked Breath*, *Love! Valour! Compassion!*, and the campier, raunchier *Party* are all in some ways artistically "classical," as they revel in the presumptive erotics of the statuesque white male nude. At the same time, Miller's work is much more deeply concerned with the effects of sexuality on a body politic, rather than simply on individual, bourgeois bodies, and is more effectively politicizing, as a result.

9. Dixon Place has since left its Bowery location, because of gentrification and rising rents, and is now located on Broadway close to Union Square.

10. Many women playwrights can now boast perfectly legitimate careers in theater in the United States. But a Broadway production ensures publication (by a play-publishing house but also by trade presses), which ensures reproduction, which ensures critical attention and wider notice. Both parts of Tony Kushner's *Angels in America* were published by Theatre Communications Group, a trade press, concurrent with its Broadway production, and McNally's *Love! Valour! Compassion!* is also available from a trade house. Lesbian plays, for the most part, must be ordered from Samuel French or Dramatists Play Service, if they're available in print at all. Rosemary Keefe Curb's edited anthology, *All-Star Amazons: Thirteen Lesbian Plays with Essays and Interviews* (New York: Applause Books, 1996), begins to ameliorate the persistent problem of availability and notice for lesbian plays.

11. Sinfield, in fact, suggests that theater is inherently queer, which is why so many gays and lesbians are drawn to it as theatre makers and spectators. He writes, "It is indeed central to my argument that *theatre generally* has been shot through with images and practices of queerness" (4).

12. Alexander Doty, *Making Things Perfectly Queer: Interpreting Mass Culture* (Minneapolis: U of Minnesota P, 1993). See in particular chapter 1, "There's Something Queer Here," in which Doty suggests that "queer positions, queer readings, and queer pleasures are part of a reception space that stands simultaneously beside and within that created by heterosexual and straight positions. These positions, readings, and pleasures also suggest that what happens in cultural reception goes beyond the traditional opposition of homo and hetero, as queer reception is often a place beyond the audience's conscious 'real-life' definition of their sexual identities and cultural positions—often, but not always, beyond such sexual identities and identity politics, that is" (15).

13. See Bette Bourne, Peggy Shaw, Paul Shaw, and Lois Weaver, *Belle Reprieve* in *Gay and Lesbian Plays Today*, ed. Terry Helbing, (Portsmouth: Heinemann, 1993): 1–39. The production was a collaboration in which the butch Peggy Shaw performed Stanley Kowalski, across from the femme man Bette Bourne's Blanche, while the femme lesbian Weaver played Stella, and the femme gay man Paul Shaw played Mitch. The production was a true gender/sexuality deconstruction of Williams's play.

14. For an excellent explication of the complicated ways in which discussions of sexuality and theater too often forget how performances by lesbians and gay men

are always already racially marked, see Kate Davy, "Outing Whiteness: A Feminist/Lesbian Project," *Theatre Journal* 47.2 (May 1995):189–205.

15. Jane Chambers was one of the first out lesbian playwrights to be produced in New York and around the country. Her work was generally realist in form, and domestic in style, although structurally, it, too, suffered from its own gendered presumptions, particularly about butch lesbians. See, for example, *Last Summer at Bluefish Cove* (New York: JH P, 1982). See also my chapter, "'Lesbian' Subjectivity in Realism: Dragging at the Margins of Structure and Ideology," in *Presence and Desire: Essays on Gender, Sexuality, Performance* (Ann Arbor: U of Michigan P, 1993): 159–177.

16. Joan Nestle, *A Restricted Country* (Ithaca: Firebrand Books, 1987): 9–10.

17. I'd like to thank Erin Hurley for sharing these observations with me.

18. See Sue-Ellen Case, ed., *Split Britches: Lesbian Practice/Feminist Performance* (New York: Routledge, 1996), for texts of Split Britches's work. See also Holly Hughes, *Clit Notes* (New York: Grove, 1996), and Lynda Hart, ed., *Of All the Nerve: Deb Margolin Solo* (New York: Cassell/Continuum, 1999), for texts of their solo work.

19. Kobena Mercer, "Skin Head Sex Thing: Racial Difference and the Homoerotic Imaginary," in *How Do I Look? Queer Film and Video*, ed. Bad Object-Choices (Seattle: Bay, 1991) 205. Mercer says, "In a material context of restricted access to the means of representation, minoritized subjects are charged with an impossible 'burden of representation.' Where subordinate subjects acquire the right to speak only one at a time, their discourse is circumscribed by the assumption that they speak as 'representatives' of the entire community from which they come" (205). He later says, "One can lift the burden off so-called minority practitioners by spreading responsibility for the representation of difference" (218).

20. Mercer, 204.

21. Cindy Patton, "Safe Sex and the Pornographic Vernacular," in Bad Object-Choices, 45. Patton writes, "Sexual vernaculars are learned contextually: members of various language communities experience cultural recognition not through visual identification, but when performances—*what is said*—are meaningfully decoded by another person. Sexual vernaculars are the identifying characteristics of liminal sexualities" (45). I'm fascinated by the contextual, local implications of the vernacular, and the ways in which (community-based?) theater might exploit its specificity.

22. Patton, 31.

23. See Richard Schechner, *Essays on Performance Theory, 1970–1976* (New York: Drama Book Specialists, 1977) 79. Schechner writes, "[R]itual is an event upon which its participants depend; theatre is an event which depends on its participants."

24. Miller and Román; and Lynda Hart and Peggy Phelan, "Queerer Than Thou: Being and Deb Margolin," *Theatre Journal* 47.2 (May 1995): 269–282, all illustrate the complex material, intellectual, artistic, and erotic ways in which gay/lesbian/queer critics, theorists, and performers inform and draw from one another's work. Both articles in some ways model a kind of community building, as they are

written collaboratively, from positions within theater experiences as well as performance and theater theory, history, and criticism.

25. Doty, xix. He writes, "[N]ew queer spaces open up (or are revealed) whenever someone moves away from using only one specific sexual identity category—gay, lesbian, bisexual, or straight—to understand and to describe mass culture, and recognizes that texts and people's responses to them are more sexually transmutable than any one category could signify—excepting, perhaps, that of 'queer'" (xix).

26. I'd like to thank Stacy Wolf, Erin Hurley, Jay Plum, Kate Davy, and Alisa Solomon, all of whom commented on earlier drafts of the keynote address.

27. See, for example, my description of the Women's Project and Productions November 1997 conference, "Mapping the Sources of Power," in chapter 1.

28. One of the best things about the conference program was in fact its variety. Here is a partial listing of the people who spoke, performed, or participated: Tony Kushner, Larry Kramer, Paula Vogel, Holly Hughes, Lisa Kron, Moe Angelos, Sue Finque, Deb Parks-Satterfield, Sue-Ellen Case, Karen Williams, Lipsynka, Moe Meyers, José Muñoz, Randy Gener, David Román, Tim Miller, Peggy Phelan, Joan Jett Blakk, Richard Elovich, Chris Durang, Carmelita Tropicana (Alina Troyano), the Five Lesbian Brothers, Jennifer Brody, George Haggerty, Laurence Senelick, and Amy Robinson.

29. See Robin Kelley, *Yo' Mama's Disfunktional!* (Boston: Beacon, 1997) 36–41.

30. See Michael Bronski, *The Pleasure Principle: Sex, Backlash, and the Struggle for Gay Freedom* (New York: St. Martin's, 1998).

31. See Peggy Phelan, *Unmarked* (New York: Routledge, 1993).

32. See the debate between Sue-Ellen Case and Holly Hughes, which began in Rebecca Schneider's interview with Hughes, "Holly Hughes: Polymorphous Perversity and the Lesbian Scientist," *TDR* 33.1 (spring 1989): 171–183, and continued with the exchange of letters between Case and Hughes in "A Case Concerning Hughes: Letters from Sue-Ellen Case and Holly Hughes," *TDR* 33.4 (winter 1989): 10–17.

33. See, for example, David Román and Alberto Sandoval Sanchez, "Caught in the Web: Latinidad, AIDS, and Allegory in *Kiss of the Spiderwoman: The Musical*," in *Every Nightlife: Culture and Dance in Latin/o America,* ed. Celeste Frazier Delgado and José Estaban Muñoz (Durham: Duke UP, 1997); Alberto Sandoval Sanchez, *José, Can You See? Latinos on and off Broadway* (Madison: U of Wisconsin P, 1999); and David Román, "Not about AIDS," *GLQ* 6.1 (summer 2000); 1–28.

34. See in addition to work by Muñoz, Román, Sandoval Sanchez, Alicia Arrizón, *Latina Performance: Traversing the Stage* (Bloomington: Indiana UP, 1999).

35. See David Román, *Acts of Intervention: Performance, Gay Culture, and AIDS* (Bloomington: Indiana UP, 1998), especially the last chapter, in which he details his response to *Rent*.

36. See Sarah Schulman, *Stagestruck: Theater, AIDS, and the Marketing of Gay America* (Durham: Duke UP, 1998).

37. See, for instance, Terrence McNally's plays off and on Broadway, *Party, Naked Boys Singing, Will and Grace, In and Out, Buffy the Vampire Slayer, Ellen, My*

Best Friend's Wedding, Next Best Thing, and many more examples of mainstream representations of gay men and a few lesbians.

38. See Michael Warner, *The Trouble with Normal: Sex, Politics, and the Ethics of Queer Life* (New York: Free, 1999); and Bronski.

39. The fact that Lisa Kron's piece *2.5 Minute Ride* was presented in June 2000 at Center Stage, the notable regional theater in Baltimore, is a very good sign.

40. See Alina Troyano, with Ela Troyano and Uzi Parnes, *I, Carmelita Tropicana: Performing between Cultures,* ed. Chon A. Noriega (Boston: Beacon, 2000).

41. I gave this lecture on 27 April 2000 in the Department of Theatre at University of Maryland–College Park. I'd like to thank Catherine Schuler for making possible the spirited discussion I had there around many of the issues laid out in these final ruminations.

Chapter 6

1. Scholars and teachers trained in fields such as educational policy, education, and curriculum and instruction, of course, have generated a large body of research on pedagogy. The literature on progressive pedagogy inspires much of my thinking here. See, for example, Henry Giroux, ed., *Post-Modernism, Feminism, and Cultural Politics* (Albany: State U of New York P, 1991); Henry Giroux, *Border Crossings: Cultural Workers and the Politics of Education* (New York: Routledge 1992); and Peter McLaren, *Critical Pedagogy and Predatory Culture: Oppositional Politics in a Postmodern Era* (New York: Routledge, 1995). But it's noteworthy that many other established disciplines fail to address the practices of teaching as a matter of course, at conferences or in their publications. This maintains in theater studies, except for our semiannual journal, *Theatre Topics*, which explicitly addresses pedagogy on a regular basis. In gay and lesbian studies, see, for example, Linda Garber, ed., *Tilting the Tower: Lesbians Teaching Queer Subjects* (New York: Routledge, 1994); Toni A. H. McNaron, *Poisoned Ivy: Lesbian and Gay Academics Confronting Homophobia* (Philadelphia: Temple UP, 1997); and George E. Haggerty and Bonnie Zimmerman, eds., *Professions of Desire: Lesbian and Gay Studies in Literature* (New York: Modern Language Association, 1995).

2. Scholars such as Michael Bérubé, Cary Nelson, and John Wilson, are the exceptions to this rule. The now defunct Teachers for a Democratic Culture, which was established by Gerald Graff at the University of Chicago, spent a few years trying to organize progressive faculty. But the challenges of grassroots activism in an academic context finally overcame the group's efforts. For elegant counterarguments to the Right's critique, see Bérubé and Nelson's *Higher Education under Fire: Politics, Economics, and the Crisis of the Humanities* (New York: Routledge, 1995); Nelson's *Manifesto of a Tenured Radical* (New York: New York UP, 1997); and Wilson's *The Myth of Political Correctness: The Conservative Attack on Higher Education* (Durham: Duke UP, 1995).

3. Wendy Brown, in "The Impossibility of Women's Studies," *differences: A Journal of Feminist Cultural Studies* 9.3 (fall 1997), notes the frustration of faculty trying to teach students subjects that span several disciplines when they have little or no knowledge of any of them. She suggests provocatively that women's studies would

be quite different if training in interdisciplinary feminist theory happened within disciplines that could provide the necessary intellectual background knowledge for students to grasp the antecedents and references of the fields with which feminist and women's studies are in conversation (81, 98).

4. For a set of excellent articles that addresses the institutionalization of the field, see Joan Wallach Scott, guest ed., "Women's Studies on the Edge," *differences: A Journal of Feminist Cultural Studies* 9.3 (fall 1997), many of which I reference here.

5. See, for example, Lawrence Levine's compelling argument about the canon's historicity in *The Opening of the American Mind: Canons, Culture, and History* (Boston: Beacon, 1996).

6. The women in that support group included Judy Rosenthal, Trudy Scott, Anne Wyma, and Celia Wiesman. The journal we inaugurated, *Women and Performance: A Journal of Feminist Theory*, is still published under the auspices of the department.

7. As Leora Auslander says, in "Do Women's + Feminist + Men's + Lesbian and Gay + Queer Studies = Gender Studies?" *differences: A Journal of Feminist Cultural Studies* 9.3 (fall 1997), women's studies, as it's become institutionalized, has suffered "some of the inevitable loss of energy that follows the shift from insurgency to institutional legitimation" (4). In the late eighties, this seemed true of women's studies at UW–Madison.

8. Brown asks, appropriately, "Why are many senior feminist scholars, once movers and shakers in the making of women's studies programs, no longer involved with them? How did women's studies lose its cachet? Is it a casualty of rapidly changing trends and hot spots in academe, or has it outlived its time or its value in some profound sense? . . . What is the relationship between its political and its intellectual mission?" (80).

9. See Ellen Messer-Davidow, "Know-How," in *(En)Gendering Knowledge: Feminists in Academe*, ed. Messer-Davidow and Joan E. Hartman (Knoxville: U of Tennessee P, 1991), who suggests that many feminist academics find themselves surprised to be at the center of institutional action. Such surprise is borne out, for example, in the introduction to Jane Gallop's collection of essays on feminist literary critical anthologies, *Around 1981* (New York: Routledge, 1992), and in the roundtable discussion among Gallop, Marianne Hirsh, and Nancy K. Miller, "Criticizing Feminist Criticism," that ends *Conflicts in Feminism*, ed. Marianne Hirsh and Evelyn Fox Keller (New York: Routledge, 1990) 349–369. Although much of this anxiety and surprise was expressed in the early nineties, I would suggest that the awkwardness of being an institutionalized, powerful, once resistant movement continues to trouble politically oriented academic feminists.

10. Brown argues, "Faculty, curriculum, and students in women's studies programs are in a relentless, compensatory cycle of guilt and blame about race, a cycle structured by women's studies original, nominalist, and conceptual subordination of race (and all other forms of social stratification) to gender" (93).

11. See Dana Heller, ed., *Cross Purposes: Lesbians, Feminists, and the Limits of Alliance* (Bloomington: Indiana UP, 1997).

12. See, for example, Sue-Ellen Case, "Toward a Butch-Feminist Retro Future," in Heller, 205–220, as well as her *Domain-Matrix: Performing Lesbian at the End of Print Culture* (Bloomington: Indiana UP, 1997); Teresa de Lauretis, "Fem/Les Scramble," in Heller, 42–48; and Biddy Martin, *Femininity Played Straight: The Significance of Being Lesbian* (New York: Routledge, 1996). See also Sherrie Inness, *The Lesbian Menace* (Amherst: U of Massachusetts P, 1997), who argues that "queer" is mostly an East and West Coast phenomenon and not widely resonant or applicable in the rest of the United States.

13. Joan Wallach Scott, "Women's Studies on the Edge: Introduction," *differences: A Journal of Feminist Cultural Studies* 9.3 (fall 1997): ii.

14. As Beverly Guy-Sheftall points out in her interview with Evelynn M. Hammonds, the "institutionalization of women's studies . . . is at a very different point in historically black colleges. . . . Even the question about the institutionalization of white women's studies is a complicated one. . . . [D]espite the fact that there are over six hundred women's studies programs in the U.S. academy, . . . women's studies is still institutionally fragile, in the sense that most women's studies programs are without their own faculty lines and have inadequate budgets and very little control over their curricula because they depend on departmental courses or joint appointments," "Whither Black Women's Studies: Interview," *differences: A Journal of Feminist Cultural Studies* 9.3 (fall 1997): 38–39.

15. See Candace de Russy, Revolting Behavior: The Irresponsible Exercise of "Academic Freedom," *Chronicle of Higher Education* 6 March 1998, B9, for one of the SUNY trustees' reading of this event. De Russy was largely responsible for inspiring the furor over the conference and has been nationally visible in her attempt to reassert conservative values on college campuses. See also SUNY trustee Paul Perez's letter to the editor, *New York Times* 14 February 1998, A12, in which he derides the system of faculty governance that allowed the conference to happen. The City University of New York is suffering its own ideological skirmishes with its trustees. For analyses of developments at SUNY and CUNY, see Patrick Healy and Peter Schmidt, "In New York, A 'Standards Revolution' or the Gutting of Public Colleges," *Chronicle of Higher Education* 10 July 1998, A21–23. For a progressive analysis of these events, see Alisa Solomon with Deirdre Hussey, "Enemies of Public Education: Who Is Behind the Attacks on CUNY and SUNY," *Village Voice* educational supplement 21 April 1998, 2–7, and Alisa Solomon, "CUNY Trustees Vote to End Remedial Courses," *News from CLAGS* 8.2 (summer 1998): 3–4.

16. Auslander, 18.

17. Biddy Martin, "Success and its Failures," *differences: A Journal of Feminist Cultural Studies* 9.3 (fall 1997): 108. Martin ventures this suggestion within a discussion of the isolation of the humanities from the sciences, but it pertains between identity area studies and other interdisciplinary and disciplinary areas as well.

18. Jane Gallop addressed the question of teaching and mentoring students as advocacy in a paper she presented at "Anxious Pleasures: The Erotics of Pedagogy," a symposium organized by the Center for Lesbian and Gay Studies at the CUNY Graduate Center, 14 February 1998. Gallop was quite persuasive about the ways in

which all good teaching requires advocating for students, and for strongly held ideological positions.

19. As my colleague Harriet Malinowitz pointed out when she read this chapter, it's important to note that I've only taught in four-year research universities, with students fairly well prepared for higher education. In a community college, a two-year college, or a university in which students needed a great deal of remedial work, some of these strategies would clearly need to be rethought and retooled.

20. See Chris Weedon, *Feminist Practice and Post-Structuralist Theory* (London: Basil Blackwell, 1987); Michel Foucault, *The History of Sexuality*, vol. 1, *An Introduction* (New York: Vintage, 1980); Joan Nestle's *A Restricted Country* (Ithaca: Firebrand Books, 1987); Cherríe Moraga and Gloria Anzaldúa, eds., *This Bridge Called My Back: Writings by Radical Women of Color* (Watertown: Persephone, 1981); Gloria Anzaldúa, ed., *Making Face, Making Soul: Creative and Critical Perspectives by Women of Color* (San Francisco: Aunt Lute Foundation Books, 1990); and Audre Lorde, *Zami: A New Spelling of My Name, A Biomythography* (Freedom: Crossing, 1982).

21. Barbara Christian, "The Race for Theory," *Feminist Studies* 14.1 (spring 1988): 67–80.

22. See Holly Hughes, *The Lady Dick* in *Clit Notes: A Sapphic Sampler* (New York: Grove, 1996); Sue-Ellen Case, ed., *Split Britches: Lesbian Practice/Feminist Performance* (New York: Routledge, 1996); John D'Emilio and Estelle B. Freedman, *Intimate Matters* (New York: Harper and Row, 1988); Sue-Ellen Case, "Towards a Butch/Femme Aesthetic," in *Making a Spectacle: Contemporary Feminist Performance*, ed. Lynda Hart (Ann Arbor: U of Michigan P, 1989) 282–299; Teresa de Lauretis, "Sexual Indifference and Lesbian Representation," in *Performing Feminisms: Feminist Critical Theory and Theatre*, ed. Sue-Ellen Case (Baltimore: Johns Hopkins UP, 1990) 17–39; Esther Newton, "The Mythic Mannish Lesbian: Radclyffe Hall and the New Woman," in *Hidden from History: Reclaiming the Gay and Lesbian Past*, ed. Martin Bauml Duberman, Martha Vicinus, and George Chauncey Jr. (New York: New American Library, 1989) 281–293; Lillian Faderman, *Odd Girls and Twilight Lovers: A History of Lesbian Life in the Twentieth Century* (New York: Columbia UP, 1991); Judith Butler, *Gender Trouble* (New York: Routledge, 1990); and Diana Fuss, ed., *Inside/Out: Lesbian Theories, Gay Theories* (New York: Routledge, 1991).

23. Ann Bannon, *Beebo Brinker* (Tallahassee: Naiad , 1962).

24. William Zinsser, *On Writing Well* (1976; New York: Harper and Row, 1988); William Strunk Jr. and E. B. White, *Elements of Style*, 3rd ed. (New York: Macmillan, 1979).

25. Anna Quindlen, *Living Out Loud* (New York: Ivy Books, 1988).

26. Joan Schenkar, *Signs of Life*, in *Signs of Life: Six Comedies of Menace*, ed. Vivian Patraka (Middleton: Wesleyan UP, 1998); Susan Yankowitz, *The Slaughterhouse Play*, in *New American Plays*, vol. 4, ed. William M. Hoffman (New York: Hill and Wang, 1971) 1–70; Cherríe Moraga, *Giving Up the Ghost* (Los Angeles: West End, 1986); Sue-Ellen Case, ed., *Performing Feminisms* (Baltimore: Johns Hopkins UP, 1990); Lynda Hart, ed., *Making a Spectacle*; Hart and Peggy Phelan, eds., *Acting*

Out (Ann Arbor: U of Michigan P, 1993); and Peggy Phelan, *Unmarked* (New York: Routledge, 1993).

27. Susan Bennett, *Theatre Audiences*, 2nd ed. (1996; New York: Routledge, 1990), and Henry Louis Gates, "'Authenticity' or the Lesson of Little Tree," *New York Times Book Review* 24 November 1991, 1, 26–28.

28. Alexis DeVeaux, *The Tapestry*, in *9 Plays by Black Women,* ed. Margaret B. Wilkerson (New York: New American Library, 1986) 141–195.

29. See Holly Hughes, *Dress Suits to Hire*, cocreated with Lois Weaver and Peggy Shaw, in *On and Beyond the Stage: A Sourcebook of Feminist Theatre and Performance,* ed. Carol Martin (New York: Routledge, 1996) 267–292.

30. Tony Kushner, *Angels in America: A Gay Fantasia on National Themes, Part One: Millennium Approaches* (1992; New York: Theatre Communications Group, 1993); *Part Two: Perestroika* (1992; New York: Theatre Communications Group, 1992, 1994). See also Robert Vorlicky, ed., *Tony Kushner in Conversation* (Ann Arbor: U of Michigan P, 1998), and Deborah Geis and Steven Kruger, eds., *Approaching the Millennium: Essays on Angels in America* (Ann Arbor: U of Michigan P, 1997).

31. The version of the course I'm describing here was its best iteration; other times, the performances were less risky, less compelling, the learning environment less charged with possibility and danger. The class in this example met in spring 1994, which was also my last semester on the faculty at the University of Wisconsin–Madison. I think my own strong feelings about ending my time at UW contributed to the keen emotions I felt and inspired in that class. Also, I should note that thinking about race and ethnicity with only or mostly white students in class is complex, but probably less fraught than doing so in groups of mixed race and ethnicity. See, for example, Wendy Coleman and Stacy Wolf, "Rehearsing for Revolution: Practice, Theory, Race, and Pedagogy (When Failure Works)," *Theatre Topics* 8.1 (March 1998): 13–32.

Epilogue

The epigraph is taken from Robin Kelley, *Yo' Mama's Disfunktional!* (Boston: Beacon Press, 1997) 101.

1. See Ann Pellegrini, "Critical Response (to Jane Gallop) II: Pedagogy's Turn: Observations on Students, Teachers, and Transference-Love," *Critical Inquiry* 25.3 (spring 1999): 617–625, on the operation of transference in teaching.

2. I'm borrowing here from the end of Tony's Kushner's *Angels in America,* part 2, *Peristroika* (New York: Theatre Communications Group, 1994).

bibliography

Abelove, Henry, Michele Aina Barale, and David H. Halperin, eds. *The Lesbian and Gay Studies Reader*. New York: Routledge, 1993.

Allen, Robert. *Horrible Prettiness: Burlesque and American Culture*. Chapel Hill: U of North Carolina P, 1991.

Anzaldúa, Gloria, ed. *Making Face, Making Soul: Creative and Critical Perspectives by Women of Color*. San Francisco: Aunt Lute Foundation Books, 1990.

Appadurai, Arjun. *Modernity at Large: Cultural Dimensions of Globalization*. Minneapolis: U of Minnesota P, 1997.

Aronowitz, Stanley. *The Knowledge Factory: Dismantling the Corporate University and Creating True Learning*. Boston: Beacon, 2000.

Arrizón, Alicia. *Latina Performance: Traversing the Stage*. Bloomington: Indiana UP, 1999.

Auslander, Leora. "Do Women's + Feminist + Men's + Lesbian and Gay + Queer = Gender Studies?" *differences: A Journal of Feminist Cultural Studies* 9.3 (fall 1997): 1–30.

Auslander, Philip. *From Acting to Performance: Essays in Modernism and Post-Modernism*. New York: Routledge, 1997.

——. *Liveness: Performance in a Mediatized Culture*. New York: Routledge, 1999.

Bacon, Wallace A. Editor's Comment. *Text and Performance Quarterly* 9.1 (1989): n.p.

Balme, Christopher B. "Staging the Pacific: Framing Authenticity in Performances of Tourists at the Polynesian Cultural Center." *Theatre Journal* 50.1 (March 1998): 53–70.

Bannon, Ann. *Beebo Brinker*. Tallahassee: Naiad, 1962.

Becker, Carol. "A New Generation of Artists and Arts Schools." *Chronicle of Higher Education* 8 November 1996, B8–9.

——, ed. *The Subversive Imagination: Artists, Society, and Social Responsibility*. New York: Routledge, 1994.

——. *Zones of Contention: Essays on Art, Institutions, Gender, and Anxiety*. Albany: State U of New York P, 1996.

Bennett, Susan. "Subject to the Tourist Gaze." *TDR* 37.1 (spring 1993): 9–13.

——. *Theatre Audiences*. 2nd ed. 1990. New York: Routledge, 1996.

Bennett, William J. *The Death of Outrage: Bill Clinton and the Assault on American Ideals*. New York: Free, 1998.

Berson, Misha, ed. *Between Worlds: Contemporary Asian-American Plays*. New York: Theatre Communications Group, 1990.

Bérubé, Michael. *The Employment of English: Theory, Jobs, and the Future*. New York: New York UP, 1998.

Bérubé, Michael, and Cary Nelson, eds. *Higher Education under Fire: Politics, Economics, and the Crisis of the Humanities*. New York: Routledge,1995.

Bourdieu, Pierre. *Distinction: A Social Critique of the Judgement of Taste*. Trans. Richard Nice. Cambridge: Harvard UP, 1984.

Bourne, Bette, Peggy Shaw, Paul Shaw, and Louise Weaver. *Belle Reprieve*. In *Gay and Lesbian Plays Today*, ed. Terry Helbing. Portsmouth: Heinemann, 1993.

Bronski, Michael. *The Pleasure Principle: Sex, Backlash, and the Struggle for Gay Freedom*. New York: St. Martin's, 1998.

Brown, Wendy. "The Impossibility of Women's Studies." *differences: A Journal of Feminist Cultural Studies* 9.3 (fall 1997): 79–101.

Butler, Judith. "A 'Bad Writer' Bites Back." Op-ed. *New York Times* 20 March 1999, 15.

_____. *Bodies That Matter: On the Discursive Limits of "Sex."* New York: Routledge, 1993.

_____. *Gender Trouble: Feminism and the Subversion of Identity*. New York: Routledge, 1990.

_____. "Performative Acts and Gender Constitution: An Essay in Phenomenology and Feminist Theory." In *Performing Feminisms: Feminist Critical Theory and Theatre*, ed. Sue-Ellen Case. Baltimore: Johns Hopkins UP, 1990.

Cahan, Susan, and Zoya Kocur, eds. *Contemporary Art and Multicultural Education*. New York: New Museum of Contemporary Art; London: Routledge, 1996.

Califia, Pat. Column. *Girlfriends* March/April 1996, 38.

Carlson, Marvin. *Performance: A Critical Introduction*. New York: Routledge, 1996.

_____. *Places of Performance: The Semiotics of Theatre Architecture*. Ithaca: Cornell UP, 1989.

_____. "Theatre History, Methodology, and Distinctive Features." *Theatre Research International* 20.2 (summer 1995): 90–96.

_____. *Theatre Semiotics: Signs of Life*. Bloomington: Indiana UP, 1990.

Case, Sue-Ellen. *The Domain-Matrix: Performing Lesbian at the End of Print Culture*. Bloomington: Indiana UP, 1996.

_____, ed. *Performing Feminisms: Feminist Critical Theory and Theatre*. Baltimore: Johns Hopkins UP, 1990.

_____, ed. *Split Britches: Lesbian Practice/Feminist Performance*. New York: Routledge, 1996.

_____. "Toward a Butch/Femme Aesthetic." In *Making a Spectacle: Contemporary Feminist Performance*, ed. Lynda Hart. Ann Arbor: U of Michigan P, 1989.

_____. "Toward a Butch-Feminist Retro Future." In *Crossed Purposes: Lesbians, Feminists and the Limits of Alliance*, ed. Dana Heller. Bloomington: Indiana UP, 1997: 205–220.

Case, Sue-Ellen, and Janelle Reinelt, eds. *The Performance of Power: Theatrical Discourse and Politics*. Iowa City: U of Iowa P, 1991.

Chambers, Jane. *Last Summer at Bluefish Cove*. New York: JH Press, 1982.

Champagne, Leonora, ed. *Out from Under: Texts by Women Performance Artists*. New York: Theatre Communications Group, 1990.

Chauncey, George. "The Ridicule of Gay and Lesbian Studies Threatens All Academic Inquiry." *Chronicle of Higher Education* 3 July 1993, A40.

Cheney, Lynne V. *Fifty Hours: A Core Curriculum for College Students*. Washington, D.C: GPO, 1989.

——. *Telling the Truth: Why Our Culture and Our Country Stopped Making Sense*. New York: Simon and Schuster, 1995.

Clifford, James. *Routes: Travel and Translation in the Late Twentieth Century*. Cambridge: Harvard UP, 1997.

Cohen, Cathy. "Punks, Bulldaggers, and Welfare Queens: The Radical Potential of Queer Politics?" *GLQ* 3.4 (1997): 437–465.

Cole, David. *Acting as Reading*. Ann Arbor: U of Michigan P, 1992.

Coleman, Wendy, and Stacy Wolf. "Rehearsing for Revolution: Practice, Theory, Race, and Pedagogy." *Theatre Topics* 8.1 (March 1998): 13–32.

Conquergood, Dwight. "Poetics, Play, Process, and Power: The Performative Turn in Anthropology." *Text and Performance Quarterly* 9.1 (1989): 82–88.

——. "Rethinking Ethnography: Towards a Critical Cultural Politics." *Communication Monographs* 58 (1991): 179–194.

Creekmur, Corey K., and Alexander Doty, eds. *Out in Culture: Gay, Lesbian, and Queer Essays on Popular Culture*. Durham: Duke UP, 1995.

Davis, Thulani. *All Things Considered*, National Public Radio, June 1992.

Davy, Kate. "Outing Whiteness: A Feminist/Lesbian Project." *Theatre Journal* 47.2 (May 1995): 189–205.

D'Emilio, John. *Making Trouble: Essays on Gay History, Politics, and the University*. New York: Routledge, 1992.

De Lauretis, Teresa, ed. *Feminist Studies/Critical Studies*. Bloomington: Indiana UP, 1986.

——. "The Technology of Gender." In *Technologies of Gender: Essays on Theory, Film, and Fiction*. Bloomington: Indiana UP, 1987.

De Russy, Candance. "Revolting Behavior: The Irresponsible Exercise of Academic Freedom." *Chronicle of Higher Education* 6 March 1998; B9.

DeVeaux, Alexis. *The Tapestry*. In *Nine Plays by Black Women*, ed. Margaret Wilkerson. New York: New American Library, 1986.

Desmond, Jane. "Invoking 'the Native': Body Politics in Contemporary Hawaiian Tourist Shows." *TDR* 41.4 (winter 1997): 83–109.

Diamond, Elin. ed. *Performance and Cultural Politics*. New York: Routledge, 1996.

——. "The Violence of 'We': Politicizing Identification." In *Critical Theory and Performance*, ed. Janelle Reinelt and Joseph Roach. Ann Arbor: U of Michigan P, 1992.

Dolan, Jill. "Building a Theatrical Vernacular: Responsibility, Ambivalence, and Queer Theatre." *Modern Drama* 39.1 (spring 1996): 1–15.

——. *The Feminist Spectator as Critic*. Ann Arbor: U of Michigan P, 1989.

——. "Gay and Lesbian Professors Out on Campus." *Academe* 84.5 (September/October 1998): 40–5.

———. *Presence and Desire: Essays on Gender, Sexuality, Performance*. Ann Arbor: U of Michigan P, 1993.

Donkin, Ellen, and Sue Clement, eds. *Upstaging Big Daddy: Directing as if Gender and Race Matter*. Ann Arbor: U of Michigan P, 1993.

Doty, Alexander. *Making Things Perfectly Queer: Interpreting Mass Culture*. Minneapolis: U of Minnesota P, 1993.

Drukman, Steven. "Writers and Their Work: Holly Hughes Interviewed by Steven Drukman." *Dramatists' Guild Quarterly*. (summer 1996): 40.

Duderstadt, James J. *A University for the Twenty-First Century*. Ann Arbor: U of Michigan P, 2000.

Duggan, Lisa, and Nan Hunter. *Sex Wars: Sexual Dissent and Political Culture*. New York: Routledge, 1995.

During, Simon, ed. *The Cultural Studies Reader*. New York: Routledge, 1993.

Eagleton, Terry. *Marxism and Literary Criticism*. Berkeley: U of California P, 1976.

Elam, Harry. *Taking It to the Streets: The Social Protest Theatre of Luis Valdez and Amiri Baraka*. Ann Arbor: U of Michigan P, 1997.

Escoffier, Jeffrey. *American Homo: Community and Perversity*. Berkeley: U of California P, 1998.

Faderman, Lillian. *Odd Girls and Twilight Lovers: A History of Lesbian Life in the Twentieth Century*. New York: Columbia UP, 1991.

Faludi, Susan. *Backlash: The Undeclared War against American Women*. New York: Crown, 1991.

Ferris, Lesley, ed. *Crossing the Stage: Controversies on Cross-dressing*. New York: Routledge, 1993.

Fiske, John. "British Cultural Studies and Television." In *Channels of Discourse: Television and Contemporary Criticism*, ed. Robert Allen. Chapel Hill: U of North Carolina P, 1987.

Foucault, Michel. *The History of Sexuality*, Vol. I, *An Introduction*. New York: Vintage, 1980.

Freire, Paolo. *Pedagogy of the Oppressed*. New York: Continuum, 1970.

Fuss, Diana, ed. *Inside/Out: Lesbian Theories, Gay Theories*. New York: Routledge, 1991.

Gallop, Jane. *Around 1981: Academic Feminist Literary Theory*. New York: Routledge, 1992.

———. *Feminist Accused of Sexual Harassment*. Durham: Duke UP, 1998.

———. "Resisting Reasonableness." *Critical Inquiry* 25.3 (spring 1999): 599–609.

Gallop, Jane, Marianne Hirsh, and Nancy K. Miller. "Criticizing Feminist Criticism." Roundtable discussion in *Conflicts in Feminism*, ed. Marianne Hirsh and Evelyn Fox Keller. New York: Routledge, 1990.

Garber, Linda, ed. *Tilting the Tower: Lesbians Teaching Queer Subjects*. New York: Routledge, 1994.

Garber, Marjorie. *Vested Interests: Cross-Dressing and Cultural Anxiety*. New York: Routledge, 1992.

Geis, Deborah, and Steven Kruger, eds. *Approaching the Millennium: Essays on Angels in America*. Ann Arbor: U of Michigan P, 1997.

Gilroy, Paul. *The Black Atlantic: Modernity and Double Consciousness*. Cambridge: Harvard UP, 1993.

Giroux, Henry. *Border Crossings: Cultural Workers and the Politics of Education*. New York: Routledge, 1992.

_____, ed. *Postmodernism, Feminism, and Cultural Politics*. Albany: State U of New York P, 1991.

Gitlin, Todd. *Twilight of Common Dreams: Why America Is Wracked by the Culture Wars*. New York: Metropolitan Books, 1995.

Graff, Gerald. *Beyond the Culture Wars: How Teaching the Conflicts Can Revitalize American Education*. New York: Norton, 1992.

Grimes, William. "Face-to-Face Encounter on Race in Theatre." *New York Times* 29 January 1997, C9.

Grossberg, Lawrence, Cary Nelson, and Paula Treichler, eds. *Cultural Studies*. New York: Routledge, 1992.

Guy-Sheftall, Beverly, with Evelyn M. Hammonds. "Whither Black Women's Studies. Interview." *differences: A Journal of Feminist Cultural Studies* 9.3 (fall 1997): 31–45.

Haggerty, George E., and Bonnie Zimmerman, eds. *Professions of Desire: Lesbian and Gay Studies in Literature*. New York: Modern Language Association, 1995.

Hart, Lynda. *Fatal Women: Lesbian Sexuality and the Mark of Aggression*. Princeton: Princeton UP, 1994.

_____, ed. *Of All the Nerve: Deb Margolin Solo*. New York: Cassell/Continuum, 1999.

Hart, Lynda, and Peggy Phelan. "Queerer Than Thou: Being Deb Margolin." *Theatre Journal* 7.2 (May 1995): 269–282.

_____, eds. *Acting Out: Feminist Performances*. Ann Arbor: U of Michigan P, 1993.

Healy, Patrick, and Peter Schmidt. "In New York, A 'Standards Revolution' or the Gutting of Public Colleges." *Chronicle of Higher Education* 10 July 1998, A21–23.

Hebdige, Dick. *Subculture: The Meaning of Style*. London: Methuen, 1979.

Heller, Dana, ed. *Cross Purposes: Lesbians, Feminists, and the Limits of Alliance*. Bloomington: Indiana UP, 1997.

hooks, bell. *Ain't I a Woman? Black Women and Feminism*. Boston: South End, 1981.

_____. *Feminist Theory: From Margin to Center*. Boston: South End, 1984.

Hughes, Holly. *Preaching to the Perverted*. Performance in progress, Dixon Place, New York City, 10 July 1999.

_____. *Clit Notes*. New York: Grove, 1996.

_____. Interview by Jill Dolan. Graduate Center, City U of New York, New York City. 23 February 1997.

_____. Hughes, Holly, with Lois Weaver and Peggy Shaw. *Dress Suits to Hire*. In *On and Beyond the Stage: A Sourcebook of Feminist Theatre and Performance*, ed. Carol Martin. New York: Routledge, 1996: 267–292.

Inness, Sherrie. *The Lesbian Menace*. Amherst: U of Massachusetts P, 1997.

Kakutani, Michiko. "Portrait of the Artist as a Focus Group." *New York Times Sunday Magazine* 1 March 1998, 26.

Kaplan, E. Ann, and George Levine, eds. *The Politics of Research*. New Brunswick: Rutgers UP, 1997.

Keefe Curb, Rosemary, ed. *All-Star Amazons: Thirteen Lesbian Plays with Essays and Interviews*. New York: Applause Books, 1996.

Kimball, Roger. *Tenured Radicals: How Politics Has Corrupted Our Higher Education*. New York: Harper and Row, 1990.

Kincaid, James. "Critical Response I (to Jane Gallop): Power, Bliss, Jane, and Me." *Critical Inquiry* 25.3 (spring 1999): 610–616.

Kushner, Tony. *Angels in America: A Gay Fantasia on National Themes, Part I: Millennium Approaches*. 1992. New York: Theatre Communications Group, 1993. *Part II: Perestroika*. 1992. New York: Theatre Communications Group, 1994.

Lee, Josephine. "Disciplining Theatre and Drama in the English Department: Reflections on 'Performance' and Institutional History." *Text and Performance Quarterly* 19.2 (April 1999): 145–158.

Levine, Arnold. "The Soul of a New University." *New York Times* 13 March 2000, A25.

Levine, Lawrence W. *Highbrow/Lowbrow: The Emergence of Cultural Hierarchy in America*. Cambridge: Harvard UP, 1988.

_____. *The Opening of the American Mind: Canons, Culture, and History*. Boston: Beacon, 1996.

Lorde, Audre. *Zami: A New Spelling of My Name, A Biomythography*. Freedom: Crossing, 1982.

MacAloon, John, ed. *Rite, Drama, Festival, Spectacle: Rehearsals Toward a Theory of Cultural Performance*. Philadelphia: Institute for the Study of Human Issues, 1984.

McConachie, Bruce. *Melodramatic Formations: American Theatre and Society, 1820–1870*. Iowa City: U of Iowa P, 1992.

McLaren, Peter. *Critical Pedagogy and Predatory Culture: Oppositional Politics in a Postmodern Era*. New York: Routledge, 1995.

McNally, Terrence. *Love! Valour! Compassion!* and *A Perfect Ganesh*. New York: Plume, 1995.

McNaron, Tony A.H. *Poisoned Ivy: Lesbian and Gay Academics Confronting Homophobia*. Philadelphia: Temple UP, 1997.

Marcus, George, ed. *Rereading Cultural Anthropology*. Durham: Duke UP, 1992.

Marranca, Bonnie. "Performance World, Performance Culture." *Performing Arts Journal* 10.3 (1987): 21–30.

_____. "Theatre in the University at the End of the Twentieth Century." *Performing Arts Journal* 50/51.2/3 (May/September 1995): 55–71.

Martin, Biddy. *Femininity Played Straight: The Significance of Being Lesbian*. New York: Routledge, 1996.

_____. "Success and Its Failures." *differences: A Journal of Feminist Cultural Studies* 9.3 (fall 1997): 102–131.

_____. "Teaching Literature, Changing Cultures." *PMLA* 12:1 (January 1997): 7.

Martin, Biddy, and Chandra Talpade Mohanty. "Feminist Politics: What's Home

Got to Do With It?" In *Feminist Studies/Critical Studies*, ed. Teresa de Lauretis. Bloomington: Indiana UP, 1986.

Mercer, Kobena. "Skin Head Sex Thing: Racial Difference and the Homoerotic Imaginary." In *How Do I Look? Queer Film and Video*, ed. Bad Object-Choices. Seattle: Bay, 1991.

Messer-Davidow, Ellen. "Know-How." In *(En)gendering Knowledge: Feminists in Academe*, ed. Ellen Messer-Davidow and Joan E. Hartman. Knoxville: U of Tennessee P, 1991.

Meyer Spacks, Patricia, ed. *Advocacy in the Classroom: Problems and Possibilities*. New York: St. Martin's, 1996.

Meyers, Moe. *The Politics and Poetics of Camp*. New York: Routledge, 1994.

Miller, K. Nancy. *Bequest and Betrayal: Memoir of a Parent's Death*. New York: Oxford UP, 1996.

_____. *Getting Personal: Feminist Occasions and Other Autobiographical Acts*. New York: Routledge, 1991.

Miller, Tim. *Shirts and Skins*. Boston: Alyson, 1997.

Miller, Tim, and David Román. "Preaching to the Converted." *Theatre Journal* 47.2 (May 1995): 169–188.

Mintz, Beth, and Esther D. Rothblum, eds. *Lesbians in Academia: Degrees of Freedom*. New York: Routledge, 1997.

Moraga, Cherríe. *Giving Up the Ghost*. Los Angeles: West End, 1986.

Moraga, Cherríe, and Gloria Anzaldúa, eds. *This Bridge Called My Back: Writings by Radical Women of Color*. Watertown: Persephone, 1981.

Moy, James. "The Anthropological Gaze and the Touristic Siting of Chinese America." *Modern Drama* 35.1 (1992): 82–89.

——. *Marginal Sights: Staging the Chinese in America*. Iowa City: U of Iowa P, 1993.

Muñoz, José E. *Disidentifications: Queers of Color and the Performance of Politics*. Minneapolis: U of Minnesota P, 1999.

Murfee, Elizabeth. *Eloquent Evidence: Arts at the Core of Learning*. Washington, D.C.: National Endowment for the Arts, 1995.

National Gay and Lesbian Task Force. *Campus Packet*. Washington, D.C.: National Gay and Lesbian Task Force, 1998.

Nelson, Cary. *Manifesto of a Tenured Radical*. New York: New York UP, 1997.

_____, ed. *Will Teach for Food: Academic Labor in Crisis*. Minneapolis: U of Minnesota P, 1997.

Nelson, Cary, and Stephen Watt, eds. *Academic Keywords: A Devil's Dictionary for Higher Education*. New York: Routledge, 1999.

Nestle, Joan. *A Restricted Country*. Ithaca: Fireband Books, 1987.

Newton, Esther. "Dickless Tracy and the Homecoming Queen: Lesbian Power and Representation in Gay Male Cherry Grove." In *Inventing Lesbian Cultures in America*, ed. Ellen Lewin. Boston: Beacon, 1997.

_____. "The Mythic Mannish Lesbian: Radclyffe Hall and the New Woman." In *Hidden from History: Reclaiming the Gay and Lesbian Past*, ed. Martin Bauml

Duberman, Martha Vicinus, and George Chauncey Jr. New York: New American Library, 1989.

Nussbaum, Martha. "The Professor of Parody: The Hip Defeatism of Judith Butler." *New Republic* 23 February 1999, 37+.

Osborn, M. Elizabeth, ed. *On New Ground: Contemporary Hispanic-American Plays*. New York: Theatre Communications Group, 1987.

Paglia, Camille. *Sexual Personae*. New Haven: Yale UP, 1990.

Patton, Cindy. "Safe Sex and the Pornographic Vernacular." In *How Do I Look? Queer Film and Video*, ed. Bad Object-Choices. Seattle: Bay, 1991.

Pellegrini, Ann. "Critical Response II (to Jane Gallop): Pedagogy's Turn: Observations on Students, Teachers, and Transference-Love." *Critical Inquiry* 25.3 (spring 1999): 616–625.

_____. *Performance Anxiety: Staging Psychoanalysis, Staging Race*. New York: Routledge, 1997.

Perez, Paul. Letter. *New York Times* 14 February 1998, A12.

Phelan, Peggy. "Serrano, Mapplethorpe, the NEA and You: 'Money Talks.'" *TDR* 34.1 (spring 1990): 4–15.

——. "Tim Miller's *My Queer Body*: An Anatomy in Six Sections." *Theater* 24.2 (1993): 30–34.

_____. *Unmarked: The Politics of Performance*. New York: Routledge, 1993.

Postlewait, Thomas, and Bruce McConachie, eds. *Interpreting the Theatrical Past*. Iowa City: U of Iowa P, 1989.

Pratt, Minnie Bruce. "Identity: Skin Blood Heart." Rev. version in *Rebellion: Essays 1980–1991*. Ithaca: Fireband Books, 1991.

Quindlen, Anna. *Living Out Loud*. New York: Ivy Books, 1988.

Reinelt, Janelle. "Staging the Invisible: The Crisis of Visibility in Theatrical Representation." *Text and Performance Quarterly* 14.2 (April 1994): 97–107.

Reinelt, Janelle, and Joseph Roach, eds. *Critical Theory and Performance*. Ann Arbor: U of Michigan P, 1992.

Richards, Sandra. "Writing the Absent Potential: Drama, Performance, and the Canon of African-American Literature." In *Performance and Performativity*, ed. Andrew Parker and Eve Kosofsky Sedgwick. New York: Routledge, 1995.

Ristock, Janice L., and Catherine G. Taylor, eds. *Inside the Academy and Out: Lesbian/Gay/Queer Studies and Social Action*. Toronto: U of Toronto P, 1998.

Roach, Joseph. *Cities of the Dead: Circum-Atlantic Performance*. New York: Columbia UP, 1996.

_____. "Economies of Abundance." *TDR* 39.4 (fall 1995): 164–165.

——. "Reconstructing Theatre/History." *Theatre Topics* 9.1 (March 1999): 3–10.

Roiphe, Katie. *The Morning After: Sex, Fear, and Feminism on Campus*. Boston: Little, Brown, 1993.

Román, David. *Acts of Intervention: Performance, Gay Culture, and AIDS*. Bloomington: Indiana UP, 1998.

_____. "Performing All Our Lives: AIDS, Performance, Community." In *Critical Theory and Performance*, ed. Janelle Reinelt and Joseph Roach. Ann Arbor: U of Michigan P, 1992.

Roof, Judith, and Robyn Wiegman, eds. *Who Can Speak? Authority and Critical Identity*. Urbana: U of Illinois P, 1995.

Rooney, Ellen. "Discipline and Vanish: Feminism, the Resistance to Theory, and the Politics of Cultural Studies." In *differences: A Journal of Feminist Cultural Studies* 2.3 (1990): 14–28.

Rorty, Richard. *Achieving Our Country: Leftist Thought in Twentieth-Century America*. Cambridge: Harvard UP, 1998.

Rotello, Gabriel. *Sexual Ecology: AIDS and the Destiny of Gay Men*. New York: Dutton, 1997.

Rubin, Gayle. "Sexual Traffic." Interview with Judith Butler. *differences: A Journal of Feminist Cultural Studies* 6:2/3 (1994): 62–99.

Sandoval Sanchez, Alberto. *José, Can You See? Latinos On and Off Broadway*. Madison: U of Wisconsin P, 1999.

Savran, David. "Ambivalence, Utopia, and a Queer Sort of Materialism: How *Angels in America* Reconstructs the Nation." *Theatre Journal* 47.2 (May 1995): 207–227.

Schechner, Richard. *Between Theatre and Anthropology*. Philadelphia: U of Pennsylvania P, 1985.

_____. *Essays on Performance Theory, 1970–1976*. New York: Drama Book Specialists, 1977.

———. *Performance Theory*. Revised edition. New York: Routledge, 1988.

———. "Transforming Theatre Departments." *TDR* 39:2 (Summer 1995): 8.

Schechner, Richard. and Willa Appel, eds. *By Means of Performance: Intercultural Studies of Theatre and Ritual*. Cambridge: Cambridge UP, 1990.

Schenkar, Joan. *Signs of Life*. In *Signs of Life: Six Comedies of Menace*, ed. Vicki Patraka. Middleton: Wesleyan UP, 1998.

Schneider, Rebecca. *The Explicit Body in Performance*. New York: Routledge, 1997.

Scott, Joan Wallach, ed. "Women's Studies on the Edge. Introduction." *differences: A Journal of Feminist Cultural Studies* 9.3 (fall 1997): i–v.

Sedgwick, Eve Kosofsky. *Epistemology of the Closet*. Berkeley: U of California P, 1990.

_____. *Tendencies*. Durham: Duke UP, 1993.

Senelick, Lawrence, ed. *Gender in Performance: The Presentation of Identity*. Hanover: U Presses of New England, 1992.

Shewey, Don, ed. *Out Front: Contemporary Gay and Lesbian Plays*. New York: Grove, 1988.

Signorile, Michelangelo. *Life Outside: The Signorile Report on Gay Men: Sex, Drugs, Muscles, and the Passages of Life*. New York: HarperCollins, 1997.

Sinfield, Alan. *Out on Stage: Lesbian and Gay Theatre in the Twentieth Century*. New Haven: Yale UP, 1999.

Smith, Anna Deveare. *All Things Considered*, National Public Radio. June 1992.

———. "Not So Special Vehicles." *Performing Arts Journal* 50/51.2/3 (May/September 1995): 77–92.

Solomon, Alisa. "CUNY Trustees Vote to End Remedial Courses." *News from CLAGS* 8.2 (summer 1998): 3–4.

_____. "Queen for a Day: Marjorie Garber's Drag Race." *Village Voice* Literary Supplement, June 1992: 23.

Solomon, Alisa, and Deidre Hussey. "Enemies of Public Education: Who Is Behind the Attacks on CUNY and SUNY." *Village Voice* Educational Supplement, 21 April 1998, 2–7.

Steiner, Wendy. *The Scandal of Pleasure*. Chicago: U of Chicago P, 1995.

Stimpson, Catharine R. "Activist Trustees Wield Power Gone Awry." *Chronicle of Higher Education* 16 January 1998, B4–5.

Strunk, William Jr., and E. D. B. White. *The Elements of Style*. 3rd ed. New York: Macmillan, 1979.

Sullivan, Andrew. *Virtually Normal: An Argument about Homosexuality*. New York: Random House, 1995.

Theatre Studies in Higher Education: Learning for a Lifetime. Denver: Association for Theatre in Higher Education, 1997.

Thompson Drewal, Margaret. "The State of Research on Performance in Africa." *African Studies Review* 34.3 (December 1991): 1–64.

Tomasky, Michael. "Academic Labor Movement." *Lingua Franca* (February 1997): 41–47.

Uncovering the Right on Campus: A Guide to Resisting Conservative Attacks on Equality and Social Justice. Cambridge: Center for Campus Organizing, 1997.

Vaid, Urvashi. *Virtual Equality: The Mainstreaming of Gay and Lesbian Liberation*. New York: Anchor Books, 1995.

Vorlicky, Robert, ed. *Tony Kushner in Conversation*. Ann Arbor: U of Michigan P, 1998.

Walters, Suzanna. "From Here to Queer: Radical Feminism, Post-Modernism, and the Lesbian Menace (Or, Why Can't a Woman Be More Like a Fag?)." *SIGNS: Journal of Women in Culture and Society* (summer 1996): 830–869.

Warner, Michael, ed. *Fear of a Queer Planet*. Minneapolis: U of Minnesota P, 1993.

_____. "From Queer to Eternity: An Army of Theorists Cannot Fail." *Village Voice* Literary Supplement, June 1992, 18–19.

_____. *The Trouble with Normal: Sex, Politics, and the Ethics of Queer Life*. New York: Free, 1999.

Weedon, Chris. *Feminist Practice and Post-Structuralist Theory*. London: Basil Blackwell, 1987.

Williams, Jeffrey, ed. *PC Wars: Politics and Theory in Academy*. New York: Routledge, 1995.

Wilson, John. *The Myth of Political Correctness: The Conservative Attack on Higher Education*. Durham: Duke UP, 1995.

Wolf, Stacy. "Civilizing and Selling Spectators: Audiences at the Madison Civic Center." *Theatre Survey* 39.2 (November 1998): 7–23.

——. "Theatre as Social Practice: Local Ethnographies of Audience Reception." Diss., University of Wisconsin–Madison, 1994.

Worthen, W. B. "Drama, Performativity, and Performance." *PMLA* 113.5 (October 1998): 1093–1107.

Yang, Alan. *From Wrongs to Rights: Public Opinion on Gay and Lesbian Americans'*

Moves toward Equality. Washington, D.C.: Policy Institute of the National Gay and Lesbian Task Force, 1998.

Yankowitz, Susan. *The Slaughterhouse Play*. In *New American Plays*, vol. 4, ed. William M. Hoffman. New York: Hill and Wang, 1971.

Young, Iris Marion. "The Ideal of Community and the Politics of Difference." In *Feminism/Postmodernism*, ed. Linda Nicholson. New York: Routledge, 1990.

Zarrilli, Phillip. "Toward a Definition of Performance Studies, Part I." *Theatre Journal*. 38.3 (October 1986): 372–376.

Zinsser, William. *On Writing Well*. 1976. New York: Harper and Row, 1988.

resource list

ACT-UP
  AIDS Coalition to Unleash Power
  332 Bleecker Street, Suite G5
  New York, NY 10014
  Voice mail/fax: (212) 966-4873
  E-mail: actupny@panix.com
  http://www.actupny.org
  ACT-UP is a direct action organization dedicated to education on and public
  intervention in HIV/AIDS issues throughout the country. ACT-UP trains communities to gain media access through demonstrations, acts of civil disobedience, and media documentation initiatives such as the Diva TV project, which
  documents AIDS activism and news from local communities.

American Association of University Professors
  1012 14th Street NW, Suite 500
  Washington DC 20005-3465
  Telephone: (202) 737-5900
  Fax: (202) 737-5526
  E-mail: aaup@aaup.org
  http://www.aaup.org
  Founded in 1915, the American Association of University Professors defends ac-
  ademic freedom and tenure, advocates collegial governance, and develops poli-
  cies ensuring due process.

American Association of University Women
  Educational Foundation
  1111 16th Street NW
  Washington, DC 20036
  Telephone: (202) 728-7613
  Fax: (202) 872-1425
  http://www.aauw.org/7000/foundation.html
  The American Association of University Women is a nonprofit organization
  dedicated to advancing the position of women in academic institutions across
  the nation. The AAUW promotes programs that expand opportunities for
  women in academia, lobby against gender discrimination in the workplace, and
  provide opportunities for young women to succeed in their pursuit of careers
  in higher education.

American Civil Liberties Union
125 Broad Street, 18th Floor
New York, NY 10004-2400
Telephone: (212) 344-3005
http://www.aclu.org
The American Civil Liberties Union is a nonprofit advocacy organization dedicated to the defense of individual rights and democracy in the United States. The ACLU promotes litigation, legislation, and education to the public on a broad array of issues including gay and lesbian rights, antiracist politics, and HIV/AIDS.

American College Personnel Association's Standing Committee for Lesbian, Gay, Bisexual and Transgender Awareness
http://www.cas.ucsf.edu/sclgbta
The Standing Committee for Lesbian, Gay, Bisexual and Transgender Awareness is a working committee of the American College Personnel Association operating since 1985. SCLGBTA promotes efforts to protect and advocate for the basic human rights of lesbian, gay, bisexual, and transgender students and colleagues at college and university campuses nationwide.

American Educational Research Association
1230 17th Street NW
Washington, DC 20036-3078
Telephone: (202) 223-9485
Fax: (202) 775-1824
http://www.aera.net
Founded in 1916, the American Educational Research Association is concerned with improving the educational process by promoting scholarly inquiry and dissemination and the practical application of research results in the field of education. AERA's 22,000-person membership comprises educators; administrators; directors of research; testing or evaluation in federal, state, and local agencies; counselors; evaluators; graduate students; and behavioral scientists. Special interest groups (SIGs) include Critical Examination of Race, Ethnicity, Class, and Gender in Education; Disability Studies in Education; Indigenous Peoples of the Americas; International Perspectives on the Visual and Performing Arts in Education; and Lesbian and Gay Studies.

American Studies Association
1120 19th Street NW, Suite 301
Washington, DC 20036
Telephone: (202) 467-4783
Fax: (202) 467-4786
E-mail: asastaff@erols.com
Founded in 1951, the American Studies Association is a multidisciplinary organization that encourages and promotes the study of American culture. ASA

hosts an annual meeting as well as regional conferences and publishes a journal and a newsletter. In recent years, ASA has fostered some of the most exciting interdisciplinary work in the academy and has provided a stimulating site for academic activists to share their work. As of spring 2000, a performance studies caucus was in the early planning stages.

Asian/Pacific-Islander Lesbian and Bisexual Network
APLBN
P.O. Box 210698
San Francisco, CA 94121
Telephone: (650) 697-0375
APLBN is a national organization founded in 1987 and dedicated to bridging the Asian lesbian, bisexual, and transgender communities throughout the United States and abroad.

Association for Theatre in Higher Education
P.O. Box 4537
Boulder, CO 80306-4537
Telephone: (888) 284-3737 or (303) 440-0851
Fax: (303) 440-0852
E-mail: Nericksn@aol.com
http://www.hawaii.edu/athe
The Association for Theatre in Higher Education is an organization of individuals and theater departments that provides vision and leadership for the study of theater and its practice. ATHE promotes theater education of the highest quality by actively supporting theater scholarship, research, teaching, practice, and production. It serves as a collective voice for its members through its publications (*Theatre Journal* and *Theatre Topics*), conferences, advocacy work, special projects, and collaborations with other organizations and institutions. Comprising twenty-four focus groups and eleven committees—among the focus groups are Theatre as Social Change, Women and Theatre, Lesbian/Gay Theatre, Theory, Dramaturgy, Black Theatre Association, Association of Asian Performance, and among the commmittees are Advocacy, Professional Development, and Electronic Technology—ATHE is committed to a democratic, grassroots governance process, while it increasingly provides a voice for national issues in arts advocacy and education. ATHE is committed to integrating theater theory and practice.

Astraea Foundation
116 East 16th Street, 7th Floor
New York, NY 10003
Telephone: (212) 529-8021
Fax: (212) 982-3321
E-mail: info@astraea.org
The Astraea National Lesbian Action Foundation is a national nonprofit public

charity founded in 1977 to support community and institutional efforts that serve the lesbian community through the organization of networks, and allocation of funding, education, and technical assistance for resource development. Astraea benefits lesbians, women, gay men, bisexual and transgender communities nationally and internationally.

Audre Lorde Project
85 South Oxford Street
Brooklyn, NY 11217
Telephone: (718) 596-0342
Fax: (718) 596-1328
E-Mail: alpinfo@alp.org
The Audre Lorde Project is a center for lgbt communities of color. The center supports health outreach and services, promotes lgbt activism by communities of color in the New York City area, and houses a variety of community archival efforts, as well as artistic and social gatherings that mark their presence in New York and the country at large.

Center for Campus Organizing
165 Friend Street, M/S 1
Boston, MA 02114-2025
Telephone: (617) 725-2886
Fax: (617) 725-2873
E-mail: cco@igc.org
http://www.cco.org
The Center for Campus Organizing is a national organization dedicated to building progressive movements on college campuses. It believes that progressive campus movements in the United States can and should contribute more effectively to larger struggles for social justice. Its programs function to bolster, aid, and instigate these contributions.

The Center for Critical Thinking
Sonoma State University
c/o POB 220
Dillon Beach, CA 94929
Telephone: (707) 878-9100
Fax: (707) 878-9111
The Center for Critical Thinking conducts advanced research, disseminates information on critical thinking, and sponsors an annual International Conference on Critical Thinking and Educational Reform. The center works with local, state, and national educational organizations to facilitate the implementation of critical thinking instruction.

The Center for Lesbian and Gay Studies
The Graduate School and University Center

City University of New York
365 Fifth Avenue, Room 7.104
New York, NY 10016
Telephone: (212) 817-1955
E-mail: clags@gc.cuny.edu
http://web.gsuc.cuny.edu/clags
The Center for Lesbian and Gay Studies is the first and only university-based research center in the United States dedicated to the study of historical, cultural, and political issues of vital concern to lesbian, gay, bisexual, and transgender individuals. By sponsoring public programs and conferences, offering fellowships to individual scholars, and functioning as an indispensable conduit of information, CLAGS serves as a national center for the promotion of scholarship that fosters social change.

Center for Mexican American Studies
University of Texas–Austin
West Mall Building 5.102
Austin, TX 78712
Telephone: (512) 471-4557
Fax: (512) 471-9639
E-mail: cmas@uts.cc.utexas.edu
The Center for Mexican American Studies of the University of Texas–Austin supports the funding and development of research, teaching, and publication of scholarship pertaining to populations of Mexican origin in the United States. CMAS also works to bridge the university with the community at large through the organization of lecture series, conferences and symposia, and *Latino USA*, a weekly public radio journal of news and culture. Through the Advanced Graduate Seminar in Chicano Research, CMAS brings together a multidisciplinary group of graduate students and professors to explore current research on Latino studies and to discuss issues of activism, critical pedagogy, and the academy.

Center for Puerto Rican Studies
Hunter College
695 Park Avenue
New York, NY 10021
Telephone: (212) 772-5690
Fax: (212) 650-3673
http://centropr.org
Founded in 1973, the Center for Puerto Rican Studies is a research-based institute dedicated to interdisciplinary study of the Puerto Rican experience. The center serves as a research and educational resource network, guiding and mentoring students, assisting and advising community organizations, and serving on policy-related committees at the local, state, and national levels.

Center for Social Justice
489 College Street, Suite 303
Toronto, ON Canada M6G 1A5
Telephone: (416) 927-0777
Toll-free: (888) 803-8881
Fax: (416) 927-7771
E-mail: justice@socialjustice.org
The Center for Social Justice was founded in 1997 as a partnership of activists from universities and unions, faith communities and social movements. The center is committed to the democratic values of equality, justice and respect for human rights through progressive research and analysis, and the distribution of activist knowledge through education.

Center for the Arts in the Basic Curriculum
1319 P Street NW, Suite 900
Washington, DC 20004-1152
Telephone: (202) 638-5196
http://www.newhorizons.org/ofc_cabc.html
Founded in 1989, the Center for the Arts in the Basic Curriculum is dedicated to the development and distribution of strategies to develop arts-integrated schools that recognize diversity. CABC engages teachers, administrators, and the public in dialogue about the benefits of an arts-integrated curriculum.

Dixon Place
309 East 26th Street
New York, NY 10010
Telephone: (212) 532-1546
Fax: (212) 532-1094
E-mail: contact@dixonplace.org
Dixon Place is a nonprofit organization dedicated to providing a space for literary and performing artists to create and develop new work in front of a live audience.

Esperanza Peace and Justice Center
922 San Pedro
San Antonio, TX 78212
Telephone: (210) 228-0201
Fax: (210) 228-0000
E-mail: esperanza@esperanzacenter.org
The Esperanza Center is a progressive grassroots cultural organization founded in 1987 to advocate for people of color, women, lesbians and gay men, the working class, and poor. Esperanza Center offers diverse programming that includes film, the visual arts, music, literature and performance, as well as grassroots organizing, leadership workshops, and direct intervention activism.

Gay and Lesbian Alliance Against Defamation

National Office
8455 Beverly Blvd., Suite 305
Los Angeles, CA 90048
Telephone: (323) 658-6775
Hotline: (323) 874-5223
Fax: (323) 658-6776
Telephone: (800) GAY-MEDIA
E-mail: glaad@glaad.org
http://www.glaad.org

Regional Offices
1360 Mission Street, Suite 200
San Francisco, CA 94103
Telephone: (415) 861-2244
Hotline: (415) 861-4588
Fax (415) 861-4893

1825 Connecticut Avenue NW, 5th Floor
Washington, DC 20009
Telephone: (202) 986-1360
Fax: (202) 667-0902

1447 Peachtree Street NE, Suite 1004
Atlanta, GA 30309-3707
Telephone: (404) 876-1398
Fax: (404) 876-1399

1509 Westport Road
Kansas City, MO 64111
Telephone: (816) 756-5991
Fax: (816) 756-5993

New York, New York
150 West 26th Street, Suite 503
New York, NY 10001
Telephone: (212) 807-1700
Fax: (212) 807-1806

Formed in New York in 1985, the Gay and Lesbian Alliance Against Defamation is a national organization dedicated to the promotion of fair, accurate, and inclusive representations of individuals and events in all media as a means of eliminating homophobia and discrimination based on gender identity and sexual orientation. GLAAD leads and supports lobbying efforts, media training programs, and media research and analysis projects that concern the lgbt community nationally.

Gay Asian Pacific Islander Men of NYC
P.O. Box 1608
Old Chelsea Station
New York, NY 10113
Telephone: (212) 802-RICE (7423)
E-mail: gapimny@gapimny.org
http://www.gapimny.org
The Gay Asian Pacific Islander Men of NYC, now in its tenth year of opera-
tion, provides a social, political, and educational forum for gay and bisexual
Asian and Pacific Islander men in New York City.

The Gay, Lesbian, and Straight Education Network

GLSEN National Office
121 West 27th Street, Suite 804
New York, NY 10001
Telephone: (212) 727-0135
Fax: (212) 727-0254
E-mail: glsen@glsen.org
http://www.glsen.org

GLSEN Western Field Office
1360 Mission Street, Suite 200
San Francisco, CA 94103
Telephone: (415) 551-9788
Fax: (415) 551-9789
E-mail: glsenwest@glsen.org

GLSEN Southern Field Office
1447 Peachtree Street, Suite 1004
Atlanta, GA 30309
Telephone: (404) 815-0551
Fax: (404) 815-1739
E-mail: glsensouth@glsen.org

Founded in 1990, the Gay, Lesbian, and Straight Education Network
(GLSEN) is dedicated to education and advocacy in K–12 schools in order to
create safe and affirming learning environments for all students regardless of
sexual orientation or gender identity. Through a network of eighty-five chapters
in thirty-five states, GLSEN creates and distributes teacher-training materials
and lgbt-inclusive curricular resources to elementary and secondary schools
across the country. GLSEN is involved in federal, state, and local advocacy
through programs such as the annual Back-to-School Campaign, which documents programs and policies protecting lgbt youth in schools.

The Gill Foundation
Headquarters and Out-Giving Project

2215 Market Street, Suite 205
Denver, CO 80205
Telephone: (303) 292-4455
Fax: (303) 292-2155
The Gill Foundation supports community efforts that advocate for the equal
rights of gay men and lesbians and that showcase their contributions to American society. The Gill Foundation offers funding through grants, technical assistance, and other social, activist, and cultural programs.

Highways Performance Space
Highways Performance Space
1651 18th Street
Santa Monica, CA 90404
Telephone: (310) 453-1755
http://www.highwaysperformance.org
Highways's mission is to develop and present innovative performance and
visual art, foster critical dialogue among artists that address social and
community issues, and promote interaction among people of diverse cultural
identities. It meets its mission through performance programming, which
includes festivals, community rituals, and gallery exhibitions, and
through Performance University Workshops, which provide training in
performance, writing, and movement techniques. A particular commitment is
to provide educational and residency programs that engage community
members in the arts and provide them with access to professionally directed
instruction.

Human Rights Campaign
919 18th Street NW
Washington, DC 20006
Telephone: (202) 628-4160
Fax: (202) 347-5323
E-mail: hrc@hrc.org
http://www.hrc.org
The Human Rights Campaign is a national political organization dedicated to
the promotion of equal rights for lgbt citizens in the United States. The HRC
supports a federal government lobbying team on lgbt issues, participates in
election campaigns, organizes volunteers and action networks, and trains communities to advocate for their rights at the local and state levels.

International Foundation for Gender Education
P.O. Box 540229
Waltham, MA 02454-0229
Telephone: (781) 899-2212
Fax: (781) 899-5703
E-mail: info@ifge.org

http://www.ifge.org
Founded in 1987, the International Foundation for Gender Education is a national advocacy organization. Functioning as a clearinghouse and information center on the free expression of gender identity, IFGE houses a bookstore on transgenderism out of their national headquarters in Waltham, Massachusetts, and publishes a magazine that offers a space for transgender communities to communicate nationally.

Jews for Racial and Economic Justice
140 West 22nd Street, Suite 302
New York, NY 10011
Telephone: (212) 647-8966
Fax: (212) 637-7124
E-mail: jfrej@igc.org
Jews for Racial and Economic Justice is a nonprofit organization for the mobilization against racial and ethnic tension, violence, and economic disparities in New York City. JFREJ supports educational, community organization, and media intervention efforts by progressive Jewish citizens, in collaboration with African American, Latino/a, Asian American, lgbt, and labor groups.

Lambda Legal Defense and Education Fund
National Headquarters
120 Wall Street, Suite 1500
New York, NY 10005
Telephone: (212) 809-8585
Fax: (212) 809-0055
http://www.lambdalegal.org
Organized in 1972, the Lambda Legal Defense and Education Fund is a national organization dedicated to litigation, education, and public policy work for lgbt people and people with HIV/AIDS nationally. Lambda maintains a national network of law professionals committed to lgbt issues. Their litigation often includes free speech cases at educational institutions, ranging from curricular censorship to student activity programming.

Lambda 10 Project–GLB Greek Issues
Indiana University
705 East Seventh Street
Bloomington, IN 47405
Telephone: (812) 855-4463
Fax: (812) 855-4465
E-mail: lambda10@indiana.edu
http://www.lambda10.org
Developed in 1995, the Lambda 10 Project–National Clearinghouse for Gay, Lesbian, Bisexual Greek Issues works to heighten the visibility of gay, lesbian, and bisexual members of the college fraternity by serving as a clearinghouse for

educational resources and educational materials related to sexual orientation and the fraternity/sorority experience.

Latinos and Latinas de Ambiente–NY (LLANY)
1 Little West 12th Street
New York, NY 10014
Telephone: (212) 465-3114
Fax: (212) 741-0010
Latinos and Latinas de Ambiente is a community-based advocacy organization dedicated to the social and cultural needs of the Latina/o lgbt community in New York City. LLANY organizes activist efforts as well as cultural and social events.

Lincoln Center Institute
70 Lincoln Center Plaza, 7th Floor
New York, NY 10023-6594
Telephone: (212) 875-5535
Fax: (212) 875-5539
http://www.lincolncenter.org/institut
Since its foundation in 1975, the Lincoln Center Institute has fostered the development of aesthetic education as an important part of learning. In association with the Teachers College of Columbia University, and with The Museum of Modern Art and The Brooklyn Museum of Art, the Center offers a variety of arts education programs in order to develop a greater understanding of the arts, the artist's process, and how these understandings apply to life in general.

LLEGO: The National Latina/o Lesbian, Gay, Bisexual and Transgender Organization
1612 K Street NW, Suite 500
Washington, DC 20006
Telephone: (202) 466-8240
Fax: (202) 466-8530
http://www.llego.org
The National Latina/o Lesbian, Gay, Bisexual and Transgender Organization (LLEGO) is a service, education, and advocacy organization committed to the development of Latina/o lgbt communities from the grassroots to national levels. LLEGO organizes efforts for the cultural and political development of lgbt Latina/os, facilitates their access to medical and wellness services, and mobilizes lgbt communities, as well as the Latina/o community at large, to address issues of homophobia, racism, and gender discrimination.

Modern Language Association of America
10 Astor Place
New York, NY 10003-6981
Telephone: (212) 475-9500
Fax: (212) 477-9863

http://www.mla.org
Founded in 1883, the Modern Language Association of America is a national
organization dedicated to the exchange of scholarship, pedagogical practices
and institutional challenges in the fields of language and literature. It sponsors
a lively annual conference, publications, journals, and other resources for academics in English and foreign languages departments. Its caucuses and divisions include those focusing on gay/lesbian scholarship and institutional issues,
and women's issues in the academy, and many others.

The Multicultural Pavilion

http://curry.edschool.virginia.edu/go/multicultural
The Multicultural Pavilion is a Web site created and maintained by Paul Groski,
Coordinator, Diversity Works and Student Intercultural Learning Center at the
University of Maryland, to provide resources and a forum for educators to ex-
plore and discuss multicultural education. The site provides a useful list of pro-
gressive educational organizations in the United States.

National Art Education Association

1916 Association Drive
Reston, VA 20191-1590
Telephone: (703) 860-8000
Fax: (703) 860-2960
E-mail: naea@dgs.dgsys.com
http://www.naea-reston.org
Established in 1947, the National Art Education Association organizes over seventeen thousand art educators from elementary to university levels, as well as
education departments at cultural institutions and editors in the arts publishing
industry interested in promoting art education through professional development, service, advancement of knowledge, and leadership. NAEA provides
grant support for a variety of art education programs and sponsors student initiatives such as the National Art Honor Society and National Junior Art Honor
Society.

National Association for Multicultural Education

NAME National Office
733 15th Street NW, Suite 430
Washington, DC 20005
Telephone: (202) 628-6263
Fax: (202) 628-6264
E-mail: nameorg@erols.com
http://www.inform.umd.edu/name
The National Organization for Multicultural Education is committed to the
project of multicultural education at all levels of academic instruction and areas
of disciplinary inquiry, and to diverse educational institutions. NAME serves as
a national clearinghouse for the distribution of multicultural educational re-

source materials and advocates for institutional adoptions of policies in support of multicultural education.

National Association of Scholars
221 Witherspoon Street, 2nd Floor
Princeton, NJ 08542-3215
Telephone: (609) 683-7878
Fax: (609) 683-0316
http://www.nas.org
The NAS says it is "the only organization dedicated to the restoration of intellectual substance, individual merit, and academic freedom in the university." Check the Web site to see how conservative academics are organizing.

National Campaign for the Freedom of Expression
1429 G Street NW, PMB, Suite 416
Washington, DC 20005-2009
Telephone: (202) 393-2787
E-mail: ncfe@ncfe.net
http://www.ncfe.net
The National Campaign for Freedom of Expression is an educational and advocacy network of artists, arts organizations, audience members and citizens committed to the protection of freedom in artistic expression and to fighting censorship at the local, state, and national levels.

National Center for Curriculum Transformation Resources on Women
Towson University
Towson, MD 21252
http://www.towson.edu/ncctrw
The National Center for Curriculum Transformation Resources on Women focuses on curricular change projects and activities. NCCTRW provides information on resources and organizational materials for faculty and project directors at secondary and postsecondary educational institutions interested in curricular changes that reflect the experiences of women in society.

National Consortium of Directors of Lesbian Gay Bisexual and Transgender Resources in Higher Education
http://www.uic.edu/orgs/lgbt
The National Council of Directors of Lesbian Gay Bisexual and Transgender Resources in Higher Education was established in 1997 to advocate for the rights of lgbt students, faculty, administrators, staff, and alumnae to higher education equity. The Consortium provides support to educators serving lgbt communities in higher education; consults with higher education administrators in the interest of improving the campus climate and services for lgbt faculty, staff, students, administrators, and alumnae; and advocates for institutional policy changes and program development that recognize the needs of lgbt communities.

National Council Against Censorship
275 7th Avenue
New York, NY 10001
Telephone: (212) 807-6222
Fax: (212) 807-6245
E-mail: ncac@ncac.org
http://www.ncac.org
Founded in 1974, the National Coalition Against Censorship is an umbrella organization that brings together a diversity of national nonprofit literary, artistic, religious, educational, professional, labor, and civil liberties organizations. The NCAC works to educate the public about "freedom of thought" rights and advocates for grassroots efforts to defend them.

National Directory of Lesbian, Gay, Bisexual, and Transgender Community Centers
A Project of the National Association of Lesbian and Gay Community Centers
Published by the Lesbian and Gay Community Services Center of New York
1 Little West 12th Street
New York, NY 10014-2000
Telephone: (212) 620-7310
email: info@gaycenter.org
http://www.gaycenter.org
The National Association of Lesbian and Gay Community Centers (NALGCC) is a national organization that networks lgbt community centers to foster their growth around the country and to share ideas and program models. The directory, published by the New York affiliate, provides contact information for all members of the NALGCC.

National Education Association Gay and Lesbian Caucus
http://users.supernet.com/pages/jtesterman
The Gay and Lesbian Caucus is a volunteer organization within the National Education Association dedicated to the elimination of institutional discrimination and homophobia in academic institutions. The NEA-GLC participates in all NEA organizational efforts, policies, and events to ensure the inclusion of gay and lesbian students, educators, and administrators in the mission of the organization. The National Education Association is devoted to the improvement of education at the national level. Additional information is available at the NEA Web site (http://www.nea.org).

National Gay and Lesbian Task Force
1700 Kalorama Road NW
Washington, DC 20009-2624
Telephone: (202) 332-6483
Fax: (202) 332-0207
TTY (202) 332-6219
http://www.ngltf.org

The National Gay and Lesbian Task Force is a national organization devoted to working for the civil rights of gay, lesbian, bisexual and transgender people. NGLTF provides leadership training to lgbt activists, promotes research in lgbt policy issues, and initiates as well as supports lgbt policy efforts at the local, state, and national levels. NGLTF sponsors "Creating Change," an annual conference of lgbt activists and policy makers.

National Guild of Community Schools of the Arts
40 North Van Brunt Street, Suite 32
P.O. Box 8018
Englewood, NJ 07631
Telephone: (201) 871-3337
Fax: (201) 871-7639
http://www.natguild.org
The National Guild of Community Schools of Art provides service, advocacy, and leadership for community arts organizations. Currently, the Guild has 283 member institutions, which serve over 300,000 students in 361 communities across the country. NGCSA schools provide open access to affordable, quality arts instruction by skilled professional faculty.

National Organization for Women
P.O. Box 96824
Washington, DC 20090-6824
Telephone: (202) 628-8669
Fax: (202) 785-8576
E-mail: now@now.org
http://www.now.org
Established in 1966, the National Organization for Women advocates for legal, political, social, and economic changes that eliminate sexism and end other forms of oppression. NOW intervenes through direct mass actions (including marches, rallies, pickets, counterdemonstrations, nonviolent civil disobedience), intensive lobbying , grassroots political organizing, and litigation. Their political agenda includes antiracist and antihomophobic action.

National Jewish Democratic Council
P.O. Box 75308
Washington, DC 20013-5308
Fax: (202) 216-9061
E-mail: NDJC@ndjc.org
http://www.njdc.org
The National Jewish Democratic Council is a nonprofit national organization of Jewish Democrats. The NJDC advocates for quality public education. The NJDC conducts grassroots political training seminars and policy forums throughout the country and to empower communities in defense from the extreme right. The NJDC promotes active engagement with electoral politics as

well as strategic use of the media. They educate and inform members to give them the knowledge to gain access to talk radio and newspapers.

National Queer Student Caucus
An Affiliate of the United States Student Association
1413 K Street, NW, 10th Floor
Washington, DC 20006
Telephone: (202) 347-USSA
Fax: (202) 393-5885
E-mail: ussa@essential.org
The National Queer Student Caucus was founded in 1971. NQSC is a student-run organization dedicated to the support of networking, organizing political efforts, and local, state, and national advocacy campaigns for lgbt students across the country.

National Women's Studies Association
University of Maryland
7100 Baltimore Boulevard, Suite 500
College Park, MD 20740
Telephone: (301) 403-0525,
Fax: (301) 403-4137
E-mail: nwsa@umail.umd.edu
http://www.nwsa.org
The National Women's Studies Association was founded in 1977 to support and promote "feminist/womanist" teaching, learning, research, and professional and community service at the prekindergarten through postsecondary levels and serves as a locus of information about the interdisciplinary field of women's studies for those outside the profession.

National Youth Advocacy Coalition
1638 R Street NW, Suite 300
Washington, DC 20009
Telephone: (202) 319-7596
Fax: (202) 319-7365
E-mail: nyac@nyacyouth.org
http://www.nyacyouth.org
The National Youth Advocacy Coalition advocates for and with young people who are gay, lesbian, bisexual, or transgender in an effort to end discrimination against these youth and to ensure their physical and emotional well being.

Parents, Families, and Friends of Lesbians and Gays
1726 M Street NW, Suite 400
Washington, DC 20036
Telephone: (202) 467-8180
Fax: (202) 467-8194

E-mail: pflagntl@aol.com

http://www.pflag.org

Parents, Families, and Friends of Lesbians and Gays is a national nonprofit organization with worldwide affiliates dedicated to promoting the health and
well-being of lgbt persons, their families, and friends. PFLAG provides support, education, and advocacy, to end discrimination and to secure equal civil
rights for lgbt communities.

Pedagogy and Theatre of the Oppressed

P.O. Box 31623

Omaha, NE 68131-0623

Telephone: (402) 554-3471

E-mail: clloyd@unomaha.edu

http://cid.unomaha.edu/~pto

This organization developed out of the Pedagogy and Theatre of the Oppressed Conference held for the first time in Omaha in 1995. The conference
evolved from the work of Paulo Freire and Augusto Boal in their efforts to help
oppressed peoples of the world develop critical literacies to overcome social
systems of oppression.

People for the American Way

2000 M Street NW, Suite 400

Washington, DC 20036

Telephone: (202) 467-4999 or (800) 326-7329

pfaw@pfaw.org

http://www.pfaw.org

The People for the American Way is a national civil liberties organization devoted to defending progressive politics throughout the United States. PFAWF
supports research, legislation, and educational campaigns. PFAWF is committed to the development of community activism on the left and advocates for efforts in areas such as education, free expression, and religious freedom.

Performance Space 122

150 First Avenue

New York, NY 10009

Telephone: (212) 477-5829

Fax: (212) 353-1315

E-mail: ps122@ps122.org

P.S. 122 is a nonprofit theater- and performance-producing organization dedicated to housing experimental performance and dance.

P.E.R.S.O.N. Project: Public Education Regarding Sexual Orientation Nationally

E-mail: jessea@uclink4.berkeley.edu

http://www.youth.org/loco/PERSONProject

The P.E.R.S.O.N. Project is an activist network dedicated to advocacy for lgbt-inclusive curricular policies in public education. The P.E.R.S.O.N. Project lobbies state and local boards of education and educational policy makers at all levels of government about educational equity issues, and distributes information on resources for addressing lgbt issues in the classroom.

South Asian Lesbian and Gay Association of New York (SALGA-NY)
    P.O. Box 1491
    Old Chelsea Station
    New York, NY 10113
    Telephone: (212) 358-5132
    E-mail: salganyc@hotmail.com
    The South Asian Lesbian and Gay Association of New York is a social and political group for lesbians, gay men, bisexual and transgender South Asian and South Asian–descent communities.

Southern Poverty Law Center
    400 Washington Avenue
    Montgomery, AL 36104-0286
    Telephone: (205) 264-3121
    E-mail: nct@splcenter.org
    http://www.splcenter.org
    The Southern Poverty Law Center is a nonprofit organization dedicated to the fight against racism and discrimination. The center operates through education and litigation to ensure racial tolerance in communities across the country. The Tolerance Project, SPLC's educational program, provides resources for addressing issues of race and cultural diversity in the classroom.

Theatre Communications Group
    355 Lexington Avenue
    New York, NY 10017
    Telephone: (212) 697-5230
    Fax: (212) 983-4847
    E-mail: tcg@tcg.org
    http://www.tcg.org
    Theatre Communications Group is a national theatre service organization dedicated to supporting not-for-profit theatre in the United States. TCG sponsors a variety of residencies, career development efforts, publication series, community outreach programs, and arts advocacy campaigns. It also publishes *American Theatre*, the trade monthly.

WOW Cafe
    59 East Fourth Street,
    New York, NY 10003
    Telephone: (212) 777-4280
    E-mail: sil_1210@hotmail.com

http://www.geocities.com/Wellesley/2056

Founded in 1980, WOW is a nonprofit theater space dedicated to the production of work by, about, and for women. WOW is run by a volunteer collective and its primary focus is on the development of new works and the training of volunteers in the many different aspects of theatre production.

Library of Congress Cataloging-in-Publication Data

Dolan, Jill, 1957–
    Geographies of Learning : theory and practice, activism and
performance / Jill Dolan.
        p. cm.
    Includes bibliographical references.
    ISBN 0-8195-6467-2 (cloth)—ISBN 0-8195-6468-0 (pbk.)
        1. Gay theater—United States.   2. Feminist theater—United States.
3. Gay and lesbian studies—United States.   4. Women's studies—
United States.   1. Title.
PN2270.G39 D65 2001
792'.086'640973—dc21   00-051328